"Yesterday I received a copy of [the] book *Born Dancing*. . . . What a remarkable achievement it really is. I stayed up late last night reading it and I can tell you that both as a parent and a professional I profited and feel it to be superb! It is surely a unique contribution. The manner in which [Thoman and Browder] tap into the major questions, worries, and queries parents have, and then go on to answer or put into research perspective the issues—in such an easy style to boot—is truly remarkable. . . . In short, there is no other book like [it]—nor could there ever be."

—James J. McKenna, associate professor and chairman,
Department of Sociology and Anthropology, Pomona College

"I received a complimentary copy of [the] book *Born Dancing* and have read it from cover to cover with pleasure. . . . I have never been able to explain successfully the development of relationships and their importance to either parents or pediatricians. [Thoman and Browder] have succeeded admirably. I have always wanted to write a book for parents, but I find I don't have the ability to write in the style [they] have achieved. Parents and pediatricians will be thankful for [the] book. Congratulations!"

—A. H. Parmalee, M.D., professor of pediatrics
and head, Division of Child Development, University of California,
Los Angeles

PERENNIAL LIBRARY

HARPER & ROW, PUBLISHERS • New York

Cambridge, Philadelphia, San Francisco, Washington

London, Mexico City

São Paulo, Singapore, Sydney

BORN DANCING

How Intuitive Parents Understand
Their Baby's Unspoken Language
and Natural Rhythms

**EVELYN B. THOMAN, Ph.D.,
and SUE BROWDER**

Grateful acknowledgement is made for permission to reprint "Nothing in Heaven Functions as It Ought?" from *Cross Ties,* by X. J. Kennedy. Copyright © 1985 by X. J. Kennedy. Reprinted by permission of the University of Georgia Press.

Line from "The Turf of Flowers" from *The Poetry of Robert Frost,* edited by Edward Connery Latham. Copyright © 1934, © 1969 by Holt, Rinehart & Winston. Copyright © 1962 by Robert Frost. Reprinted by permission of Henry Holt and Company.

"Invitation," from *Where the Sidewalk Ends,* by Shel Silverstein. Copyright © 1974 by Snake Eye Music, Inc. Reprinted by permission of Harper & Row, Publishers, Inc.

Chart on p. 184 from *Child Development.* Copyright © 1972 by The Society for Research in Child Development, Inc.

Excerpts from *Parenting in a Multicultural Society,* by Mario D. Fantini and Rene Cardenas. Reprinted by permission of Longman, Inc.

First PERENNIAL LIBRARY edition published 1988.

Designer: Ruth Bornschlegel

Copyeditor: Marjorie Horvitz

Indexer: Brian Hotchkiss

Library of Congress Cataloging-in-Publication Data
Thoman, Evelyn B.
   Born dancing.
   "Perennial Library."
   1. Child rearing.   2. Parenting.   3. Nonverbal communication (Psychology)   I. Browder, Sue.
II. Title.
HQ769.T486   1988   649'.1   86-45702
ISBN 0-06-091463-7 (pbk.)

88 89 90 91 92 MPC 10 9 8 7 6 5 4 3 2 1

We dedicate this book to:

*My mother, Lila, my first and lifelong
dancing partner; to the six beautiful
young people with whom I have been
privileged to dance since their birth: Lila
Anne, Linda, Kim, Ruthie, Roger, and
Eric; and to Vic, who continues to teach
me new steps.*

—E.B.T.

*And to Walt, who was dancing
beautifully long before he'd ever heard
about the dance.*

—S.E.B.

There is only the dance.

—T. S. ELIOT

CONTENTS

ACKNOWLEDGMENTS

You'll notice we've used the first-person personal pronoun throughout the book. This obviously refers to Dr. Thoman. *Born Dancing* is based on her research. This book, though, has been very much a collaboration, and a very enriching one at that.

In this spirit we would like to thank Maggie Freese, Patricia Becker, Chris Acebo, Diane Davis, and Rosemary Glazier, who joined me in spending long hours in the homes of mothers and their babies, helping to carry out studies that others said were not possible, and the families who welcomed us into their homes during those many hours and days so that we could record and describe how babies and mothers spend their time together in the real world.

We'd also like to thank our ever-supportive, enthusiastic editor, Brad Miner, who believed in the book from the beginning; our agent, Julian Bach, who was behind us all the way when we had only a "good idea"; and the many distinguished scientists whose years of painstaking research have made this book possible.

Finally, of course, few books are written without the patience and support of those we love. Our deepest thanks go to Vic, Walter, Dustin, and Erin, who devoted years of understanding to this project.

PREFACE

In this century, man's whole vision of himself and of reality has changed irrevocably. Physicists, beginning with Albert Einstein, revealed that on the level of the electron and even beyond—at the very essence of reality—the world is incredibly more complex than anyone during the Renaissance or nineteenth-century ever imagined.

You can take two paired electrons (one spinning right, the other left) and separate them so far from one another that it's impossible for them to "communicate" in any way. Yet at the instant—the very *instant*—you reverse one electron's spin, its partner will reverse *its* spin, as if the two were inextricably connected by some invisible cosmic force. Think about it. How could it happen? How can these two electrons each instantaneously "know" what the other is up to?

I remember hearing about this new physics while sitting one day at the kitchen table in my Connecticut home, listening to two physicists talk. And I thought to myself, "Wow! When the man and woman in the street finally begin to understand what Einstein and the new physicists were saying, it will change their whole awareness of the world. Nothing will ever again be the same. Our whole approach to life will change forever."

That change is coming. That change is happening now. Because physics studies the very essence of reality, it tends to orient all the sciences—and the new physics has had a tradition-shattering effect on all of science in this century, not only in this country but around the globe.

In psychology (which of course encompasses child-rearing theory), a parallel development to the new physics is the new systems theory, which explains complex human relationships—like the one between you and your baby. We're going beyond the old cause-effect ideas of Newtonian physics (which still work but are more limited than we ever thought) and into the optimistic new world of Einsteinian physics and the new physics called quantum mechanics. Once we fully grasp all the enormous implications of the new physics and the parallel new systems theory, our views of behavior, child rearing, men, women, babies, and in fact all human relationships, will never be the same again.

This book is the first step in what I believe will be the most revolutionary change in child-rearing advice to occur in this century. I haven't invented the ideas about physics that are presented in this book. Thinkers far greater than I have done that. But this book is the first to apply the mind-boggling new vision of reality to you and your baby at home.

I haven't discussed the new *theories* in this book perhaps as much as some scientists would hope. If you want an in-depth analysis of the new systems theory, see my bibliography for a list of books and articles you might read. What I hope to do is give you, a thoughtful mother or father, a new perspective on child rearing so you can just relax and raise your baby in the natural way you were meant to. I don't want this book to be like Dr. Spock's *Baby and Child Care* in that you keep it close at hand so you can consult it whenever you encounter a specific parenting stumbling block. Rather, I hope the ideas in this book will become so much a part of you that in a pinch you feel confident enough to rely on yourself. Thus, I'm not saying this book *replaces* Dr. Spock. After reading the new ideas contained here, you may go back to Spock again. But you'll use him in a new way—more as a consultant than as an expert who knows much more than you do.

This book is written in four parts. Part I—Getting Rid of the "Shoulds"—looks at much current child-rearing advice (based on the old cause-effect views of you and your baby) and shows why this advice can be misleading. Part II—Epilogue and Prologue—

is a bridge between the traditional views of child rearing and the new vision, which I call Danceparenting. Part III—Getting Ready to Dance—discusses three aspects of your baby that will help you dance better with him (his capabilities, his feelings, and his rhythms). And Part IV—Let the Dance Begin—describes how you and your baby can dance (and are probably *already* dancing) beautifully together, a flexible, ever-changing dance that can go on all your lives.

I don't want to fix you up, change you, or turn you into a different "type" of parent. I only want to dazzle you with a new awareness based on science as it has been building for the last three-quarters of a century, an awareness that takes parenting away from the experts and gives it back to you. The new child-rearing science shows us that you can learn more about raising your baby than even the top child-rearing experts in the world can teach you. So let's begin.

Introduction: What This Book Will Do for You

We know very little at the present time about how [parent] competence is acquired. Conventional wisdom is that teachers learn to teach in the classroom; I suspect that parents learn to be parents in their encounters with their children.

—DR. ROBERT D. HESS
Stanford University psychologist

The experts have gotten parenthood down and broken its arm.

—A FRUSTRATED FATHER

Here you are, about to have a baby. And because you want to be the Best Parent Ever, you're reading everything intriguing about babies you can get your hands on.

At first *all* the advice looks authoritative. But then you begin noticing the experts often disagree. This doctor says, "Pick up your baby whenever she cries." That one warns, "Let your baby fuss ten minutes first or you'll spoil her." A Yale psychologist insists your baby's IQ is pretty much set at birth. A Philadelphia expert claims that if you teach your baby to read, you'll raise his IQ, maybe even turn him into a genius. One expert says, "Don't let your baby suck his thumb." Another cautions, "If you stop your baby's thumb sucking, you'll make him neurotic."

Now, how can anyone possibly decipher all this conflicting advice? If experts know so much, why can't they agree on even something as simple as thumb sucking? (Good question.) Since they seem so confused, can you trust any of the experts at all?

Well, yes and no.

What how-to-parent books often never bother to tell you (but what you're obviously beginning to suspect) is that there is no one set of rules or rigid formula you "should" follow to raise your baby. Experts can tell you solid facts about babies in general (at what age most babies walk or talk, for example). And they can give you fairly reliable advice on mechanics like how to mix a formula or fold a diaper. But when it comes to your special baby and more subjective questions—Will your baby get spoiled? Should you let your baby sleep in your room? What's the best way to soothe your baby when he's cranky?—rules about babies in general simply don't work. You have to get to know your special baby. You have to treat him or her only as he or she needs to be treated.

Babies are simply too individual and complex for you to answer most questions about them with a simplistic "yes," "no," or "should." If you always pick up your baby the instant he fusses, will you spoil him? That depends. On what? Your baby. You can't spoil a newborn, but some older babies will get spoiled. Others will just feel loved.

My first of three major goals in this book, then, is to help you decipher a lot of conflicting child-rearing advice you've heard and free you from many anxiety-causing "shoulds" and myths that are floating around. As an infant-development specialist (I've been studying babies for more than twenty years), I especially want to help you sort out the jumbled advice you're hearing about infants. Now that babies are bearing the brunt of so much new research and scientists have at last discovered how "smart" babies are, many pseudo experts are saying that if you truly want to be a good parent, you should treat your baby according to special new prescriptions.

How-to-raise-a-genius advocates say if you really want to do your baby justice, you'll teach him to read, multiply, and memorize the countries Dan Rather talks about on the evening news. Do this, they promise, and you'll "multiply your baby's intelligence." Ignore this sage advice, and you'll supposedly squander your baby's best years.

I don't believe that. And in this book I'll tell you why. In fact, I'll answer many questions you may have about your baby's intelligence: How much does your baby know? *Can* you raise your baby's IQ or turn him into a genius? (Should you try?) Does a baby need to learn to read? But more important, I'll tell you about your baby's feelings. What does your baby feel? What does he have feelings about? And how can you make your baby feel most loved?

My second major goal in this book is to help you view your baby in a way in which you may never have seen him before—a way that makes parenthood a lot less anxious and a lot more fun. There is an illusion (created mostly by misguided experts) that a baby is somehow unfinished. Many experts talk about a baby as if he were: (1) a computer into which you, the all-powerful parent, must program hopes, goals, fears, knowledge, and values; (2) a fragile Dresden doll you can easily shatter (or at least make terribly neurotic); or (3) an incomplete adult, rather like a dot-to-dot drawing you have to complete before your baby can be fully human (in other words, an adult).

The result of all these misleading views of babies is that when your infant is born you see him as a being you can either make or break. This attitude, in turn, often transforms parenthood from the joyous process you deserve into a guilt-laden goal. If you're Supermom or Superdad, self-styled experts often imply, your child will become another Mozart or Madame Curie. If you're a flop (say, you flub a critical step like potty training), sorry: Your baby will probably wind up stealing hubcaps. *It all depends on you.*

Whew! No wonder so many bright young couples today decide not to have children. With burdens like this dumped on you, it's amazing you have the nerve even to consider parenthood. When reading most how-to-parent books, you're constantly reminded you can ruin or fail your baby. And that's sad. In fact, it's beyond sad—it's tragic. Why? Because these views of babies as empty computers, breakable dolls, or dot-to-dot adults are much too simple.

By now you may be thinking, "I know that. Babies are people—like the rest of us." If that's your attitude, good for you. You'd be amazed how many of even our top scientists don't know that. Even world-renowned Harvard developmental psychologist Dr. Jerome Bruner recently said in *The New York Review of Books* that Kenneth Kaye's book *Mental and Social Life of Babies: How Parents Create Persons* at last answers that all-important question: "How babies become persons." I know and respect Jerome Bruner. But his comment in this case is off base. Experience raising my own six children and my twenty-plus years of professional experience watching babies both in the lab and (more important) in the home, interacting naturally with their mothers, has taught me your baby is already a total person. At birth, your baby isn't a moldable, imperfect creature you have to change, control, and improve, but a total, complete, viable person with his own likes and dislikes, who deserves to be trusted, respected, and understood.

Like any real person, your baby has feelings. For years, scientists insisted babies felt only two emotional responses: pleasure and pain. Even today, many experts believe that until your baby can think logically, he feels very little. This belief that a baby lives in an emotional vacuum stems, in large part, from the fact that scientists have had no tools to study emotions with. Until recently. Thanks to techniques developed by such researchers as Paul Ekman (at the University of California Medical School in San Francisco) and Harriet Oster (at the University of Pennsylvania), we can now begin to understand how a baby feels. New findings, including some drawn from my studies at the University of Connecticut, reveal that your baby comes into this world with a wealth of emotions. Babies have feelings every bit as real as yours. In fact, feelings (not thoughts) are what make you and your baby most alike. Respond to your baby's feelings, and you can greatly enhance his emotional life (thereby providing the rich emotional soil he needs to grow mentally).

How can you best respond to what your baby feels?

That brings me to my third goal for this book: I want to give you a simple, effective program for raising your baby, a program not directly designed to boost his IQ (which, as you'll see in Chapter 1, is unnecessary) but designed to make him feel good. This program—which I call Danceparenting—will be based not on formulas, black-and-white answers, or rigid dogma, but on mutual understanding, respect, and trust between you and your baby. That's another place where some how-to-parent books go astray: They picture a baby as a totally demanding, ungiving tyrant, a diapered dictator who just takes and never gives. Not so. The best baby-parent relationships aren't one-way. Your baby needs to understand and respect *your* needs too. And he comes into this world equipped to learn how.

The program in this book is unlike any other you've read in a child-care book before, because it's based not on simplistic solutions but on options. There are many "good" ways to raise a baby; I want to help you find the one that best suits your baby and you. In my program, I'll help you chart your own parenting path—not a straight, rigid, narrow one, staked out by an expert you've never met, but a winding, twisty, lovely path that meanders wherever you and your baby want it to. This path will be created just for—and by—you and your baby.

Without a precise formula or rigid list of rules to follow, however will you lay out a path you and your baby can safely follow? Relax. The judgment you gain as you go along will guide you. And so will your baby.

Aha, I sense some skepticism. "How can my baby help me?" you may very well ask. "He can't even talk." That's what is so remarkable—in a way, he can. Babies are a lot more intricate and capable than you may have been led to believe. Thanks to slow-motion films made in the lab, composed of thirty or more pictures a second, scientists have learned that babies even have their own "language."

In fact, babies are born dancing.

Whatever do I mean by that? Later I'll explain in great detail. But I obviously don't mean babies come into this world waltzing to Strauss's "Blue Danube." The kind of dance I'm talking about is a timeless form of communication, infinitely more complex, subtle, and meaningful than a polite ballroom waltz. The baby's dance—which is actually communication at its most basic—comprises rhythmic arm movements, eye shifts, head tilts, coos, cries, fusses, gazes, and dozens of other behaviors. How your baby breathes is part of his dance (and tells you a great deal about him). Another part of his dance is the look in his eyes.

We tend to think dancing has to be set to music. Not so. A baby dances, instead, to his own internal rhythms. Even the single cell oscillates. Your baby's sleeping, eating, breathing, sucking, and crying are rhythmic. As a recent *Science News* article notes, "The body is a symphony of rhythms—the rate of cell division, the timing of hormone production, and the patterns of brain waves all change throughout the day and night." And the newborn, because he's the closest he'll ever be to his biological heritage, grooves into these rhythms to tell you his deepest feelings about himself.

A baby dances his moods as a bee dances the location of a honey tree or clover field—with his whole being. But a baby's dance is incredibly more complex and meaningful. He's telling you about himself and how he feels about this fascinating new world he's in.

By now you may be wondering, Does only the baby dance?

Of course not. You dance too. You have an extensive repertoire of steps (voice tone, facial expressions, head movements, body language, etc.) with which you "talk" to your baby and to which your baby responds. I call your ability to understand and share your baby's dance "biological wisdom." (As you'll see throughout this book, bringing up baby isn't a growth process just for him but also for you.)

When talking with your baby—if you just relax and tune in to him—you just naturally raise your eyebrows in mock surprise, exaggerate your facial expressions, talk in a baby-pleasing tonal quality, and use many other split-second signals to tell your baby you understand and adore him. And your baby uses his wordless dance to respond. At times he dances so subtly you don't consciously notice it (as when he moves his body in rhythmic synchrony with the cadence of your voice). But many other times you can clearly see and understand your baby's steps (as when he gives you his curious, alert look meaning, "Ready to play, if you are!").

In Parts III and IV of this book, I'll help you understand your baby's conversational dance. I'll also outline a simple, flexible program to help you and your baby dance rhythmically and joyously together.

First, though, we need to banish some common child-rearing myths that may make you so anxious or uncertain that they negate your wisdom and disrupt your dance. We'll start with the ridiculous notion that if you teach your baby thousands of facts, you'll make him "better."

PART 1

GETTING RID OF THE "SHOULDS"

It's too hard, and life is too short, to spend your time doing something because someone else has said it's important. You must feel the thing yourself.

—ISIDOR I. RABI
Nobel Prize–winning physicist

The Real Truth About Superbabies

I have no patience with this "better baby" business.

—DR. EDWARD ZIGLER
Sterling Professor of Psychology
Yale University

Parents have always understood how smart babies are. Just watch a mother talk, smile, and coo at her new daughter. Ask if she thinks her baby understands her, and she'll likely reply, "Of *course* she does—don't you, Katie?" And on she goes, "conversing" with her baby.

But now scientists have at last discovered what parents always knew: that babies are bright, clever, and competent.[1] And it's big news. Magazines like *Time* and *Reader's Digest* display adorable babies on their covers and ask, "What Does a Baby Know?"[2] The answer: More than scientists ever dreamed they did.

So now that researchers have at last learned how capable babies are, what should you as a parent *do?* Experts have oodles of answers. "Teach your baby to read," some say. "Show him how to add 2 + 7. Make him memorize where Bangladesh is on the globe so he can understand Dan Rather on the nightly news."

Computer companies are selling software for babies. Bookstore shelves are laden with emotionally persuasive books like *How to Give Your Baby Encyclopedic Knowledge,* in which Glenn Doman, director of the Better Baby Institute in Philadelphia, claims you should teach your baby thousands of facts—from how to tell a grosbeak from a blue jay to how to read Japanese.[3] (Doman promises that if you follow his prescription, you'll "multiply your baby's intelligence," a seduction hard for any loving parent to resist.) And prenursery schools with enticing names like Crème de la Crème charge hundreds of dollars a week to teach your two-year-old to count, read, and speak French.

If you're like many well-meaning parents, you may believe your baby needs all the schooling he can get to cope in today's fast-paced, competitive world. As one Houston father says, "I think Tara needs to absorb all she can as early as possible. She can decide later what she'll do with it." Naturally, you want the best for your baby. And when you're achievement-oriented and know how tough it is to get ahead, it seems that the earlier you get your baby started in the race of life the better. (The truth is, by training a baby in some tasks too early, you may actually slow him down so he'll be behind the child who didn't have lessons. But we'll get to that in a minute.)

If you're still unconvinced your baby needs lessons, the tales of Superbabies might sway you. It seems every other baby you hear about these days is well on his way to becoming another Mozart (who began picking out thirds and sixths on the harpsichord at age three) or John Stuart Mill (who at three could read Greek). An eleven-month-old in Akron, Ohio, is learning to speak both English and French. "Next we'll start her on Latin," her proud mother says, beaming. An eighteen-month-old in Los Angeles is reputedly doing long division. And even your best friend's four-month-old may be going to baby school or at least learning to swim. After regaling you with tales of her diapered prodigy's latest feats, your friend may then sweetly ask, "So what's your baby up to?"

An intimidating question.

If your baby is only cooing at mobiles, you may feel uneasy, if not downright inept. At the very least, you may suffer lingering doubts. As Maria, an art director and the mother of a ten-month-old, told me, "My best friend's eight-month-old is working on his ABCs and knows eighty words. My little Susie's only piddling with the pots and pans. Days when I'm feeling confident and secure, I think, 'Oh, what balderdash. What does a baby need with spelling lessons?' But on more anxious days, I wonder. Am I missing Susie's most formative months? Am I letting her down?"

What I told Maria I'd also like to tell you. Don't let the pressure to keep up with the baby Joneses get to you. No, you're not failing your baby by letting her play and be a baby. By letting her explore her world at her own pace, you're giving her room to grow. Contrary to popular myth, babies taught a lot of facts and pushed to excel don't all become geniuses. Many just become stressed and confused.

John Stuart Mill, possibly because he *was* pushed hard as a child, suffered a mental breakdown at twenty-one. Luckily, Mill recovered. But not all manufactured prodigies do.

A good example of a child who was pushed intellectually at the expense of his feelings was William James Sidis, who was born near the start of this century. When he was born, his father, Boris (a Boston psychiatrist), vowed he'd turn his son into a genius. And he seemed to have succeeded. By eighteen months of age, William was reading *The New York Times*. By the time he got to school, he stunned his elementary school teachers and captured newspaper headlines by blitzing through seven years of schooling in three months. By age eleven, he dismayed Harvard professors by lecturing to them on his complex original theories about four-dimensional bodies.

Yet shortly after receiving his Ph.D., at age seventeen, William suffered an emotional breakdown. Shortly after being dismissed from a college position for failure to get along with his colleagues, William disappeared from the public eye.

He wasn't discovered again until he was forty, when writer James Thurber of *The New Yorker* found him living alone in a shabby rooming house in a Boston slum. Thurber described Sidis as a shy, burned-out, antisocial clerk, whose life had been spent drifting from one dead end job to the next. His only great ambitions? To find a job in which he could use an adding machine and to pursue his esoteric hobby of collecting subway transfers from all over the world. Sidis's only claim to fame as an adult occurred when he sued *The New Yorker* for invasion of privacy—and lost.[4] To be "turned" into a genius by his parents, Sidis may have paid an incredibly high emotional price.

In the end, the tales of manufactured prodigies—even those few, like John Stuart Mill, who did fulfill their early promise—are just that: tales. One story about one father or mother who "created" one genius isn't sound enough evidence to build a baby's life on. How many would-be genius-builders fail and just wind up making their kids miserable? How many geniuses supposedly created by their parents would have been geniuses anyway had they simply been helped to develop at their own rates? What kind of home *does* help a child become a superachiever?

These questions must be answered by looking at *dozens* of achievers, not just one or two. Benjamin Bloom at the University of Chicago recently did just that. Dr. Bloom studied 126 gifted and talented people, from Olympic swimmers, tennis players, and concert pianists to world-renowned scientists, to find out what their childhoods had been like. Virtually *all* these superachievers who'd made major contributions before they were forty came from traditional, loving, non-pushy families. Their parents believed a baby should have time to play and develop his whole being—not just that tiny part of him we call his IQ.[5]

Babies aren't meant to perform for adults or to be status symbols. They're meant to be themselves. And speaking of performing for adults, that reminds me of one program you and I need to talk about.

THE BETTER BABY INSTITUTE: WHAT YOU NEED TO KNOW

It's not my purpose to criticize each early-learning advocate individually. But there's one who deserves special mention simply because he's sold millions of books, so he's influencing millions of parents. I'm referring to Glenn Doman, head of the Better Baby Institute outside Philadelphia, whose program for giving babies formal lessons has received massive media attention.

In his books and at his institutes, Doman displays babies who can multiply, identify chemical elements, and read words in three languages. He then tells parents all babies are potential geniuses at birth and unless children exercise their potential (by reading, doing math, and memorizing encyclopedic facts), "this genius *descends* until age six, when it is virtually gone."[6]

Nonsense. As a child-development researcher for more than twenty years, I have not seen even one controlled scientific study published in a reputable journal that proves this claim.

Genius is a very tricky word, of course, because even its definition differs for different people. Some people consider any adult (or child) with an IQ of 150 or higher a genius (even if that person does nothing more with his or her great brain than solve crossword puzzles). Other people insist a person isn't a true genius until he or she makes a major contribution to mankind, such as composing a great symphony or discovering a cure for cancer.

Doman's definition of genius seems to be equally uncertain. On pages 139 and 140 of his book *How to Multiply Your Baby's Intelligence,* for example, he promises:

> If you read this book and truly *understand* it and don't do any of the techniques included in the "How To" section (reading, encyclopedic knowledge, and math), then you'll deal with him in a totally different way through all those vital first six years of life, and he ought to arrive at six years of ability by the time he is four years old chronologically. That will give him an I.Q. of 150.
>
> If you read this book and truly *understand* it, and deal with him in a totally different way through all those vital six years of life and *also* teach him how to read and how to gain encyclopedic knowledge and how to do math, then he ought to have gained the six years of ability that an average six-year-old has no *later* than at three years of age. That will give him an I.Q. of 200 or above, depending on how much before three years of age he reaches that all-important sixth year of life.[7]

In these paragraphs, Doman is promising a great deal. If you just follow his program, he's insisting your child's IQ will skyrocket.

Yet only one or two pages later, Doman tells you the test of true genius isn't your child's IQ anyway, but what he *does* with his brain (specifically, whether he swims, plays the violin, reads, or speaks Japanese, for example). He states, "GENIUS IS AS GENIUS DOES. No *more* and no *less.*"

Amazingly, no matter how you personally happen to define a genius (whether you focus on a 150 or higher IQ or the fact that your child can read and multiply at age three), Doman insists that using his program will help turn your baby into one. At the Better Baby Institute, infants as young as eight months are exposed to flash cards of words or dots. When enrolled in this program, you and your baby start with three short sessions in reading and three in math and work up until you're spending as much as an hour a day on each subject. At the Institute, you can learn Doman's techniques for teaching your baby thousands of facts in a week-long course costing hundreds of dollars; when you graduate, you receive a diploma proclaiming you a "professional parent."

I want to pay special attention to this program because it's so emotionally appealing (Doman calls his plan "the gentle revolution") yet I and many of my colleagues are deeply concerned that it's potentially harmful to parents and babies. Many of Doman's claims simply aren't supported by the bulk of current infant research. I don't want to spend pages talking about Doman's misconceptions (though I could). So let's take just a few good examples. Here are some notions he actually calls "facts" on page 37 of *Teach Your Baby Math*:[8]

• *Domanism 1.* "Tiny children *want* to learn math." Who says? If left to explore the world on their own, very *few* babies will be attracted by the number 2. Just watch your baby play. I'll bet you'll find he'd much rather ring a bell, shake a rattle, or clang a pan with a spoon than sit in his crib and do arithmetic.

• *Domanism 2.* "Tiny children *can* learn math . . ." I'll go along with this—to a point. Children can learn a lot, and they're especially quick at rote memorization. (Whether a two-year-old actually "learns" math in the sense that he understands mathematical logic is much more questionable.) Then Doman adds: "and the younger the child, the easier it is [for him to learn math]." Where are his controlled scientific studies to back up this claim? If he has any, neither I nor the distinguished child-development researchers I know have ever seen them. He certainly doesn't include any specific research findings in his book or tell you where any studies he's done have been published so you can look them up for yourself. Contrary to Doman's claims, Jean Piaget, the famed Swiss psychologist who revolutionized our ideas about child development, said it was easier for a child to learn logical concepts like math when he reached his "concrete operational period" at about age six or seven[9]—in other words, at about the age most kids normally start school.

• *Domanism 3.* "Tiny children *should* do math (because it is an advantage to do math better and more easily)." Math may be advantageous to an adult, but what use is it to a baby? What does a baby need to count—his diapers? This third Domanism can be the most insidious because it contains that guilt-producing "should." If tiny children "should" learn math, many mothers may feel the implication is, "So why are you failing as a parent and not teaching *your* baby?"

Doman also insists that "Doing math is one of the highest functions of the human brain" and "Doing math is one of the most important functions of life." Come on, now. Math? What happened to love, joy, laughter, play, painting, poetry, music?

What happened to *dance*?

And that brings us to my main concern about Doman's approach (and other plans like his): If you follow all his "shoulds" and put too much pressure on your baby to perform, you may disrupt the dance between you. Your baby may come to see himself not as a person loved and respected for himself, but as worthy of your love only if he performs adequately. Developmental psychologist Dr. Edward Zigler at Yale, who probably knows as much about child development as any scientist in America, says of Doman's program, "This is not a healthy parent-child relationship. It's giving children the message, 'I love you only because you're smart.' "[10]

Worse, what happens to tiny children who *can't* master the lessons? Tufts University psychologist Dr. David Elkind says in *The Hurried Child*, "Children who are confronted with demands to do math or read before they have the requisite mental abilities may experience a series of demoralizing failures and begin to conceive of themselves as worthless."[11]

This sense of inferiority may be so great a child could (though certainly not all children *will*) slip into what University of Pennsylvania psychologist Martin Seligman calls "learned helplessness." Learned helplessness is a phenomenon wherein people repeatedly exposed to situations they can't control literally "give up." They become passive, lose interest, and stop trying. In short, they burn out.[12]

Sadly, a study by psychologist Tiffany Field, director of the Nursery Program at the Mailman Center for Child Development in Miami, suggests that overstimulating a baby—as there's a great danger of doing in a program like Doman's—*does* make some babies quite passive. She found that if a mother bombards her child with stimuli, the infant often comes to initiate fewer activities himself. As Dr. Field points out, "Children learn by taking the initiative and exploring their environment on their own." She shares my deep concern when she adds that by giving a baby intensive lessons in one area (math, for instance), "We may be interfering with some other development that's going on."[13]

Even if you *could* raise your baby's IQ to 150 or 200 by pumping him full of facts, emphasizing that tiny part of your baby we call his IQ makes no sense. And here's why.

WHY YOU NEEDN'T FRET ABOUT YOUR BABY'S IQ

When people talk about Superbabies, they emphasize only what the baby knows. Nobody ever says, "That's a Superbaby—look at her great sense of humor" (though perhaps we should; a great sense of humor isn't easy to come by). But does the fact that some babies have higher IQs make them "better" than other babies? No.

Superiority on IQ tests in infancy means a lot less than you've been told. A baby with the equivalent of a 150 IQ who can read and talk could be behind yours in creeping, climbing stairs, developing a sense of generosity, or hundreds or other tasks (many of them perhaps much more complex than reading). I have very often seen babies who can crawl and climb but can't pick up a tiny crumb with two fingers. Babies have many skills and concepts to learn; those measured by IQ tests are only a few of them.

Studies have confirmed that a high IQ score in infancy has little or no connection with high IQ in later life. One of the first studies to show this was reported in 1933 by psychologist Nancy Bayley at the University of California at Berkeley. Dr. Bayley, who developed the famous Bayley Infant Developmental Scales (as popular for testing a baby's intelligence as the Stanford-Binet test is for testing adult IQ), gave sixty-one babies repeated intelligence tests during their first three years of life. Her conclusion: A baby's IQ during his first year has little or no relation to his intelligence when he's two or three years old.[14]

So let's say your child is two or three. *Now* can you predict his future IQ? No. Again, many studies have shown this.[15] But among the most scientifically sound and complete were those done by Robert B. McCall, a senior psychologist at Boys Town Center in Nebraska. Dr. McCall used several different tests to see if he could predict a child's IQ from his test scores as a baby. He couldn't. McCall concluded in a 1972 issue of *American Psychologist:* "In the first three years of life, there is relatively poor prediction in infant tests of intelligence to I.Q. scores assessed in middle or late childhood."[16]

"Ah," you may ask, "but do IQ tests measure *true* intelligence?"

"Of course not," replies Dr. Victor Denenberg, a University of Connecticut psychobiologist and editor of *Education of the Infant and Young Child.*[17] "We have no way of indexing true intelligence. We don't even agree on what intelligence is."[18]

The IQ test as we know it today was devised and revised between 1905 and 1911 by French psychologist Alfred Binet, who was trying to find a way to determine which children should be placed in schools for the mentally retarded. In other words, the IQ test was originally created not to predict genius but to pinpoint children who weren't intelligent enough to attend regular schools.[19] Binet was opposed to the idea of reducing all the scores on his test to a single "IQ score." He feared people might start trying to compare one score with another in an attempt to see who was most intelligent.[20] Unfortunately for all of us, that of course is precisely what has happened.

The point is, nobody—certainly not Superbaby advocates—knows what makes a "highly intelligent" baby. No one knows fully what a baby *should* be learning at six or eight months of age. Is eight-month-old Kimberly, who babbles sixty words, superintelligent? Is she brighter or "better," say, than Lisa, who only knows how to say "goo-goo" and "Mama"? Or is Lisa the more intellectually advanced, because she's spent her time and effort learning to play a great game of Peek-a-boo?

Since no scientist yet fully understands what a baby is "supposed" to learn at any given stage, the current rage for giving babies lessons seems even more bizarre. Lessons in *what*? I'm far from alone in believing that giving babies formal lessons is useless and may interfere with more valuable learning at this age. Dr. Zigler at Yale (who correctly calls all this talk about Superbabies "nonsense") says, "The constant finding has been that the relationship between intellectual performance in the first year of life and after age seven or eight is zero. So even if you could get a baby to do a little bit more, what *difference* would it make?"[21] Psychologist Tiffany Field says, "We know that babies are coming into the world with a lot more sophisticated skills than we had previously thought, but I do not think reading, writing and arithmetic should be in their curriculum."[22] University of Denver psychologist Kurt Fischer says of your baby's first year, "Don't worry about teaching as much as providing a rich and emotionally supportive atmosphere."[23] He's precisely right. In fact, much evidence I'll cite throughout this book shows it's not formal lessons but socially interacting with *you* that makes your baby bright.

KNOWING ABCs DOESN'T MAKE A BABY "BETTER"

"Forget IQ tests," you may say. "I never believed IQ measured full human intelligence, anyway. Let's get back to those Superbabies we've all heard about. They can read. Certainly that ability alone will give them a head start in school and maybe even later in life, right?"

Not necessarily. I call this the "earlier is better" myth.

We tend to suspect early readers are smarter and will read better the rest of their lives. But the world is full of high-IQ adults who read late. Einstein didn't talk until he was four or read until he was seven. The Quiz Kids, a group of prodigies who appeared on radio and TV in the forties and early fifties, didn't all read before kindergarten. Ruth Duskin Feldman points out in *Whatever Happened to the Quiz Kids: Perils and Profits of Growing Up Gifted:* "Although many Quiz Kids did learn to read before kindergarten, James Watson, the future Nobel Laureate, was not among them. Yet by ten, Watson was reading himself to sleep with the World Almanac. Another Quiz Kid, Warren Cavior, was the only first grader in his class who could not spell his name; at 11, he startled his camp counselor by reading Marx and Engels."[24] Reading early simply does not mean a child is a genius. Nor does reading late mean he's not.

I'm not suggesting that if your child wants to read you should stop him. The dogma from the past that "only teachers should teach" and you should wait until a child gets to school or reaches age six and a half before he learns to read has long been discarded. If your child eagerly asks, "What's this letter?" or "What does that word say?" certainly you don't want to frustrate his curiosity by saying, "Wait till you get to school." But in such a case, your child is reaching out on his own, not being rushed. Few six-month or year-old babies want or try to read. Only an unenlightened expert would suggest that they do. Let me put it this way: If your baby crawls over to you and says, "Show me how to write my name," show him!

Experts who insist you should teach your baby or toddler to read sometimes mention a University of Illinois education professor named Dolores Durkin. (At least, those early-learning advocates who cite a few references mention her; many self-styled experts cite no studies at all.) In the early 1960s, Durkin found some children who'd learned to read before entering kindergarten. Comparing these early learners with kids who'd waited until first grade to read, she found that over the next three years, early readers consistently scored higher on IQ tests.[25]

But there are two problems with this study if you take it seriously (as does Joan Beck in How to Raise a Brighter Child[26]) as "proof" that you as a parent had better get busy and teach your child to read. One, the study didn't last long enough. Durkin followed her subjects only through third grade—not quite long enough for the so-called late readers to catch up. As Dr. Zigler, a founder of Head Start and the first director, in 1970, of the Federal Office of Child Development, points out, "Children from the middle and upper-middle classes don't benefit from earlier instruction. As a parent, if you just take your time and wait until your children get to school, by the age of ten you will not know the difference between your child and one who has been instructed earlier."[27] Age ten, Dr. Zigler says. Durkin's study ended when the children were eight. (In later studies, Durkin did follow early and late readers through fourth grade. Guess what? By fourth grade, the late readers had caught up.[28])

Problem two: Durkin never asked, "Were early readers as happy as late readers? Did they enjoy reading at a later age more than other children did?"

Unlike Durkin, famed educator Carleton Washburn did ask how happy early and late readers were. He also followed his subjects into adolescence. In the 1930s, in the public schools of Winnetka, Illinois, Washburn compared classes of kids who were introduced to formal reading instruction in first grade with those taught to read in second grade. By fourth grade, there was no difference in reading skills between the two groups. Even more intriguing, when these children reached junior high, Washburn asked outside observers (who had no idea which group had read first) to watch the two groups and see if they could detect any difference between them. They could: The kids who'd read later read more enthusiastically and spontaneously than those taught to read in first grade.[29]

If you want to make the effort, you may be able to teach your baby to read, as some experts claim. But even if you could, would you want to?[30]

What's really important is not how early your child reads but whether reading becomes a part of his life. As the late Benjamin Fine, former education editor for *The New York Times* and headmaster of Sands Point Country Day School for the gifted, wrote in his book *Stretching Their Minds:* "The parent who pushes and prods can squeeze creativity and curiosity out of a child. . . . [But] it will not truly matter, when your youngster is thirty years old, whether he learned to read at four, five, or seven. It will matter whether he learned that reading is a source of delight, information, knowledge, strength."[31]

Evidence clearly shows that your baby has far, far more important things to learn than his ABCs, anyway, as I'll demonstrate throughout this book. But before we leave this overemphasis on IQ and reading behind, let me stress one more fact.

PRECOCITY IN SOME SKILLS MAY EVEN BE A HANDICAP

Not only has no connection been shown between a baby's earlier and later IQ, but "superior" performance early can even mean poor performance later. In studies at the Infant Laboratory at the Center for Psychological Studies at Princeton University, psychologists Michael Lewis and Harry McGurk tested the IQs of twenty babies. During their first two years, these babies took intelligence tests at three, six, nine, twelve, eighteen, and twenty-four months of age. Not only did Drs. Lewis and McGurk come to the same conclusion as Bayley, McCall, and the vast majority of other researchers (in babies there's no way to predict future IQ), but they discovered that on some tests, many babies who scored high at three months scored low at nine months. In short, earlier is not necessarily better. Being advanced in some skills may even handicap a baby.[32]

Well-known Harvard psychiatrist Peter Wolff at Boston Children's Hospital pointed out years ago in a paper in the journal *Pediatrics* that as Swiss psychologist Jean Piaget explained, children develop in definite thinking (or what scientists call cognitive) stages. Your child literally thinks differently at age one than he does at five. Therefore, trying to hasten a child through any stage by boosting him tremendously high in one or two skills like reading or counting *could* interfere with the natural sequence of stages later.[33] That's one reason so many thoughtful pediatricians, including Dr. Benjamin Spock, and psychologists, including Dr. Zigler, are especially nervous about all this emphasis on lessons.[34]

Some evidence already suggests that giving a baby formal lessons at six months can put him behind his peers at age four. University of Edinburgh researchers T. G. R. Bower and Jennifer C. Wishart have found that between the ages of six months and two years, your baby learns a primitive form of counting. If shown two sets of dots, your baby can master the concept and then point out which set contains more, which less. It's not that babies *can* learn this skill; they *do* learn it. On their own. Without prodding. But a baby can't put this knowledge into words yet. He can only physically point at the right answer with his tiny index finger. By the age of two years seven months, almost all children can verbally tell you which set contains more dots. They get the correct answers almost 100 percent of the time.

But a strange thing happens.

Sometime after two years seven months of age, Drs. Wishart and Bower find, children somehow "forget" what they once knew. By the time he's three years eleven months old, a child is very confused about which set contains more dots. He can tell you the correct answer only about 20 percent of the time.

Bower and Wishart wondered, Can we improve these scores? What would happen if, when a baby first learned this primitive form of counting, you gave him lots of practice at it (much as you would in a course like Doman's)? Would he then remember it better later? So they took a group of six-month-olds and made them "practice" pointing to the right set of dots over and over again. When these children got to be three years eleven months old, guess what? They could almost *never* give the right answer.

They didn't even do as well as untutored children, who scored 20 percent. In other words, by practicing his skill *more* at first, a baby may somehow know *less* later.[35]

Now, if you've already given your baby reading or counting lessons, don't panic. There's a great difference between *intensive* lessons and lessons used as a game, where your baby learns much more than reading and counting (he learns to communicate with attentive, fun-loving *you*). If the goal of giving your baby lessons is just to give you a fun activity to do together and you really don't care that much whether your baby learns to read or count, fine. But in this case, you're focusing on the play, not on how well you're teaching.

WHAT YOUR BABY LEARNS WITHOUT FORMAL LESSONS

All this emphasis on enrolling your baby in school or trying to "teach" him to enjoy learning is a lot like trying to teach a duckling to like water. "Children learn for the same reason that birds fly," Dr. Zigler says. "They're programmed to learn, and they do it beautifully. You can't stop children from learning—and you certainly don't have to push them to."[36] Your baby learns naturally—all the time. As Yale psychology professor William Kessen, who has been studying infants for more than thirty years, says in admiration of the newborn's zestful approach to life, "He's eating up the world."[37]

Formulas for teaching your baby specific learning tasks (ABCs, counting to 100, etc.) presume that infant development experts all agree on precisely what a baby needs to know. Yes, your baby is brilliantly competent, no doubt about that. Yes, your baby learns rapidly. But some experts would have you focus this brilliance on mundane textbook tasks like reading and math. In fact, your baby is already learning profounder tasks than $2 + 2 = 4$.

Such as?

Well, take Euclidean geometry, for example. No, your baby's not learning geometry. Yet in a sense, he's getting ready to.

At the University of Edinburgh in Scotland, researchers have stumbled upon a remarkable finding: If a baby can't see during his first two years, when he becomes an adolescent he'll be unable to solve the simplest Euclidean geometry problem. In studies of blind children, Drs. Bower and Wishart have found a striking difference between babies born blind (who later, after operations, gain their sight) and babies who can see at birth but go blind later. Babies who can see during their first two years, even if they can't see afterward, can still solve Euclidean geometry problems in college; those born blind, though they can memorize theorems brilliantly, can never do the simplest problem.

Strange as it seems, some experience when a child is a baby will determine whether he can solve geometry problems ten or twenty years later.[38]

Notes Dr. Wishart, "It seems ridiculous that experience in infancy could have any possible effect on the acquisition of Euclidean geometry, but it does seem that without certain experience in infancy, there's *just no way* that the concepts involved in Euclidean geometry can be understood."[39] Somehow—without formal lessons—your baby is absorbing experiences that will one day help him do geometry.

Another thing your baby may learn during his first year is altruism. Babies have been traditionally considered too self-centered and selfish to feel empathy for others. But in her remarkable studies, Marian Radke Yarrow, chief of the Laboratory of Developmental Psychology at the National Institute of Mental Health, has found that as early as one year, some babies actually try to comfort people who are crying or in pain. They snuggle up to them, pat them, hug them—even attempt to help.

At the doctor's office, one mother with a sore throat was having her throat swabbed and made a strangling sound. At once, her small son—only fifty weeks old—tried to knock the swab from the nurse's hand to defend his mother. Dr. Yarrow's conclusion: Somehow, even in their earliest months, babies can learn to become "Good Samaritans."[40] How hard is it to learn altruism? Well, let's put it this way: It's a rare human who can never learn to read. But haven't you met a lot of people who missed out on altruism?

Most important of all, in his first months of life, your baby learns to relate to you. He develops a sense of trust. He discovers how great it is to feel loved. He's coming to grips with the world inside and outside himself. He's learning what this beautiful new world looks, smells, tastes, feels, and sounds like. And that's *a lot* to do.

Suppose you bombard your baby with reading lessons. Fine, you may teach him to read. But are you distracting him from profounder pursuits? Will he concentrate so hard on his ABCs that he misses altruism or that ineffable Euclidean geometry stuff? He just might.

Equally important, being concerned only about your baby's IQ and how he performs on textbook tasks focuses *your* attention exclusively on what your baby knows or does rather than on how he feels and who he is. Enthusiastically teaching your baby a lot of facts can not only be boring but distract you from the truly important things your baby is designed to learn at this age (such as playing creatively and happily with you). Too much emphasis on what scientists call cognition may lead to too little concern for your baby's precious feelings. Yet your baby is both a thinking and a feeling being. And, as you'll see in Chapter 8, feelings come first.

Every baby comes into this world with a special biological makeup that's exclusively his. Never before and never again will there be a baby quite like yours. He has things to learn on his own, at his own beautiful rate—not at some regimented rate prescribed in a textbook by a self-styled expert who never even met your baby.

People who insist you should turn your baby into a *better* baby simply misunderstand. Your baby is already super. He's already the best baby he can be. Giving your baby lessons not only can rob him of his babyhood and distract him from profounder pursuits but can take away a lot of the joy you as a parent deserve. There are many real challenges that come with raising a baby. Why add pseudo challenges like reading lessons to the list?

So the next time someone tries to tell you of a baby that does great things (implying yours doesn't), you have an answer. You can say you feel your baby isn't ready to specialize yet, that he has far more important skills to learn than reading, and that he's already mastering profounder tasks than long division—without special lessons.

Now that you've seen why Superbabies aren't worth worrying about, let's see why you don't have to worry about being a Supermom, either.

2 The All-Powerful Supermom Trap

I don't know what I did, but I did it, I know. . . . Everything you do has something to do with me.

—*Mother talking to her suicidal daughter
in Marsha Norman's* 'night, Mother

What's a perfect mother? We hear too much about loving mothers making homosexuals, and neglectful mothers making crooks, and commonplace mothers stifling intelligence. The whole mother business needs radical reexamination.

—*From Robertson Davies' novel* The Rebel Angels

Everywhere I turn today, mothers are torn with anxiety and guilt. When she finds marijuana in her teenage son's room or learns her sixteen-year-old daughter is taking the pill, a mother invariably recites a litany of her own failures: "I knew I should have been stricter (or more lenient), never gone to work, refused to let her date that creepy boy, etc., etc."

Even when her child has relatively minor problems, Mother suspects she's somehow to blame. One mother whose fourteen-year-old son, Patrick, got an F in freshman algebra, said, "Why didn't I buy him that computer? Why didn't I send him to summer math camp? Now he'll never get into college—and it's all my fault."

As Jerome Kagan, professor of human development at Harvard, so aptly puts it, "Today we live in a complex society in which 25-year-olds try to explain why they didn't get into law school or why they got divorced. And we have a simple answer: 'Your mother did it to you.' "[1]

Are mothers to blame for everything that happens to their children? Are mothers the cause of all the neuroses on earth?

No. And it's about time somebody told you so.

THE SCAPEGOATING OF MOTHERS

It's hardly surprising if you *think* you're to blame for all your child's problems. After all, self-styled child-rearing experts have been scapegoating mothers for decades. When Paula J. Caplan, Ph.D., and Ian Hall-McCorquodale of the Ontario Institute for Studies in Education recently looked at the phenomenon of mother blaming in major psychological and psychiatric journals, they found that in the 125 articles studied, mothers were blamed for a whopping seventy-two different kinds of psychopathology. The problems mothers allegedly "caused" their children to suffer included: aggressiveness, agitation, agoraphobia, anorexia nervosa, arson, bad dreams, chronic vomiting, delinquency, failure to mourn (also premature mourning), hyperactivity, marijuana use, minimal brain damage, moodiness, poor concentration, sibling jealousy, suicidal behavior, tantrums, timidity, truancy, and something called "self-induced television epilepsy."

Dr. Caplan and her colleagues observed, "In no article was the mother's relationship with the child described as simply healthy, nor was she ever described only in positive terms."[2]

In another article, the same researchers state,

As long as mothers are held to be primarily responsible for their children's emotional adjustment, a dangerous source of intense anxiety, self-deprecation, and fear will be brought to the relationships many mothers have with their infants. For many women, the pervasiveness of mother-blaming means that when they give birth or adopt a baby, they put themselves in a spotlight where, should anything go wrong, they will almost surely be accused. In view of this it is perhaps remarkable than any mothers can relax at all. There are very few jobs in which one individual will be blamed for anything that goes wrong, and fewer still in which what can go wrong, and the feeling of being blamed, are so devastating.[3]

Dr. Caplan and her colleague's conclusion? This scapegoating of mothers must stop.

As a mother, you're *not* the master builder of your child's entire future. Certainly your role is important. You do play a major part in your baby's growth. But there are many other influences in this complex world that help determine how your child will grow up: television, peers, school, teachers, *Time* magazine, Hollywood, the child's father, siblings, and other close relatives . . . not to mention the child himself. What mother-blaming experts continually overlook is that how your child grows depends, to a great extent, on the choices *he* or *she* makes. Two children exposed to the same experience will not react identically. Let's say a child fails to win a major prize after working six months for it. Energetic Doralin may take this setback in stride and vow to try even harder next time. Less assertive, more sensitive Myron may be devastated for three months. Mothers have very little control over many events that happen to children . . . and to blame you for *all* your child's problems is highly unrealistic—and unfair.

THE RESULT OF SCAPEGOATING: THE SUPERMOM TRAP

Unfortunately, too many mothers have been convinced they have total control over their child's destiny. They then begin trying too hard. They fall into what I call the Supermom Trap. You know you've been caught in the Supermom Trap when you find yourself thinking, "I'm going to take all the right steps with my baby. I'll never make a mistake."

What's wrong with this? There's nothing wrong with the *motive*. It's admirable you want to do the best for your baby. What's wrong is the anxiety that follows: How, exactly, will you do "everything right"? Many experts will pretend they know all the right answers. They'll say if you just follow their formula, you'll turn your child into the Most Perfect Adult Who Ever Lived. But just *listen* to some of the crazy advice offered!

Depending on who's talking, you're told that to be a good mother, you should: Give your baby swim lessons; learn P.E.T. (parent effectiveness training); spend fifteen minutes a day doing infant exercises; go to parent school; use non-saggy diapers; stay home four months to bond with your baby; teach your baby to read and count; toilet train in a day; buy your baby a walker; buy a SIDS monitor; never spank; dare to discipline; make your own baby food; etc., etc. If you watched all the TV shows and read all the books and articles (which, luckily for you, you can't begin to manage), the ways you'd have to behave and the things you'd have to do to be a truly good mother run into the thousands.

Don't believe it.

The latest research reveals you can best help your baby thrive, not by making sure you take all the "right" steps and being Supermom, but by relaxing and being yourself. Even more reassuring, the latest research shows that among the vast majority of mothers—those who, like you, love their baby and are trying to do the best job they can—*there are no bad mothers.* You don't have to follow all the "right" prescriptions and take all the "right" steps to be a good parent because, frankly, there *is* no one right prescription or step that works. There are as many wonderful ways to raise a baby as there are babies and parents.

If the right steps you take don't determine your baby's future psychological health, why do we think they do? Mostly this "right step" mentality is left over from the first half of this century, when nearly all child-rearing experts thought that the ways we behave as adults can usually be traced back directly to some "cause" in our childhoods. A major figure (and one of the most influential in child-rearing science) was Sigmund Freud. So let's talk about his theories first.

A BRIEF SUPERMOM HISTORY

More than any other writer of his day, Freud believed your baby's early years are crucial to his future development. According to Freud's "libidinal theory," all babies went through three developmental stages (oral, anal, and genital). During each stage, Freud suggested, you had to satisfy certain needs or your baby might become locked into that stage permanently. The baby's first year or so, for example, was the "oral stage," in which he had to have all his sucking, biting, and swallowing needs fulfilled. If you gave your baby enough oral gratification during this time, he'd breeze happily on to the next growth stage. If you didn't, he'd become frustrated, "fixate" on this stage, and grow up to have an "oral personality." Among his personality quirks, he'd be overly dependent and passive and have a lot of "mouth habits," like smoking, chewing on pencils, and biting his fingernails. Similarly, if your baby got hung up in his anal stage (which he might if you potty-trained too harshly), he'd later wet his bed and become an adult with an "anal" character, meaning he'd be stubborn, stingy, and extremely fastidious—a bit like Felix Unger in Neil Simon's *The Odd Couple*.

Freud never wrote a child-rearing book and he even specifically *stated* that you couldn't necessarily use his theories to predict how a child would turn out.[4] Nevertheless, many of Freud's misguided followers tried to stretch his ideas to tell you precisely what you should and shouldn't do if you wanted to raise an emotionally healthy child.

According to so-called Freudian advice (which actually wasn't *Freud's* advice at all), to keep from doing your baby grave psychological harm you had to walk a tightrope between loving your baby too much (in which case you'd "spoil" him and he'd become a perennial adolescent) and loving him too little (in which case he'd become, in one so-called Freudian's words, one of the "great enemies of humanity"[5]). Basing their advice on the old mechanistic views of man, which began in the 1600s and are only now being abandoned (an idea I'll discuss fully in Chapter 4), these and other child-rearing experts in the first half of this century saw your effect on your baby in a very simple, cause-effect, push-button way. If you pushed Button A (toilet-trained harshly), they preached, you'd get Result B (a Felix Ungerish adult).

The child-rearing advice at that time (advice which still lingers with us today) was extremely rigid. If you missed a stage (say, for example, you failed to give your baby all the sucking he needed precisely when he needed it), it was forever too late.* Only through psychoanalysis (or if you were from another psychological school, some other form of therapy) could your child ever undo the harm you'd done. Child-rearing advice in the first half of this century was also rife with mother blaming. As a mother, you were supposedly the source of all your child's problems and character flaws,

---

* This idea that you must do it now or never is similar to the outmoded critical-periods concept some early-learning advocates still use today to try to convince you that you must teach your baby lots of facts or stimulate him just so at a certain time or it will be forever too late. For more about this critical-periods myth, see page 44.

including his fears, stuttering, aggression, daydreaming, laziness, lying, and stealing.[6]

Such advice, which pictured the baby as frail, impressionable, and helpless in the face of myriad early traumas that could make him "neurotic," placed enormous burdens on mothers. If your son turned out "badly," it was often because of some ignorant blunder you'd made before your child could even talk.

Unfortunately, many rigid child-rearing formulas from the first half of this century still bias our ideas about raising babies today. Among the misguided views we have left over from the past are: (1) the idea that the early years of your baby's life are all-critical and fraught with potential blunders; (2) the myth that mothers "cause" all the neuroses on earth; (3) the notion that babies are passive, robot-like creatures you can program for better or worse with innumerable "right" or "wrong" steps; and (4) the unrealistic concept that you can raise the perfect baby by just following a few oversimplified, sweeping, cause-effect rules, such as: "Breast-feed your baby [the cause] and you'll have a closer relationship [the effect]" and "You have to hold your baby right after birth [the cause] or you won't bond properly [the effect]." The overwhelming message that emerged from the early part of this century was that you, as an all-controlling Supermom, had better take all the "right" steps if you want your baby to grow up psychologically healthy.

BUT DO ALL THE "RIGHT" STEPS DETERMINE YOUR BABY'S FUTURE?

Do you, by all the specific ways you care for your baby, determine the baby's future psychological adjustment? Will a breast-fed baby, for instance, have lasting advantages over a bottle-fed baby? If you feed your baby on a self-demand schedule, will he turn out more confident and happy than if you force him to conform to your rigid timetable? Does traumatic potty training necessarily doom your child to be a bed-wetter and leave him with lasting emotional hang-ups? In short, does every little step you take shape your child's future?

During the 1940s and '50s, scores of scientists decided to find out. They looked at lots of individual "right" and "wrong" steps, from harsh-versus-gentle toilet training, quick-versus-gradual weaning, swaddling, and feeding schedules, to how much the babies were rocked during their first five days of life. Thorough reviews[7] of the mountains of research reached one overwhelming conclusion: Specific "right" or "wrong" steps taken during your baby's early years do *not* have a rigidly determined, lasting effect on his psychological growth. If you influence the kind of adult your baby will become (and you *do*), it's through methods other than anxiously watching over every little step you take. As Rudolph Schaffer, Ph.D., professor of psychology at the University of Strathclyde in Glasgow, Scotland, observes in *Mothering*, published by Harvard University Press, "If the child is father of the man, it is for reasons other than missing out on the breast and a too early acquaintance with the potty."[8]

WHERE DID THE OLD IDEAS GO ASTRAY?

Why didn't the old "right-step" advice hold up? For three reasons.

First, as you already know, experts in the early half of this century assumed a baby is like a robot, who has to respond on cue when Button A is pushed. Babies, of course, are real, competent persons, who have some say in how they'll respond. Let's say you *wanted* to be a lousy parent: You purposely set out to do "everything wrong." Your baby is so individual he might turn out okay, anyway! Certainly I'm not suggesting you *try* to make mistakes. Every child has an inalienable right to be loved by a parent who's trying to help him. I'm only saying babies aren't predictable in the linear, cause-effect way right-step thinkers would have you believe.

Second, experts in the first half of this century (especially misguided "Freudians") tried to trace adult emotional hang-ups back to specific ways the mother treated her baby early in his life. They ignored the overall pattern of a mother's relationship with her baby. Why did a mother wean her baby early? Did she hate breast feeding and dislike all physical touching? Was she always aloof? Or was early weaning her attempt to encourage her baby to be independent? How did her baby feel about all this? Was he content to give up the breast early? If a mother potty-trained severely, *how* severely? Did she and her baby have an otherwise happy, warm relationship? How did the baby's father fit into the picture?

By focusing only on small, fragmented steps rather than on the whole parent-baby relationship, right-step thinkers were looking at too narrow a range of behaviors. Trying to explain how you affect your baby over his entire childhood by looking at a few specific steps you took during his infancy would be a lot like trying to describe a pointillist painting by Seurat by looking at three or four colored dots in one corner. You see the small pieces accurately, but you miss the much more important way the pieces fit together. In the same way you can miss the whole pattern of a painting by focusing only on its tiniest parts, a child-rearing expert can miss the much more important overall pattern of your relationship with your baby by focusing on only a few "right" or "wrong" steps.

Third—and highly important—right-step thinkers didn't know what we now know about a baby's ability to adapt (scientists call this adaptability *plasticity*). They presumed (and many experts still do) that once your baby has any experience, that experience is indelibly etched into his brain for life and may later emerge as a neurosis. Dr. Jerome Kagan has called this idea the "tape recorder" theory of development and says it "assumes that from the first day of life every salient experience is recorded somewhere in the brain and never erased."[9] This notion puts an enormous burden on you as a parent. If every *second* of your child's life is recorded in his brain and never erased, then even your slightest "mistake" (merely one cruel word spoken in anger, for example) can damage your child's psyche forever.

Fortunately, studies in the past thirty years have shown this is simply not so. Brain researchers like Arthur H. Parmelee at the University of California in Los Angeles, Dr. P. R. Huttenlocher at the Joseph P. Kennedy Mental Retardation Center at the University of Chicago, and many others have found that your baby's brain is much less rigid and more flexible than misguided right-step thinkers realize. The connections in your baby's rapidly developing, ever-changing brain aren't made once and then kept forever, but they continually shift and change as your baby discovers the world.[10]

This brain plasticity means your baby will adjust to or even forget your minor mistakes (so long as the results aren't terribly traumatic or the mistakes aren't continually repeated). As famed neurobiologist Roger W. Sperry, who won the Nobel Prize for his brain research on right versus left brain functions, once said when talking about brain plasticity:

> One wonders if it is not more in the deep recesses of questionable psychiatric theory than in the minds of infants that the Oedipus and other such complexes really thrive. Infants and very young children would seem by nature to be comparatively resistent to psychic damage. Much more than in later years, the tendency in ages 1 to 4 is to accept and forget. *This applies to ordinary, average growth and experience, not to extremes of experiential deprivation and trauma* [italics added].[11]

In other words, brain plasticity means that if a parent did something terribly cruel to a baby (say, he or she locked the baby in a dark room for a year or totally ignored the baby except to feed or change him), naturally that horrid experience could have some strong, lasting effect (though precisely *what* effect we can't know for certain, since every baby reacts his own special way). Plasticity doesn't mean, as some misguided experts suggest, that a child is so invulnerable you can do anything to him and he'll turn out fine.[12]

What plasticity *does* mean is that your small, inadvertent, minor mistakes and each specific step you take when raising your baby are a lot less crucial than you've been told. If you're a normally warm, caring parent and just happen to slip up on Tuesday (say, you're in the shower and your baby cries an extra twenty minutes because you didn't hear him wake up), of course you may want to hug your baby to make amends. Happily, plasticity teaches us, you *can* make amends. Your baby may be more upset than usual for a few minutes (maybe even for a few hours if he's especially sensitive). But you can rest assured this small incident won't be etched in his brain forever.

In short, you're free at last from the thankless chore of straining to be Supermom and fretting that your tiniest decision will somehow mold your baby for the rest of his life. Whether you decide to breast or bottle feed or to give swim lessons or not, to cite two examples, won't make or break your baby's whole future. Rather than struggling to figure out just the "right" thing to do every second you're with your baby, you can relax and just enjoy being with him. Nature is much kinder and more flexible than right-step cause-effect thinkers would have you believe.

WHY ARTIFICIALLY ADJUSTING YOUR ATTITUDE
WON'T MAKE YOU A SUPERMOM, EITHER

Okay, maybe any given decision you make will neither make nor break your baby. But certainly your whole *attitude* toward your baby must determine his development, right?

Not necessarily.

"Attitude" is a tricky word because it has so many meanings. But in the sense I use it here, I'll limit its meaning to one definition in my Webster's dictionary: "A position assumed to serve a purpose." The purpose is to be a Supermom. And the operative word is "assumed."

You'll often hear that to be a good mother, you have to adjust your attitude to become a specific parent "type." Depending on which book you read, you may be told you should be a Democratic (as opposed to an Authoritarian) parent, an A parent (as opposed to a B one), or an Assertive parent (presumably as opposed to a milquetoast). If you dislike spanking, you're told you should "dare to discipline." If you spank, you're advised to be more understanding. In short, it seems you can only be a good parent by becoming someone you're not.

Nonsense.

This notion that you can raise a healthy, happy child only if you adopt one "right" attitude sprang originally from a series of parent attitude studies done in the 1950s and '60s. They were done by cause-effect thinkers who wouldn't give up. When their "right steps" didn't pan out, some researchers began casting about for better ways to explain how you mold your baby. They decided that cause-effect thinking was still basically correct: Mothers do create neurotics. But maybe you had to understand a mother's overall *attitude* toward her baby to see how she wielded this enormous power. Researchers were still seeking direct, linear causes and effects so they could label some mothers good and others bad. But now they were looking for broader causes: your entire set of attitudes.

One of the most famous attitude studies in the 1950s was done by Robert Sears, Eleanor Maccoby, and Harry Levin at Harvard, who asked 379 mothers of five-year-olds extremely detailed questions about how they'd raised their children. Their questions covered every practice, from feeding, weaning, and potty training to how the mothers felt about spanking and hugging, how they'd felt during their pregnancies, and whether or not they were happily married.[13]

Extensive parent attitude research was also done by Earl S. Schaefer, who devised a questionnaire that is still used today, called the Parental Attitude Research Inventory (PARI). The PARI assesses your attitudes by having you agree or disagree with such statements as "Children should realize how much parents have to give up for them" and "A child will be grateful later on for strict training."[14]

What emerged from these and other attitude studies were profiles of many parental "types." Parents were variously classed as permissive versus restrictive, emotionally involved versus calmly detached, democratic versus authoritarian, and so forth. Certain types of parents were said to produce certain kinds of kids. In the classic Sears, Maccoby, Levin study, for example, the most aggressive children were supposedly raised by extremely permissive parents who occasionally broke down and punished severely. Harsh potty training was found to damage a child most if the mother was also cold and unaffectionate. These findings quickly became child-rearing "fact" and made their way into how-to books as still more "shoulds" for you to follow.[15]

Again, the research failed to hold up. For the results of any study to be accepted scientifically, that study has to be replicated— and the same results produced—by other teams of scientists. Yet when other researchers, including Dr. Marian Radke Yarrow and her team at the National Institute of Mental Health, tried to duplicate the Sears findings, they couldn't.[16] In short, cause-effect notions, even when broadly applied to sets of attitudes, didn't hold up. Trying to adjust your attitude so you'll fit a prescribed parent profile isn't necessary, either.

Why can't you follow a formula for turning yourself into the perfect parent "type" to raise a better baby? Probably because none of us is so rigid we fit neatly into any one "type." Like your baby, you're far too individual to be simplistically categorized. You may be permissive about thumb sucking, but quite authoritarian about using the velvet chair as a trampoline. The notion that you could—or worse, should—force yourself into a narrow category is growth inhibiting and denies your uniqueness.

If neither taking right steps nor adjusting your attitude to fit a set formula explains how you shape your baby, what does? To answer that, we need to leave behind the shadowy world of simple cause-effect chains and enter the bright, new, more complex world of systems.

HOW YOU DO INFLUENCE YOUR BABY: THROUGH YOUR FAMILY SYSTEM

If you don't determine your baby's future by taking specific steps or adopting just the right attitude, must you merely sit back, do nothing, and trust nature to guide your baby's growth? Until recently, that's about the only alternative you were offered. Either you strained to be an Omnipotent Supermom (or increasingly, Superdad) by trying to control your child's entire future, or you sat back, put blind trust in nature's plan, and let your child's personhood slowly unfold like a blossoming flower.

Now you have another option. It's a choice many parents have already made; in fact, it's mostly by studying parents and their babies interacting at home that scientists have come to the new view. The difference between the old way of thinking about you and your baby and the new child-rearing approach is so profoundly revolutionary it can be likened to the difference between Newton's and Einstein's views of the universe.[17] Yet while the implications of this new vision are quite profound, the ideas behind the new view are amazingly simple. This new approach to child rearing simply says that you and your baby are a system.

What's a system? A system isn't a *thing;* it's a *process.* In the sense that I'll use the term throughout this book, a system is simply two or more people interacting with each other in an ongoing way. The "ongoing" part is important. Two strangers who meet in an elevator, ride up to the twelfth floor together, then get off and never see each other again aren't a system because they don't influence each other over time. In contrast, you and your baby do influence each other, not only from one minute to the next but over months and years. What you and your baby did yesterday will very likely be connected in many subtle ways to how you and your baby interact tomorrow. Systems explain not simple causes and effects but complex interactions between people.

As you just saw, the old child-rearing idea was that you influence your baby (supposedly a passive, robotic object) in an observable, linear, cause-effect way. By potty training severely, the old right-step thinkers insisted, *you affect your baby.* Case closed.

In an ongoing system (which allows your baby to be the active, individual person he is), simple causes and effects can't be easily traced, because you and your baby are continuously changing and affecting *each other* in many complex ways. In your family system, what counts most isn't all the individual steps you take, but your and your baby's overall "fit." It's how beautifully you and your baby "dance" together that most influences your baby's growth.

That's why even poor potty training (to use a favorite example from the past) won't necessarily harm your baby or give him a special type of personality. Suppose, just for argument's sake, that despite all your best intentions you do a really "lousy" job of potty training (which I'm sure you won't, because potty training's not *that* hard). If you and your baby have an overall warm, joyous, strong relationship (or what scientists call a stable system), it's quite likely the baby will adjust. Far from being damaged for life, your baby may well develop normally, as if nothing unusual had happened.

Some harshly potty-trained babies may (as some old-fashioned cause-effect thinkers said) go on to become emotionally troubled adults. But if so, that's because insensitive potty training often goes hand in hand with a hundred thousand other insensitivities. The mother who potty trains severely may also call her child a brat ten times a day, berate her child for being "stupid," spank for the slightest offense, etc. In short, it's the entire insensitive system, not the single innocent mistake, that eventually does the child emotional and mental harm.

That's why you can relax and not worry about every little step you take with your baby. You can mess up, and rather than suffering from guilt and possibly disrupting your dance (your system), you can decide, "Hey, I won't do that again," and go on. In a warm, loving, caring family system full of mutual trust and respect, there's plenty of time for both you and your baby to adjust. And you *will* adjust.

The importance of your *whole* parent-baby system (which is expressed through your dance) is also the reason it's not such a great idea to fret over every trivial step you take. Straining to be

Supermom forces you to pay attention only to yourself and how you're performing. Emphasizing only the right steps you take or the right attitude you have forces the spotlight away from the dance you and your baby are doing and aims it only at you. Thus, rather than dancing joyously with her baby, Supermom is dancing alone.

Of course, it's all very well for me to say, "Don't fret over every minute decision," quite another for you to know which so-called right steps to ignore. Even after knowing your baby is flexible, you may still wonder, "Yes, but what if I didn't bond with my baby right after birth?" or "Is breast milk really healthier than formula?" Some concerns you may have about your baby are certainly appropriate. It's important to make sure he's getting enough to eat, for example. But many things you may worry about are what I call TICs.

3 Banishing TICs from Your Parenting Style

What do you mean, "Don't worry about nonsense"? I've worried about nonsense since the day you were born.

—*Mother talking to her college-bound daughter*

Sometime between ages twelve and twenty, we learn that good mothers are supposed to worry. Like some emotional barometer, worry supposedly measures the level of your love. Good mothers worry a lot. So the myth goes.

Believing the myth, many of us feel downright obligated to worry about our children, just to prove we're doing the best job we can do. I'll never forget the mother I read about who was in a pediatrician's waiting room one day. She was there with her bouncy, cherubic three-year-old, named Nathan, who was obviously healthy and just seeing the doctor for his six-month checkup. At first Nathan played happily alone, trying to stack alphabet blocks in the children's play area. But soon he spotted a book—*Little Red Riding Hood*—and carried it to his mother, begging her to read him the story. Cuddling her toddler on her lap, the mother read until she reached the part where the Big Bad Wolf gobbles up Grandmother. Suddenly, the mother clutched Nathan tightly to her and said, "The Grandmother died. But don't you worry about that, sweetheart. I'll never die and leave you, okay?"

Nathan stared blankly at her for about three seconds and then replied, "So then what happened?"

Moral: When parenting, it's incredibly easy to worry about nonexistent problems. Children aren't always as emotionally fragile as you've been led to believe.

It's all very well, of course, for me to say, "Don't worry," quite another matter to sort Trivial Inconsequential Concerns (which I call TICs) from legitimate problems. It's especially difficult to ignore an issue like bonding or breast feeding when you've heard you *should* worry about this if you want your baby to become the best adult he can be.

Ours is such a media-dominated age that hardly a day passes when you don't hear of another discovery about babies or a new infant program designed to boost your baby's potential. You may then wonder, "What should I do about this? Does this finding change how I should treat my baby?"

This chapter is designed to give you information about many specific concerns and help you separate TICs from more legitimate worries.

Not all the following questions may concern you. (If you're lucky, you may not even have heard of some of these issues.) If you're not a worrier by nature, you may want to browse through this chapter just to see what other mothers worry about. Or you may want to read just those sections that deal with issues you've heard of and feel puzzled by. Though I could list hundreds of TICs here, mothers tell me the following ideas are among the most angst-provoking around. So let's examine them closer.

BIRTH-ORDER DIFFERENCES: DO THEY EXIST? SHOULD YOU TRY TO COMPENSATE?

You'll often hear that first-borns tend to become conservative, high-achieving, brilliant perfectionists, whereas last-borns grow up to be manipulative, charming, engaging show-offs. Meanwhile, middle-borns supposedly feel squeezed, dominated, and neglected and thus develop into confused, insecure adults who avoid conflict.

The idea that your baby's birth order largely determines the type of adult he'll become originated with Sigmund Freud. His comment that "a child's position in the sequence of brothers and sisters is of very great significance for the course of his later life"[1] sent researchers out to do studies . . . and they found many birth-order differences.

A few experts have even carried birth-order ideas to extremes by telling you precisely how you "should" raise your first, last, or middle child for best results. To give you just one example, in *The Birth Order Book: Why You Are the Way You Are,* psychologist Kevin Leman writes, "Each birth order is different. You have to treat each birth order with certain distinctive techniques and under-standing." He then goes on to list some fairly moderate parenting tips, such as: Don't turn your first child into an "instant babysitter"; make sure your middle child doesn't always have to wear hand-me-downs; don't underdiscipline the last-born "baby" of the family, and so forth.[2]

Even if you haven't read a book on birth-order differences (and frankly, few mothers have), you may pick up on the subtle message that you have to treat your middle-born, first, or only child "just so" if you want him to turn out okay. *Do* you have to know all about birth-order differences so you can adjust your parenting style accordingly?

No. And here's why:

There *is* much evidence that even newborns differ depending on their birth order. Not only does the mother's physiology change with a second-born[3] (so second-borns begin with different environments even in the womb), but mothers treat first-born and subsequent babies differently during their first hours together. In one of my studies years ago at Stanford, I observed both first-time and experienced mothers as they breast-fed their two-day-old infants. Compared to experienced mothers, first-timers spent more time feeding male infants, provided more stimulation for their babies, talked to their babies more (and talked to girls far more than boys), and were less sensitive to their babies' signals.[4] But such differences have to be detected in very carefully designed studies, with extremely sensitive measures of the mothers' and babies' behavior. Also, these differences only apply to babies and mothers on the *average*, not to each and every baby and mother.

In addition to myriad subtle differences at birth, each baby is born into a different family system. The number of brothers and sisters the baby has, the ages of his brothers and sisters, the sex of his siblings, etc., all combine to make an extremely complex situation in which no simple "birth-order effects" can be traced.

Thus, despite what Leman and others claim, no one can look at *any* baby, child, or adult and say with great accuracy: "That person was first born" or "That one was last." Nor is it possible in most cases to look at a mother and say whether she's caring for her first, second, or third baby. The differences are far too subtle and varied for you to work consciously to overcome them.

Some parenting compensations may be useful (I'll give birth-order enthusiasts this much). For example, you may have to work harder to find playmates for your first child. Also, your pleasures will differ from one child to the next. The intense excitement and surprises you enjoy with your first baby may give way to eager anticipation with your second. And your second baby may benefit because you may be less preoccupied with "shoulds" the second time around. Still, birth order isn't a concern to take very seriously. Your dance may be more exciting with your first baby, easier with later ones. But just because the dances differ delightfully doesn't make any dance better or worse.

BREAST VERSUS BOTTLE FEEDING: WHICH SHOULD YOU DO?

In some circles, breast feeding is so in vogue that if you want to bottle feed you may feel you're letting your baby down. That's a TIC. Breast feed only because you want to, not because you think you should.

If you haven't decided yet whether you want to breast or bottle feed, here are some answers that may help you decide:

• *Is breast milk really better or purer than prepared formulas?* Yes and no. Breast milk *does* offer some health advantages prepared formulas don't. For example, a yellowish liquid (called colostrum) secreted by the breast the first few days you nurse contains substances that provide immunity to some diseases. (This is important in underdeveloped countries, where diseases run rampant, perhaps less crucial in countries like ours, where disease is more under control.) Breast milk also has fewer calories and contains more easily digestible protein.

On the other hand, your nutrition clearly affects your breast milk. Such substances as alcohol, caffeine (found in tea and colas as well as coffee), nicotine, and even the hormones in birth control pills can be passed on to a baby through breast milk and be potentially harmful.[5] If you want to drink seven cups of coffee or smoke three packs of cigarettes a day, chances are you'll provide healthier milk for your baby by bottle feeding.

There's also little evidence for the claim that formula milk contains DDT and other poisons. Some studies have, in fact, shown that compared to cow milk, human milk contains higher concentrations of DDT (but both levels are far below the danger level and still safe).[6]

• *Does breast feeding enhance the feeling of closeness between a baby and a mother?* It depends on you. If you nurse, you'll feel a different kind of closeness with your baby. Nursing mothers, for example, often feel a sensation in their breasts when their babies cry.[7] But this difference is neither better nor worse than the intimacy bottle feeding mothers (and fathers) enjoy.

• *Isn't breast feeding more confining?* Yes and no. On one hand, it can be a hassle to boil bottles nightly if you choose Pyrex bottles (which is a certain kind of restriction). Of course, you can use prepared formula that comes in disposable bottles. On the other hand, if you're employed away from home and have to leave your baby with a sitter, you may find breast feeding quite difficult (though you can express milk from your breasts by hand or with a breast pump and store it in bottles for your baby). If you dislike the idea of breast feeding in public, then of course when you're out with your baby you'll have to find a private spot when he's hungry.

To decide whether to breast or bottle feed, you might also ask yourself: If I want to breast feed, how long? Three days, three months, or six months? Does the baby's father want to feed the baby? If so, how will we handle that? Do we want to give the baby bottles sometimes and the breast at others?

Above all, remember that though your decision to breast or bottle feed may matter to you, your baby's overall development will be more affected by *how* you feed (how you smile, talk to, cuddle, and look at your baby while he nurses) than by which method you choose. Both breast- and bottle-fed babies turn out happy, bright, healthy, and well-adjusted.[8]

PRENATAL PSYCHOLOGY: CAN YOU MAKE YOUR BABY NEUROTIC IN THE WOMB?

A relatively new TIC is the notion that if you're extremely anxious, stressed, or depressed when you're pregnant, your negative emotions will have a long-term negative impact on your baby. In *The Secret Life of the Unborn Child*, Canadian psychiatrist Thomas Verny insists that how you feel while pregnant is vital to your baby's future psychological development and warns that if you're very anxious during pregnancy, your baby could be well on his way to being schizophrenic, alcoholic, or highly compulsive.[9]

This is nonsense.

Fetuses *do* react to their uterine environment. When you're pregnant, your baby hears your voice . . . and after birth, he prefers your voice above all others. Your baby's biological rhythms are also influenced by yours. And of course what you eat or drink affects your baby (Valium crosses the placenta so fast it can put a fetus to sleep in minutes).[10] Some damage—especially physical damage—in the womb is irreversible. Mothers who took the drug Thalidomide, for example, had babies born with incompletely formed arms and legs.

But *psychological* influences in the womb are much more subtle. The notion that just because you were anxious during pregnancy your baby will be harmed, and there's little you can do about it, totally ignores all the current findings about plasticity and resilience I discussed in Chapter 2. As University of Colorado psychotherapist Charles Spezzano has aptly pointed out, "All evidence to date encourages parents to avoid pregnancy paranoia, in which they begin to fear that every wrong move they make will doom their child to an abnormal future."[11]

In short, this notion is a TIC.

AREN'T THERE CRITICAL PERIODS IN CHILD REARING?

If you haven't heard of critical periods, don't worry about them. But if you have, let's talk.

The idea of critical learning periods is used by some early-learning advocates as a major reason why you'd better get busy and teach your baby everything from how to read to how to speak Japanese. According to this idea, your baby's brain is "wired" on a rigid, set schedule and if you fail to teach precisely the "right" skills at the "right" times (the critical periods), it will be forever too late.

This notion puts enormous burdens on you as a parent. You're left feeling that your baby has dozens of make-or-break periods in his early years, so you'd better watch every step you take. If you don't, anxiety-provoking experts warn, your baby will never be as successful, bright, witty, learned, or talented as he *could* have become. Such experts then often go on to give you a rigid teaching program to follow to stimulate your baby just so at just the right times, so you won't screw him up.[12]

Does your baby have critical periods, during which you have to teach him specific skills, facts, or concepts or it will be forever too late?

No.

Some animals (particularly birds) seem to have critical periods in their early development. A baby chick, for example, has to learn to peck for food a few days after hatching, or it may never learn. Later, a chicken so deprived can stand in a roomful of grain and starve to death.[13] Likewise, some songbirds kept from hearing other birds sing during the first weeks of life may never sing well.[14]

But humans are incredibly more complex than birds. We can learn skills, facts, and concepts *all* our lives. As psychiatrist Peter Wolff at Harvard has noted in such reputable journals as *Pediatrics*[15] and *Hospital Practice*,[16] all available evidence does not support the claim that your baby has critical periods during which you have to stimulate him just so if you want him to be the best person he can be.

Your baby does have certain *sensitive* periods when he can master some skills more easily (walking and talking, for instance, are learned most easily during the early years). But these sensitive periods are not, as some experts anxiously warn, a learn-it-now-or-never time. Nor are these periods as subtle or as easily overlooked as you may have heard. The notion that you'd better get busy and teach your baby tons of facts or it will be forever too late is a TIC.

BONDING: WHAT DOES IT MEAN? HOW CRUCIAL IS IT FOR YOUR BABY'S GROWTH?

Some parents unable to hold their baby right after delivery anxiously fear they've missed their chance to "bond" early and have somehow harmed their whole future relationship. But scientists now know early bonding is much less all-critical than was once thought.

About ten years ago, many researchers *did* believe holding your baby right after birth was essential for a good relationship. After-birth bonding was said to make you a better parent, raise the odds of success at breast feeding, and enhance your baby's self-esteem, IQ, and ability to relate to others. Fortunately, the extreme, more angst-provoking aspects of bonding have now been discarded.

The early bonding studies were done mostly with mothers who had few social supports. Follow-up studies didn't show the positive effects from early togetherness that the earlier studies had.[17] In their current book, *Parent-Infant Bonding*, pediatricians Marshall H. Klaus and John H. Kennell sum up the latest bonding research when they say:

> In spite of a lack of early contact experienced by parents in hospital births in the past 20 to 30 years, almost all these parents became bonded to their babies. The human is highly adaptable and there are many fail-safe routes to attachment. Sadly, some parents who missed the bonding experience have felt that all was lost for their future relationship. This was (and is) completely incorrect.[18]

So if you don't (or didn't) have a chance to be with your baby right after birth, don't worry about it. You'll still do just fine.

SWIM LESSONS: SHOULD YOUR BABY TAKE THEM?

A recent fad is teaching three-to-six-month-olds to swim. It's been claimed that swim lessons will boost your baby's motor development, raise his IQ, give him confidence, make him swim better when he's an adult, and of course prevent drowning should he fall into a backyard pool.

Do swim lessons provide all these benefits?

No scientific evidence shows early swimming will make your baby smarter, more athletic, or even a better swimmer later. A baby who learns to swim at six months may forget how by the time he's three unless he continues practicing a lot. There's also a danger that knowing your baby can float may lull you into a false sense of security when the baby is around water. It's wise to remember that no one, not even an adult who swims well, is "drown-proof."

Another risk of swim lessons is hyponatremia, a lower than normal concentration of sodium in the bloodstream, which can occur if a baby swallows too much water. How to prevent this? Never let an instructor force your baby's head under water. If your baby swims, take him out of the water if he goes under too often (say, more than a couple of times during a lesson). And if your baby has any hyponatremia symptoms (irritable crying, vomiting, lethargy, disorientation), take him right to a hospital emergency room and tell the doctor he's just been swimming.

Babies who swim in less-than-clean pools can also get ear infections or an infection called giardiasis (a parasite transmitted by feces and sometimes found in water used by babies not yet potty trained).

Having mentioned the major risks, I'll now say swim classes are fine. If lessons are taught gently and lovingly, and involve you as well as your baby, they can be fun. The only object of swimming should be to give you and your baby a special time together. If both of you love water, swimming can be a special part of your dance.

THE BABY WORKOUT: DOES YOUR INFANT NEED EXERCISES?

Many mothers feel guilty if they're not rushing their babies off to infant gym twice weekly or at least doing special infant exercises at home. Again, the touted benefits of infant exercises often sound like old snake-oil sales pitches. Exercises will supposedly boost your baby's confidence, speed his motor development, make him more sociable, and (of course) help him read sooner.

Nonsense. Special exercises, while at times helpful or necessary for a disabled baby, won't help your normal baby any of these ways. If allowed to move and explore, your baby will just naturally master such basic skills as lifting his head, rolling over, reaching for and grasping objects, creeping, crawling, standing, and walking.

Your baby *does* need freedom to move, though. While watching mothers and babies at home, I once observed a loving mother we'll call Carolyn who kept her two babies confined all day to the small kitchen of their rambling ranch house. Why? Because Carolyn was an impeccable housekeeper and didn't want them to get the house messy. When I first saw the children (one was a year old, the other about two), both had slightly delayed motor development because they'd been consistently deprived of freedom to move. In due time, Carolyn let her babies out of their narrow world and allowed them to move freely and explore. They're now developing more normally. But this was an extreme case, in which a basically caring mother had her own hidden agendas (she *had* to have that house clean) and thus failed to recognize her healthy babies' need to crawl and play.

So *do* allow your baby room to explore. You may want to baby-proof one or more rooms by putting all breakables and any harmful substances out of reach, covering all electrical sockets, and making sure no small, swallowable objects like buttons are left on the floor. Or you may prefer keeping your baby in a playpen and allowing him to crawl freely only during those hours when you can give him your full attention. How much freedom you allow depends on you, your living space, and your baby. Some babies will pad around safely on the floor all day; others, the second your back is turned, will be on top of the sofa and doing a swan dive toward the floor. In time, you'll come to know how much freedom you can comfortably—and safely—allow your baby. But freedom to move and explore (necessary) is quite different from formal exercises (optional).

As with swim lessons, it's your choice whether or not to give your baby a regular workout. But if you do:

• Make sure the exercises suit your baby's developmental level. A small baby should never be vigorously shaken or tossed, for example, even in the name of exercise. (His developing neck muscles or even his brain can be injured.)

• Look for exercises or a gym program that allows your baby to take the initiative. Passive exercises, in which you move your baby's arms and legs for him, do nothing to tone his muscles and involve the risk of your moving your baby's limbs too quickly or energetically, spraining an arm or causing other strain.

• Remember, the goal of exercise isn't to make your baby stronger or smarter but to have fun together (it's not just exercising but interacting joyfully with you that makes your baby smarter). So consider your baby's feelings. If he cries, looks scared, or seems upset or tired, it's time to call it a day.

SIDS MONITORS: DOES YOUR BABY NEED ONE?

The possibility of sudden infant death syndrome (SIDS), a mysterious and so far unpreventable malady in which a seemingly healthy infant suddenly dies in his sleep without a cry, understandably frightens many parents. You may even see ads urging you to buy a SIDS monitor to "protect your baby from crib death." Home monitors, which come in various types, sense a baby's breathing and heartbeat as he sleeps and sound a shrill alarm if he stops breathing too long. (Note: *All* babies often stop breathing for two to ten seconds during sleep and even normal babies may have pauses as long as fifteen seconds, which are nothing to worry about.)

Should you buy your baby a monitor? Ask your pediatrician, but she'll probably say no. Monitors are often expensive: three thousand dollars or more for some models (though cheaper models are available and may work equally well). Also, false alarms are common with all types and often cause a lot of lost sleep and undue anxiety surrounding a new baby. Most SIDS researchers, including myself, liken monitors to a drug: If the patient doesn't need the drug, you don't prescribe it.

Which babies do need monitors? Even that's tricky to answer. The monitor issue is complex and growing more so. But here are some facts and figures you may find useful.

• Each year as many as ten thousand infants die from SIDS, making it perhaps the leading killer of babies between the ages of one month and one year. Yet that statistic can be deceptively scary. SIDS actually occurs in 0.2 percent of all babies. Thus SIDS, while extremely serious and tragic, is actually quite rare. The phenomenon most frequently strikes infants between three and six months of age, peaking at three months, tapering off to near-zero incidence in babies over one year old. For some mysterious reason, babies up to three weeks of age seem almost immune.

• Even the term "high-risk SIDS" can be misleading. SIDS is so rare that even high-risk babies seldom succumb. SIDS victims' brothers and sisters are more vulnerable, so naturally distraught parents who have lost one baby to SIDS are often terrified of losing another. Yet even for siblings of SIDS victims, the estimated risk is ten to twenty babies per thousand—ten to twenty times the national norm, yet still only 1 to 2 percent. Thus even parents who have had one baby die of SIDS have a 98 to 99 percent chance that their next baby will be fine.

• Extravagant claims to the contrary, monitors don't necessarily *prevent* SIDS. They only warn a parent if a baby stops breathing for a dangerously long period (usually thirty seconds or longer). To use a monitor properly, you have to learn how to troubleshoot the mechanism, handle false alarms, and administer CPR should a baby require it. All this can be needlessly time-consuming and angst-provoking—especially if your baby hasn't been identified as being at risk, and frequent false alarms can disrupt your and your baby's rhythms (and I'll talk a lot more about rhythms in Chapter 9). It's nerve-racking to be awakened frequently at night by a shrill warning sound coming from your baby's bedroom.

Despite drawbacks, a SIDS monitor may be medically advisable for a few rare babies—especially those subject to prolonged breathing pauses (called apnea). But placing a baby on a monitor requires a talk with your doctor and much careful thought. (If you'd like more information about SIDS, write the National SIDS Foundation, 2 Metro Plaza—Suite 205, 8240 Professional Place, Landover, MD 20785.)

THE QUALITY-TIME TRAP

The term "quality time" was coined by Harvard pediatrician Burton White. When comparing babies of working versus nonworking mothers, Dr. White found both groups of babies throve equally well. Why? Because when career mothers were home, they gave their babies extra-special attention (quality time).

This idea was at first reassuring. Knowing your after-work hours with your baby were so special they made up for your temporary absence, you could relax and not feel guilty about going to work.

The idea is still valid: It is the quality of time spent with your baby that counts most—whether you work or not.

So if quality time is essentially a good idea, why do I call it a trap? Because over the years, quality time has become a TIC. Afraid playing with your baby isn't nearly enough to make up for lost hours, you may feel pressured by countless "experts" to make the most of your precious moments by giving your baby the *ultimate* experience. You're made to feel it's no longer enough to play a gleeful game of Peek-a-boo. Instead, you're left feeling you should be providing a truly meaningful experience—like teaching your baby to read or multiply.

By now you know my reaction to that. *Being* with your baby is much more meaningful than any activity you can *do*. Dancing with your baby, whether you reach around to tickle his tummy every few seconds as you stir the spaghetti sauce or take twenty quiet minutes just to cuddle him closely at the end of a long day, is the highest, best quality time you can give. Your baby doesn't need fast-track lessons, a clever new toy, chocolate-chip cookies made from scratch, or any other presumably perfect family experience. He needs you. Some nights your best gift to your baby may be having a Chinese dinner delivered so you can just unwind and have time to play. Working on your own mental health can help you play more spontaneously with your baby. And relaxed, easygoing, authentic interaction is what true quality time is all about.

DO YOUR MOODS HURT YOUR BABY?

One mother recently told me, "I've felt depressed lately and now my baby seems crankier. Do my blue moods affect him?"

Some babies *are* quite sensitive to your moods. Moods, after all, involve emotions . . . and your baby comes into this world biologically designed to respond to others' feelings. Babies only a few hours old will often start wailing when they hear another newborn cry.[19] Dr. Joseph Campos, a psychologist who specializes in infant emotional development at the University of Denver, finds that some babies only thirty-six hours old can distinguish between happy, sad, or surprised faces and may even respond with happy, sad, or surprised looks of their own.[20]

Of course, each baby reacts to moods his own special way. One baby may always be so bubbly and gleeful he's unaffected when you're glum. Another will be sensitive to your every mood swing. If you have a sensitive infant and you're feeling out of sorts one day, your baby may start acting crabby too. That's normal and nothing to fret about. Negative moods are only in danger of adversely affecting your baby's development if they persist months or years. A baby who lives in a home that's *continually* tense, angry, or sad may show long-term effects. But then it's the entire depressive, angry, or tense dance you're doing, not the temporary mood shift, that hinders your baby's growth. In short, the worry that your normal mood swings might hurt your baby is a TIC.

TYPE A, TYPE B: WHICH KIND OF BABY IS YOURS?

To talk about babies, experts frequently "rubricize" them (that is, lump them all into set categories to make them easier to understand). One doctor will say your baby is one of three types: average, quiet, or active. Another insists your baby is either a competitive, impatient, hard-striving Type A (in which case he'll likely become a heart-attack-prone adult) or a more relaxed Type B baby, or an Alpha versus a Beta infant.[21] Such artificial categories, while fine and even necessary for scientists doing research, can mislead you as a parent. Your underlying feeling when reading of these various types is often: "Well, that's interesting. I wonder which type *my* baby is."

Your baby isn't any "type." He's much too special and complicated to be so easily classified. What bothers me most about lumping all babies into two or three categories is the sense some experts convey that once you determine which type your baby is, you totally understand him. Typecasting can prevent you from looking closely at your baby to see what he's *really* like.

Putting people into a few simple categories is an easy way not to think about them very deeply. We all do this at times. When we ask, "What do you do for a living?" we're trying to sum up a person quickly by knowing his or her occupation. Still, we cringe when someone tries to plunk *us* into an oversimplified category. Don't you get slightly annoyed when someone you've just met says, "Oh, now I understand—you're a Taurus." I'm often tempted to reply, "I may be a Taurus. But if you think that explains me, you're very much mistaken." We resent being rubricized because deep down we know there never has been—or will be again—another person quite like us in the universe.

Your baby is as unique as you are. The chance of another baby having even one fingerprint exactly like your baby's is said to be less than one in sixty-four billion. Even your baby's breathing patterns and sleeping and waking rhythms (as we'll see later) are as unique as his thumbprint. Only getting to know and appreciate your baby's specialness will enable you to resist classifying him (and that includes such typecasting as "He's just like me" or "That's just the way first-borns are").

HOW TO WEED OTHER TICS FROM YOUR THINKING ABOUT PARENTING

The above are just a few of many Trivial Inconsequential Concerns which can plague you throughout your parenting career. Whose advice are you to trust? Before getting anxious or worried over any future child-rearing "shoulds" you may hear, try giving that advice what I call the TIC Test.

1. Where did you hear this advice? From a friend who may be exaggerating for dramatic effect? On a TV commercial? Is this a TIC you've borrowed from your mother because she always worried so much? How reliable is this source?

2. Who is saying it? Family experts range from solid researchers with excellent training, integrity, and judgment to people with scanty information, passionate crusaders, and downright quacks. Also, remember that even the absolute truths of today may be debatable tomorrow, after more facts are in. This doesn't make all scientific knowledge untrustworthy, but it does mean you have to watch which pronouncements you live by. A handy rule of thumb: If the advice makes you anxious about how you're currently raising your baby, investigate further before you do anything to drastically alter your natural parenting style.

3. How solid is the research? Does the writer or TV expert say where the study was published, so you can go look it up? Be wary

of such statements as "A recent study found . . ." Which study? Was it published in a reputable journal? Was the scientist looking at a cross-section of *all* babies and parents? Or was he just studying a few emotionally disturbed babies or families and trying to generalize his findings to all families—including warm, caring families like yours? You can't always know the answers to all these questions by reading an article or watching a TV show, but you can put the advice into better perspective if you at least ask the questions.

4. If you're reading a book, does it contain a bibliography and footnotes, so you can look up the evidence yourself? If there is a bibliography (incredibly few baby books have one), how many solid scientific journals are listed and how many sources are just other pop child-rearing books by the same author? How long ago was the book copyrighted? In what year were the most recent articles the author cites published? When was the book revised, and if it was revised recently, how much advice was changed to keep up with current research and how much did the author just sweep through and change a few sentences so he could claim "New, Revised, Better-Than-Ever Edition"? Some books needn't be revised for years. But research on babies has changed so dramatically in the past fifteen to twenty years, I'd be quite wary of a book that came out in, say, the early 1970s or earlier and has never been updated.

5. If a study is cited to "prove" that you should now change your parenting style, have other studies shown similar results? The findings of any one study can be skewed or even invalidated by sloppy scientific methods or poorly drawn conclusions.

6. Look for what I call the "qualifiers" in child-rearing writing. Among them: *most, many, may, tend to, suggests, indicates, could, might,* and *sometimes.* Authors who use such qualifiers (and it's often the *careful* writers who use them) aren't trying to mislead you. They're trying to let you know that these findings aren't engraved in stone. Phrases like "Current evidence *suggests* that . . ." are telling you that this evidence, intriguing though it may be, isn't absolute, so don't live your life by it. Likewise, when an author states, "*Most* six-month-olds love playing Peek-a-boo," he or she is telling you not all babies love Peek-a-boo, so you still have to get to know your special baby to see which games he loves most. Often, in the haste of our busy lives, it's easy to zip quickly through an article

or book, overlooking the qualifiers. You may then come away feeling you'd better get busy and change your whole life-style to follow this latest new finding. (Did you spot the qualifier in my last sentence?)

7. Finally, be wary of dogmatic experts who give you one set, rigid formula to follow with all babies or issue a lot of blanket advice. The statement I cited in Chapter 1—"Tiny children *should* learn math"—is a good example. *Which* tiny children? All of them? Exactly how old are these children? How many studies support this sweeping statement? Where is the published research to back up this claim? Experts who cast themselves in the role of teacher and you in the subservient role of student are especially fond of such authoritarian words as *should, must, have to, never,* and *always.* Some "shoulds" are, of course, valid. When Dr. Spock writes in his section on washing bottles, nipples, and caps that "in the end you must sterilize the equipment unless you are using the single-bottle method,"[22] there probably isn't a pediatrician, scientist, or parent alive who'd dispute him. Likewise, you should pay attention to your baby and be sensitive to his signals. But when dealing with more uncertain issues—like thumb sucking, eating problems, or colic—be wary of experts who insist you should treat all babies alike. The fine art of parenting involves learning which "shoulds" are worth taking seriously and which are only TICs.

So the next time you find yourself feeling vaguely anxious or guilty or pressured to do something you don't want to do, in order to prove to the world you're a good parent, stop. Give that nagging doubt at the back of your mind the TIC Test.

Some guilt or anxiety is healthy. When your two-year-old is playing too close to the road, a little anxiety bell rings in your head and you dash out to move him to safety. Likewise, if you inadvertently hurt your child's feelings, a pang of guilt may urge you to say, "I'm sorry." But excessive anxiety over TICs and guilt over what you consider "mistakes" only make you uneasy around your baby, thereby throwing off your dance. It's not how much you worry or how guilty you feel, but how readily you can relax and dance with your baby, that communicates your love.

By now it's clear I disagree with much current child-rearing advice. Why? In the next chapter I'll tell you.

PART II

EPILOGUE AND PROLOGUE

The world view and value system that lie at the basis of our culture and that have to be carefully reexamined were formulated in their essential outlines in the sixteenth and seventeenth centuries. Between 1500 and 1700 there was a dramatic shift in the way people pictured the world and in their whole way of thinking. The new mentality and the new perception of the cosmos gave our Western civilization the features that are characteristic of the modern era. They became the basis of the paradigm that has dominated our culture for the past three hundred years and is now about to change.

—FRITJOF CAPRA
Physicist in The Turning Point

4 Why Aren't We Saying What Everyone Else Is Saying?

Much of American developmental psychology is the science of the behavior of children in strange situations with strange adults.

—DR. URIE BRONFENBRENNER
Developmental psychologist

What value is our knowledge if it is not relevant to real children growing up in real families and in real neighborhoods?

—DR. ROBERT McCALL

For the past fifty years, parenting has gradually been taken away from parents and turned over to the experts. When unsure what to do with a baby, far too many parents rush for their favorite child-rearing manual, then follow the expert's advice without question.

Why *isn't* this a good idea?

Well, let me answer that question by asking another: After fifty years of child-rearing advice, where do we stand? Since 1960, teenage suicides have risen 300 percent.[1] More than a million teenage girls a year (thirty thousand of them under age fifteen) are now getting pregnant and researchers estimate that if present trends continue, a whopping 40 percent of today's fourteen-year-old girls will be pregnant before the age of twenty.[2] An annual survey conducted by the Institute of Social Research at the University of Michigan reveals that half of all teens now use marijuana at least once in a while and cocaine use among teens has doubled in the past ten years. One out of every six teens will have sampled cocaine before senior prom night.[3] More parents are alienated from their children than ever.

If baby experts are so smart, why after all these years of parent education are parents and children in so much trouble?

It's not because parents have been ignoring the experts. According to one survey, sales figures of child-rearing books reached "an impressive 8,800,000 annually or close to a staggering 90,000,000 during the past decade."[4] Why, after fifty years of child-rearing education, during which American parents have consulted well over 200,000,000 books (a conservative estimate) and countless articles telling them how to do a "better" job, are parent-child relations still a source of guilt and uncertainty?

Certainly, we can't lay all the problems of modern society in the laps of child-rearing experts (even those who offer the silliest, most dogmatic advice). Yet as Stanford University child-education professor Robert D. Hess points out in a paper published in the book *Parenting in a Multicultural Society*, there are major flaws in much current child-rearing advice. One of the critical problems with many how-to books and other parent-education programs is that they cast the expert in the role of professional teacher and you as the incompetent, amateur parent. As Hess says:

> In a sense, programs and materials designed for parents create a para-social relationship between parents and professionals, even though there is no direct personal contact between them. In this relationship, parents are clearly amateurs. The prestige of the professional is very high, often bolstered by an institutional base—a clinic, a school, a day-care center, a welfare agency, a probation department, a community agency, or a university. The authoritative, confident tone of the child-rearing manuals contrasts vividly with the parent's awareness of his/her own struggles to deal with the complexities of raising children.
>
> Parent-education programs can induce in parents feelings of powerlessness and dependence on the advice of professionals. Awareness of their own lack of skills makes them more vulnerable to voices of authority. Dependence erodes the parent's effectiveness with her/his children and feelings of inadequacy make it difficult for parents to acquire new skills. Research on learned helplessness shows that experiences and expectation of failure depress the ability to learn, the tendency to take the initiative, and increase the desire to turn to others for assistance. Confusion and uncertainty also mar the parent's potency as a model for the child, since models are more likely to be imitated and internalized if they have high status and power.[5]

Perhaps the situation isn't quite as bleak as Dr. Hess portrays it. Certainly I know many parents who read child-care books and still manage to do just fine. But Dr. Hess's remarks should be taken in the spirit in which they're offered: A feeling of helplessness and incompetence *can* overwhelm some parents. And let's face it, after reading three or four hundred pages describing all the things you can do wrong with your baby (and the dire consequences if you goof), it might be hard for anyone to avoid feeling at least a little anxious.

Child-rearing advice of the past has also been flawed in that it's often been drawn from laboratory experiments. The result? Many of the answers dished out by experts in the past have been too simple. Let me explain.

WHY LAB RESEARCH DOESN'T NECESSARILY APPLY TO YOU AND YOUR BABY AT HOME

Much child-rearing advice of the past has been drawn from research in the lab, a highly controlled, simple environment that doesn't always reflect the complex interactions between you and your baby in real life.

Let me give you just one example of how a laboratory finding can mislead you about your baby. Many lab studies have shown that premature babies tend to be a lot crankier than infants carried to full term. Thus you may see in a book somewhere that you have to work especially hard to calm your irritable preemie once he gets home from the hospital. You may even be told about special calming techniques you "should" try because they worked especially well in the lab. Before you get home from the hospital, you may be anxiously wondering how you'll ever cope with this "especially irritable" baby.

My naturalistic studies of mothers and babies interacting at *home*, however, show that babies who were born prematurely *aren't* any crankier in their more relaxed home environment than other babies. In other words, the "prescriptions" above, although accurately drawn from findings in the lab, turn out to be way off base. Meanwhile, if you're the mother in this situation, you could have one of two reactions. Either you could trust your own observation that your baby is no fussier than any other baby and conclude, "This expert is full of baloney." Or you could continue to trust the expert and *perceive* your calm baby as "especially irritable," even though your baby is just crying for food, warmth, diaper changes, and cuddling, as all babies do. You can easily see the danger building up here: Will your undue anxiety in fact contribute to making your baby more irritable (thus fulfilling the expert's prophecy)?

I could go on with this scenario, but I'm sure you see my point. Simple laboratory findings, however intriguing, don't necessarily mirror complex reality.

How complex *is* the relationship between you and your baby? To grasp this, try to picture all relationships in the universe on a scale from 1 to 9. Noted economist Dr. Kenneth Boulding, professor emeritus at the University of Colorado, has done this and has created what he calls a "hierarchy of complexity."[6] At level 1 on Boulding's scale are the simplest relationships imaginable—like that between two rocks floating in outer space. On level 9 are relations so complex and seemingly mysterious we can't even begin to comprehend them.[7] "Transcendental experiences (God talking to a man, for example) are on level 9," Dr. Boulding says. The simple, linear, cause-effect world of most laboratory science is on level 2 of Boulding's scale. The relationship between you and your baby? At level 8. When you try to apply findings drawn from an overly simple situation (like the lab) to a highly complex one (like your home), distortions and misconceptions can result.

To overcome the potential flaws of translating laboratory findings to the home, many researchers including myself are now studying babies and parents interacting naturally at home. And guess what? We've discovered that you already possess a much greater potential to raise your baby than you can ever learn from following ten or twelve "shoulds" drawn from a study. Just by relaxing and tuning in to your baby, you can come to give him the best kind of nurturing—the kind he most needs to grow mentally, socially, and emotionally—even if you never read another "how to" manual in your life.

By observing how healthy babies and parents interact in real life, scientists have found you're a lot more competent and able to raise your baby than many mother-blaming experts have given you credit for. Evolution has endowed you with a potential biological wisdom much more profound, fluid, and flexible than anything a rigid prescription drawn from a lab experiment can offer.

I'm not knocking scientific laboratory findings here. Don't get me wrong. Many of the fascinating, useful facts we know today about you and your baby came from highly controlled lab experiments. *But* there is a very real danger in assuming that just because a fact was found to fit babies in a lab, it necessarily applies to *all* babies—or even *any* baby—in your complex home.

My observations of parents and babies interacting naturally at home have taught me to see you and your baby in many special ways. Among them, studying people like you in your home has taught me that:

1. Most mothers (and fathers) are basically good parents. Among mothers who are paying attention to their babies and are truly trying, there are no bad mothers. (My view contrasts starkly with that of the psychologist who, when asked how many of the forty mothers she'd studied were really competent and gave her no cause to worry about their physical or emotional effects on their babies, replied, "Well, I don't believe in the concept of a 'good mother,' but I'd say about three."[8])

2. At least in the early months, babies' *feelings* count more than their thoughts. Anyone who watches mothers and babies dancing at home has to be impressed by the wealth of emotions even very young infants display. Because learning is easy to quantify, isolate, control, and study in the lab, laboratory research has tended to focus almost exclusively on what your baby learns and knows (or what scientists call cognition). Home studies show us your young baby's feelings are most important, even for what your baby learns.

3. It's obvious from watching babies in the home that every baby is unique. I'm sure you know your baby has a special personality at birth. Laboratory scientists, who spend much of their time trying to study only the individual pieces of a baby (IQ is one of these pieces), don't always recognize how special each baby is.

I don't mean to imply I'm the only scientist watching mothers and babies at home. Child-development investigators at Harvard, Yale, Cornell, and other institutions are also doing what we call naturalistic research. I'm only citing the above differences in lab versus home studies to show you that when you watch babies and parents interacting naturally and spontaneously at home, you get quite a different perspective on how parents help babies grow. Or rather, how parents and babies help each other grow.

Babies aren't mechanical robots who respond on cue in a piecemeal way, but are real, whole persons. Nor do you influence your baby's overall development in a simple cause-effect laboratory-like sequence. Knowing this, you can begin to see why so much of the how-to advice dished out today doesn't work in your home according to plan. It's too simple.

That's why a growing number of child-development researchers, myself included, have been looking for new ways to explain how you influence your baby and help him grow. And we've found this new way in systems theory. To understand this new paradigm, which is changing science's whole approach to you and your baby, we have to leave child rearing for just a minute and talk—oddly enough—about physics. (Trust me. It will all make sense in a minute.)

THE NEW VISION OF REALITY

From the 1600s to the early part of this century, scientists saw the whole universe as a machine, rather like a clock, governed by exact mathematical laws.[9] But near the start of this century, something incredible happened. A brilliant man named Albert Einstein came along and he, plus a group of physicists who followed him, shook the old vision of reality to its foundation. Einstein and the physicists after him made many profound observations too complex to go into here. But one of the most important ideas to emerge from their insights was this: *The natural world isn't as mechanistic, fragmented, or simple as we often see it in the lab.* The natural world, of course, includes you and your baby.

Einstein and the others didn't say the old ideas were *wrong.* They were right—as far as they went. The old cause-effect ideas worked fine to explain the simpler aspects of the world we see around us. But the old views of nature as a simple machine didn't explain the much more complex natural world physicists found on the subatomic level. At the most basic level of reality, the new physicists discovered, the whole universe isn't made up merely of *things* (like atoms, electrons, protons, etc.) but of ineffable, ever-changing, dynamic *events.* The new physics, which has been called the "science of complexity," sees the natural world not as a static, unyielding machine composed of many disconnected wheels and gears, but as a flexible, ever-shifting, unified, rhythmic, harmonious whole that can be best summed up in the word "organic." In the words of physicist Fritjof Capra, author of *The Tao of Physics*, "Modern physics has shown us that movement and rhythm are essential properties of matter; that all matter, whether here on earth or in outer space, is involved in a continual cosmic dance."[10]

No, you don't have to understand the new physics to raise your baby. All you need to know is that near the start of this century, some incredibly profound changes occurred in Western scientific thought. Physics (which, because it studies the very nature of reality, tends to orient all the sciences) shifted from a science of simplicity to one of complexity. And the dissatisfaction physicists had felt with the overly simple answers in their field was paralleled in many other scientific disciplines. In many sciences, including psychology, biology, sociology, economics, and medicine, a parallel to the new physics (which explains the complex phenomena of matter) is the new systems theory (which explains complex, organized organic processes, including human behaviors and relationships—like the one between you and your baby).[11]

As I already pointed out in Chapter 2, a system is a bit hard to explain because you can't point to one and say, "That's a system," in quite the same way you can point to an oak tree and name it. A system isn't a *thing*, but a dynamic *process* whereby a lot of separate pieces work together as an orderly, organized whole. A single living cell is a system. The billions of cells in your brain are one system. Your heart is a system. Your whole body is a system (and it's your whole body, not each individual cell, that controls the operation of "you").

You're also part of many *social* systems (a social system merely being two or more persons interacting as a whole over time). Your family is a social system. So are you and your baby. If you're on a weekend basketball or softball team, that's another social system (and whether you're having a winning or a losing season depends a lot on how smoothly your team/system is working together as one, unified whole).

If you're happily married, you and your mate are one harmonious system. If you're divorced, you've felt how wrenching and difficult dissolving a complex social system can be. A strong social system, where everyone meshes smoothly, is joyous. Just being part of it feels good. A disjoint system, in which some or all the people frequently feel separated, isolated, and lonely, isn't any fun. People in a disjoint system (or what scientists call an asynchronous system) get on each other's nerves. *Synchrony* in a system is important because that's what makes the system strong. As I'll explain more fully later, it's dancing synchronously with your baby that makes for an optimal system and helps your baby become the best baby, child, and adult he can be.

Systems theory, then, isn't a brand-new idea scientists have created just to explain how you and your baby interact to help your baby grow. Rather, it's a view of reality that's been around for nearly half a century (the first person to formalize systems theory was a biologist named Ludwig von Bertalanffy in 1937),[12] is being applied in many fields, and has already changed our world in many ways. It's from this new systems view of man that all the popular holistic movements have sprung ("holistic" referring to the wholeness, unity, and interconnectedness of reality). It's this systems view that has led physicians to create the new field of behavioral medicine, in which doctors now recognize that when you're sick, your "healing" attitudes of joy, hope, and optimism may be as crucial to the healing process as the medicine or surgery you might receive.[13] It's this same vision of reality that has led us to see the planet Earth as a whole, interconnected, interdependent system, so that we now view hunger in Ethiopia not just as an isolated problem far across the Atlantic, which has nothing to do with you or me, but as a whole-world problem we must all work together to solve.

A number of recent books by thoughtful scientists have been based on this new vision of reality. Among them: *Lives of a Cell* by Lewis Thomas (a view of the whole earth written by a physician from a systems perspective); *The Relaxation Response* by Herbert Benson, M.D., director of the division of behavioral medicine at Boston's Beth Israel Hospital (just one of many books by physicians who share the holistic, systems view of man); and *The Turning Point* by Fritjof Capra (which in one chapter explains the new systems psychology).[14]

I could detail a lot more changes you see around you every day that have sprung from this new view of reality and man (family therapists, to cite just one more example, are now finding that to get results, they often can't treat a patient without treating that person's whole troubled family system).[15] But there's no need to belabor the point. I'm only trying to illustrate that during the first half of this century, an incredibly profound change hit science and all of Western thought—a change the likes of which hadn't hit Western thinking in nearly three hundred years.[16] Our view of the universe changed. And with that change came a new view of man. The old idea was that a person was a robotic creature— much like a clock—who was composed of fragmented pieces (mind and body) and could be "made" to react in one set, predictable way. The new systems view of man is much more exciting. As the authors of *The Process of Human Development: A Holistic Approach* (a book written from a systems perspective) note: "A general systems perspective presents a humanistic view of man as a holistic, goal-directed, self-maintaining, self-creating individual of intrinsic worth, capable of self-reflection upon his own uniqueness."[17] Evidence of this new vision of man and the universe is already around you, subtly and obviously influencing your daily life.

And now this dramatic shift in Western thought has revolutionized the way child-development researchers are starting to view parenting.

THE NEW CHILD REARING

Like scientists in other fields, from biology to medicine, many thoughtful child-rearing researchers in the latter half of this century became disillusioned with the overly simple answers of the past. The pat formulas created to turn out healthy, happy children simply weren't working. Not only were parents and children more confused and alienated than ever, but as you saw in Chapter 2, none of the "right" steps scientists had found and eagerly passed on to parents worked out very well. Strictly potty-trained infants didn't necessarily become emotionally troubled adults; permissively trained toddlers didn't turn out happier or more creative. In fact, no matter what *specific* steps parents took, many children baffled scientists by compensating for parental mistakes, coping with difficulties, sidestepping stumbling blocks, inventing fresh solutions, and seeming to grow up however they darn pleased.

The old, rigid, cause-effect formulas worked (and still work) in simple, daily, one-on-one situations. Though all children differ, it's possible you *can* train your baby to have eating problems if, every time he acts up at dinner, you give him loads of attention for it (even negative attention may be better than none at all). Likewise, if the minute your back is turned your two-year-old reaches for a hot stove burner and you paddle his bottom and say sternly, "No, hot!" you'll soon find to your great relief he doesn't reach for hot burners anymore. But these are simple parent-child interactions, involving simple cause-effect learning.

When it comes to more complex questions—How do you influence your baby's growth over the course of his childhood? How can you stimulate your baby's mind (and when should you start)? How can you raise your baby to be considerate, happy, honest, and independent? and endless others—simple cause-effect rules drawn from the old view of your baby as a machine don't provide useful answers. Your long-term influence on your baby is far too complex to be summed up in a few simple cause-effect rules.

Systems theory gives us a much more meaningful way to explain how you influence your baby. A systems perspective recognizes the true complexity of the way you interact with your baby and sees your baby not as a predictable machine but as the creative, curious, spontaneous, humorous, and unique person he is.

How you influence your baby depends not on "wrong" or "right" steps you take but on how well your total family system works. In other words, whether the way you and your baby relate affects each of you positively or negatively depends on how well you dance together. The emphasis in this new view of child rearing isn't just on what you do or don't do but on how well you and your baby "fit."[18] When the ways you look at, gesture to, talk to, and play with your baby are tailored to his needs, you not only make him brighter and happier; you help him develop his whole being. Cornell University psychiatrist Daniel Stern refers to this emotional fit between you and your baby as "attunement."[19] Other scientists who talk about this same idea speak of you and your baby as having a "good match."[20] When you and your baby are working together as one synchronous system—in other words, when you're *dancing as one*—you're doing much more to help your baby grow than you can do by watching every little step.

Dancing joyously involves coming to know your baby as a whole, unique person. It also involves coming to know, understand,

and trust yourself and your own inner wisdom. Rigid "shoulds" can make you pay more attention to expert advice than to your own inner signals (that's why I spent the first three chapters of this book urging you to get rid of them). Dancing well involves interacting with your baby in an authentic, honest, natural, spontaneous, whole-person way. It's not *doing* specific things for or to your baby that counts. It's *being* with him and dancing together. Thus, as a Dancingparent, you'll come to know it's not so much what you *do* that matters, but who you *are*.

5 Dancing with Your Baby: The New Parenting

*When the mother and infant are acting synchronously . . .
then we're forced to think that they are following a shared
program. A good analogy for this model is the waltz, where
both partners know the steps and the music by heart and
can accordingly move precisely together.*

—DANIEL STERN
Cornell University infant psychiatrist

Watch closely. You're about to observe a dance.

*Two-month-old Mark lounges in his infant seat in the sunny
kitchen of his suburban home. His mother is in the bedroom, getting
Mark's sweater for a trip to the market. Mark sits still and quiet. His
face looks sober, with a half-opened mouth, droopy cheeks, and slightly
downturned lips. Suddenly, Mark hears his mother's footsteps. His eyes
get big, bright, and alert. His hands and face move toward the direction
of the sounds.*

*Mark's mother appears at the kitchen doorway and smiles. As
his mother approaches, Mark follows her movements intently with his
head and eyes. Standing before Mark, Mother says, "Oooooooh." Her
voice is cheerier and higher pitched than if she were greeting an adult.
As she speaks, her mouth forms an open "O," her eyes open wide,
and her eyebrows rise in mock surprise. Meanwhile, as Mother goes
through her motions, Mark rhythmically dances with her: His body
tenses, his eyes get brighter and wider, and he begins to smile. As his
face becomes more animated, Mark cycles his arms toward his mother
as if he wants her to pick him up. Mother ignores this.*

*Slowly, Mark stops smiling, mouths his tongue three times, and
looks briefly down, as his mother keeps talking, making her voice more
and more "fascinating" to her baby by speeding up her tempo and
accentuating the first syllable as she repeats, in a baby-pleasing cadence,*

"Markie want to go bye-bye?" Mark continues looking down, his body tense, eyes averted, and mother touches his right arm to put on his sweater. Mark looks up and smiles widely. He narrows his eyes, brings one hand up to his mouth, hums softly, then makes a more distinct cooing sound.

Mark's arms and legs start to cycle toward his mother once again. Mother grins broadly and says—more slowly and loudly this time—*"Yeees, we're going bye-byyye."* She now picks up Mark to put on his sweater. Mark's face is turned away from his mother's, but his eyes remain alert, bright, and expectant.

Back in his infant seat, Mark coos again and Mother's face becomes amazingly animated as she again, s-l-o-w-l-y, raises her eyebrows until she reaches a full display of her *"surprise look."* After a few more seconds of play, Mark's face sobers. He looks down and pouts. Mother's eyebrows knit and lower in response, her head moves slightly down, and she purses her lips and says, *"Aaaaoooh. What's the matter, huh?"* Mother adopts a more neutral facial expression. As she picks Mark up, the baby bursts into a dazzling smile and Mother responds, *"Yeees, we're going bye-byyye."* And the two dance merrily out the door.

You've watched Mark and his mother dancing one of their myriad dialogue dances. And the above interaction shows how rich and playful even ninety seconds involving putting on a sweater can be. Every second—in fact, every millisecond—you're with your baby is filled with astonishingly orderly and rhythmic, yet ever-changing, behavior patterns which to an unenlightened observer may at first look trivial or silly, but which to you and your baby are fraught with meanings.

Dialogue dances like the one above are the "language" of emotion. Through such dialogues, which involve voice pitch, tempo, body movements, facial expressions, and a great many other steps, you tell your baby whether you're feeling happy, loving, guilty, silly, anxious, resentful, sad, or any of myriad other emotions. And your baby receives these signals and synchronously dances with movements, expressions, and sounds of his own. Through these and other incredibly complex, meaningful dances, you tell your baby you love him, thereby providing the rich emotional support he needs to grow.

Some may protest, "What's the big deal? The above mother

and baby are just playing." That's true. But we as adults tend to overestimate the value of work and underestimate the value of play. Man is basically a playful animal. We play all our lives. Why? Because playing is one of the most basic ways we learn and grow. From observing the dance, scientists now know that it's not lessons, fancy mobiles, swimming classes, fast-track baby schools, or any of the other gimmicks, that help your baby become happy and bright: It's interacting joyfully with you.

Think about it. You're the most complex, fascinating toy in the universe. Other toys may walk, talk, blink lights, or play music. But no toy can begin to offer one ten-thousandth the variety you do. No other toy can offer such intriguing, ever-changing facial expressions, sounds, and movements. You can dance, walk, talk, smile, frown, laugh, cry, make silly noises, snap your fingers, blow bubble gum, cuddle, kiss, hug, shake a rattle, and bounce a baby on your knee. You can even sing lullabies. No toy in the universe is more interesting or educational than you. Your baby is even biologically designed to seek out and look at your beautiful human face with more fascination than he looks at anything else. (He especially likes your eyes when they're bright and wide.) Experts are constantly telling you that you should stimulate your baby to make him bright. Which is true. What they often fail to tell you is that *you* are the most stimulating, imaginative toy your baby has. With some nifty toys on the market today costing fifty dollars or more, you're such a great plaything you should cost a million dollars. And that's another remarkable thing about you: You're free.

Every time you play spontaneously with your baby, whether you're playing gently, quietly, quickly, or rowdily, you can match your play style to your baby's needs. As you do so, you're expanding your baby's adaptability and awareness and telling him you love him. Babies who dance delightedly with their parents tend to feel happy and cherished. Babies whose steps are usually ignored often become frustrated, cranky, or withdrawn. The early dances you do with your baby are also the first beginnings of a highly complex communication dance that will persist between you and your baby all your lives. My studies and others have shown that by dancing joyously with your baby your first months together, you're laying the groundwork for a solid future relationship.[1] Parents and babies who dance smoothly in month three are usually dancing happily a year later (at which point babies who've been dancing well for a year are more advanced—in many ways—than those who haven't had such a dance). Somehow, by interacting socially with your baby, you're helping him grow holistically. When a baby dances happily, he grows not just intellectually but in *many* ways.[2]

Now you can see even more clearly why too much emphasis on early lessons at the expense of your baby's feelings may not be beneficial. If somehow (even if inadvertently) you've made formal lessons fun by focusing on how you're playing with your baby rather than on how well your baby performs, your baby may, in fact, become "smarter" after you've given him lessons. But if so, it wasn't just the lessons, but the happy interacting with you, that helped your baby become brighter.

How does a mother come to dance with her baby as smoothly as the mother at the start of this chapter was dancing with hers? One amazing aspect of the dance is that no one *taught* the above mother or her baby their spontaneous steps. Yet somehow they knew them. The fact that even newborns are virtuoso performers[3] has led many of us to realize that this ability to communicate emotions is largely inborn. Researchers who have studied thousands of parent-baby dances are invariably impressed by the wide repertoire of harmonious steps parents and babies execute almost from the moment they meet. Dr. Daniel Stern, who has taped thousands of these interactions, aptly refers to the dances parents and babies perform as "biologically designed choreography."[4] Dancing seems to be a *species* behavior, because nearly all caregivers—grandmothers, grandfathers, great-aunts, etc.—interact with a baby this same way. (Young girls begin to show these behaviors around a baby when they reach puberty.[5]) Somehow, your baby is born dancing . . . and you're already biologically designed to respond.

Do you just automatically know how to dance, then? Not entirely. You're *designed* to dance. But because your baby is unique, you still have to learn his particular steps so you can respond to his special needs. While some steps are common to nearly all babies (I'll discuss these in Chapter 10), no one can tell you precisely how to dance with your unique infant. Only you can feel how. Luckily, it's one of the paradoxes of natural parenting that while you can't be *taught* to dance, if you try you will *learn*. In fact, *tuning in* to your baby so you can mesh beautifully with him is what Dance-parenting is all about.

DANCEPARENTING: THE NEW VISION APPROACH

Your dance with your baby involves not only dialogue dances but everything you do together. Your total dance is how your whole system expresses itself not only from minute to minute but from one day to the next and even over your entire life span. If your parents are living and you've had a close, loving relationship, you're still dancing with them, even though your dance has changed considerably since you were one week old. Not all parents and children dance smoothly. That's when conflicts erupt. Your goals as a Dancingparent are to come to know your baby's true nature and to avoid attitudes and steps that disrupt your dance.

How does the Dancingparent's approach differ from, say, the Superparent's attitude toward a baby? There's a very clear differ-ence. Still believing in the old views of a baby, the Superparent tries to control a baby so he will grow a certain way. If the baby fails to follow a precise schedule or keep "up" with other babies, the Superparent worries.

The Dancingparent, in contrast, has a much more fluid, flex-ible, relaxed approach. The Dancingparent philosophy can best be explained, oddly enough, by a term borrowed from Chinese Taoist philosophy. That term is *wu wei.*

Used often by Taoist sages, *wu wei* literally means "nonaction" or "let be." But that literal translation is deceptive to most of us in the West because it implies total passivity (an idea which, in turn, might lead to the misconception that to be a Dancingparent you just have to sit passively and watch your baby grow without doing anything to help). That's quite wrong and misinterprets what the Chinese mean by this term.

Just as the Japanese have no word in their language that means "privacy," the Chinese can't conceive of total passivity. The idea that you could just stand impassively aside and watch nature take its course without influencing it, being a part of it, is inconceivable to the Chinese. Rather, they believe there are two *kinds* of activity:

activity in harmony with the true nature of reality and activity against the natural flow. As one writer explains:

> What the Chinese mean by *wu wei* is not abstaining from activity, but from a certain *kind* of activity, activity that is out of harmony with the ongoing cosmic process. The distinguished sinologist Joseph Needham defines *wu wei* as "refraining from action contrary to nature" and justifies his translation with a quotation from Chuan Tsu: "Nonaction does not mean doing nothing and keeping silent. [Rather it means] let everything be allowed to do what it naturally does, so that its nature will be satisfied." If one refrains from acting contrary to nature or, as Needham says, from "going against the grain of things," one is in harmony with the Tao and thus one's actions will be successful.[6]

Parenting according to the true nature of your baby (a major goal of the Dancingparent) means respecting your baby for the whole, feeling, unique person he is. It also means trusting your competent baby to reach for his own growth. A basic tenet of Dancingparents is that your child, who is born dancing, will reach toward his own mental, social, and emotional growth if you help make the steps in that direction delightful, joyous, and gratifying to him. In this sense, Danceparenting is the antithesis of many traditional child-rearing theories, which would have you concentrate your major efforts not on growth but on helping your baby *avoid* neuroses and messing up his life. Systems theory, from which Danceparenting is drawn, teaches us your baby is a striving, self-organizing little person who if given the opportunity will choose to be happy rather than sad, strong rather than weak, courageous rather than cowardly. The Dancingparent—because she understands this true nature—trusts that if given the chance, her baby will adapt, change, and reach out in an attempt to become as strong, brave, bright, creative, talented, independent, loving, and self-aware as he can be. The Dancingparent's goal is to give her baby that chance.

That's not to say your baby won't struggle at times or seem to take one step back for every two steps forward. The world, of course, is full of stumbling blocks that can frighten a small person and make him deny his own growth and self-discovery in favor of "playing it safe." These stumbling blocks aren't always under your full control. But over time, you'll grow to feel comfortable—even delighted—with the knowledge that you don't have total control of your child's destiny. You'll also come to realize that you still have enough influence over your baby (through your dance) so that you can help him grow without the enormous, totally unrealistic burden of having to assume control over his tiniest step.

Your responsibility when dancing with your baby, then, isn't to mold your child into this or that type of human being, but rather to mesh with him so he'll feel loved, respected, and eager to reach out and strive for greater and greater heights. You can help your baby feel safe and be willing to help him take the next step without forcing or pushing him to choose a direction that may be contrary to his nature.

While an outgrowth of my research and that of others, Danceparenting isn't an idea that has sprung full-blown in the 1980s. In fact, nearly twenty years ago, humanistic psychologist Abraham Maslow, one of the first New Vision psychologists in this country, hit upon somewhat the same idea when he explained how a parent can help a child choose emotional health over neurosis. If we want to help a child choose emotional growth, Maslow observed,

> all we can do is help him if he asks for help out of suffering, or else simultaneously allow him to feel safe and beckon him onward to *try* the new experience, like the mother whose open arms invite the baby to try to walk. We can't force him to grow, we can only *coax* him to, make it more possible for him, in the trust that simply experiencing the new experience will make him prefer it. *Only* he can prefer it; no one can prefer it for him. If it is to become part of him, *he* must like it. If he doesn't, we must gracefully concede that it is not for him at this moment.[7]

To reiterate this important point, then: To be a Dancingparent, you wouldn't just stand back and let your child grow up willy-nilly with no help from you (an absolute permissiveness that amounts to noncaring). A dependent little baby *does* need stimulation and help. Rather, Danceparenting means getting to know your baby's nature and then abstaining from acting contrary to that nature (not always an easy task).

Is Danceparenting easy to master, then—or hard? Frankly, it's both.

On one hand, this approach assumes self-reliance and personal growth on your part. Being a Dancingparent involves a sensitivity that simplistic "right-step" formulas just don't demand. To be a Dancingparent, you assume the responsibility of getting to know your baby better than anyone else in the world knows him (of course, that means an investment of time, effort, and love). You can learn to gently pull your baby toward learning rather than pushing him to learn something that may not be right for him (even though the path he chooses may not impress your friends or relatives). You can master ways of offering your baby a wide range of stimulating experiences, while still allowing him enough freedom to choose which experiences most intrigue and delight him. To be a Dancingparent, you don't have the comfortable option of retreating safely to a set of specific rules; sometimes you have to make a decision you're unsure of and go out on a limb. That's hard.

On the other hand, Danceparenting offers a more relaxed, playful approach than past child-rearing theories because it doesn't burden you with the fear you'll ruin your baby forever or the guilt that perhaps you already have. Danceparenting allows you to make mistakes, to goof up, to blow it—then gives you the confidence to pick yourself up and go on. Once you focus your attention and start dancing with your baby, this approach is in many ways easy. In fact, it's the way nature designed you to parent, the way you'd naturally raise your baby if you were free from guilt, anxiety, insecurity, and societal "shoulds."

OVERCOMING STUMBLING BLOCKS TO DANCING WELL

If Danceparenting is the *natural* way to raise your baby, why do you have to learn it? The paradox of this approach is that while it's the way evolution designed you to parent, dancing doesn't always come without effort. Many obstacles can get in your way and disrupt your dance. I've already dismissed many false "shoulds" that can cause you problems. But to be a natural Dancingparent, you may also have to think about yourself and your baby in ways quite different than the old child-rearing approaches taught you to think. To keep the dance running smoothly, it helps immensely if you can: (1) learn to think holistically; (2) accept your mistakes; and (3) embrace the joy of uncertainty. Let's look more closely at these three ways of thinking.

Learn to Think Holistically

To dance with your baby, it helps if you can resist thinking of your baby, yourself, and your decisions in terms of opposites and false dichotomies. It's common in our culture for us to see people and actions in terms of opposites like good/bad, right/wrong, mature/immature, and strong/weak. At times such distinctions are quite useful. We need them in order to think logically. Unfortunately, the urge to see your baby in terms of such mutually exclusive opposites as good/bad, right/wrong, or active/passive can get between you and your baby and hinder authentic communication and genuine understanding. Rather than getting to know the deepest subtleties of your whole, real baby, you can oversimplify him by putting him into a black or white category and letting it go at that.

Pressures to encourage you to think only in black or white about your baby come from many sources. Suppose your baby is sucking his thumb. Even if you have no preset opinions about thumb sucking, a well-meaning neighbor or relative may peer into your baby's crib and remark, "Tsk-tsk, you shouldn't let your baby suck his thumb—don't you know it's bad for his teeth?" This self-appointed expert may then suggest any number of home remedies, from wrapping your baby's hands in mittens to putting awful-tasting stuff on his thumb. Yet in fact, thumb sucking can have several uses. Your baby may be sucking because he's hungry or to shut out excessive, stressful stimulation. In this case, it's easier (and takes less thinking) to say, "All thumb sucking is bad," and then put a bitter liquid on a baby's thumb, than try to figure out why your particular baby is sucking his thumb now and what (if anything) to do about it. When making decisions, dichotomizing keeps you from having to face the uncertain gray areas in which most parenting decisions are made.

Likewise, trying to sum up a baby quickly as Type A/Type B, good-natured/cranky, alert/inattentive, or in any other dichotomous way, is not a goal for the Dancingparent. Rather, when you learn to think holistically, you'll come to realize that any real person—including your baby—is large enough to encompass all these opposites and thus renders the very terms meaningless. "Do I contradict myself? Very well then I contradict myself, (I am large, I contain multitudes)," poet Walt Whitman jubilantly cried. No whole person can be summed up simply, and all opposites like good/bad, right/wrong are just relative.

An example? Okay, take discipline. It may be "right" to discipline three-year-old Billy when he spreads peanut butter all over Fido, but "wrong" to send Stevie to his room for the same offense. It might also be "right" to discipline Billy in one situation (perhaps when you've already repeatedly told him no and it's obvious that he's testing your limits) but maybe not under different circumstances (when Billy was just exploring and became intensely curious about how Fido would look in peanut butter). Some parents would never discipline in this case: They'd just crack up laughing and ask Billy to help give the dog a bath. Trying to apply absolute right/wrong rules to such a situation is meaningless.

Two other dichotomies that become meaningless when you and your baby are dancing are teacher/student and mature/immature. Superbaby advocates often imply that the goal of childhood is to become "mature" as rapidly as possible. In fact, just the opposite is more true. The goal of adulthood should be to remain childlike (although not childish)* until we're a hundred. It's precisely his most childlike traits (curiosity, flexibility, open-mindedness, laughter, a sense of humor, optimism, resilience, imagination, creativity, and playfulness, to name some of our best legacies from childhood) that are man's highest attainments. Our goal in life shouldn't be to squelch these marvelous traits as quickly as possible but to become even more curious, flexible, open-minded, and so forth as we grow through life.

Through the ages, many thoughtful people have recognized this. Montaigne once said, "There is nothing more remarkable in the life of Socrates than that he found time in his old age to learn to dance and play on instruments and thought the time well spent." In his book *Growing Young*, Princeton anthropologist Ashley Montagu points out, "The truth about the human species is that in

* The distinction between these two words deserves clarification. Childish behavior, unlike child*like* behavior, is a normal part of childhood but intolerable in adults. Such behaviors as overdependence and immature whining are childish traits we *are* meant to outgrow.

body, spirit, feeling and conduct we are designed to grow and develop in ways that emphasize rather than minimize childlike traits. We are intended to remain in many ways childlike: we were never intended to grow 'up' into the kind of adults most of us have become."[8]

Fortunately, if you *have* become a bit too regimented, rigid, and serious as you've "matured," forgiving Nature has given you a second chance: She's given you a delightful baby to play with, who will remind you of your own lovely childlike traits. Besieged by work and deadlines, you may forget as you grow through life how magical a rainbow looks or how delicious it feels just to be alive on a rainy spring day. But by seeing the world through your baby's fresh, wondering eyes, you can rediscover these tiny miracles at an age when you can appreciate and savor them all the more for having once almost lost them entirely.

A Dancingparent knows that even the most obvious opposites, like teacher/student and mature/immature, aren't absolute. Helping a baby grow can help you grow too.

Accept Your Mistakes

Like many parents, you may look at your new, unblamed baby and glimpse visions of human perfection. Maybe once—at last— one human has been born who will always feel strong, happy, courageous, and well-loved, who will never flinch in fear of expressing his own best talents, who will always boldly make the right decisions and never experience defeat. I know I had such feelings with my first baby. Babies *do* seem to be born perfect (at least as perfect as any of us can be). And since you love your baby intensely, there's a strong urge to think, "I will allow this baby to be forever perfect, and I'll do it by being the perfect parent. I'll never make a mistake."

Perfection certainly *seems* worth striving for. But in fact, straining to be perfect will very likely disrupt the dance between you and your baby. To be the presumably perfect parent, you have to spend a lot of time and effort watching every little step. This, in turn, can make you so anxious and tense you wind up not dancing at all.

I'm not knocking the pursuit of excellence. Setting attainable high standards for yourself as a parent is great. Go for it. Do give parenting all you've got. Expect the best from yourself. Love your baby with all the energy and joy you can muster. But I'm simply suggesting that you temper this admirable urge with lots of realistic self-forgiveness. You will make mistakes. You will have times when you think you can't take any more 2 A.M. feedings, crying, dirty diapers. Such thoughts don't make you a "bad" parent, only human.

Though it's one of our society's best-kept secrets, nearly every mother has moments when she wishes she'd never see another diaper and could just run off to Timbuktu. Accept these normal feelings as nature's way of saying, "You're pushing yourself too hard—slow down." Maybe you can't escape to a far-distant land (and of course in calmer moments you wouldn't want to). But you might be able to hire a sitter and spend an afternoon alone at a museum, the movies, or the beach. As a sensitive Dancingparent, you'll love spending time with your baby. But you also love and deserve the time you have for yourself. If you let yourself relax, you'll be more able to rebound after a hard day and start naturally flowing with your baby again the next day.

Also, remember dialogue dances are the language of *emotion*. So if you're continually tense from straining to be perfect, your baby will feel your tension. He won't "know" what's wrong. He'll only sense that whenever you're with him, you're uneasy. To dance joyously with your baby most times, you have to admit honestly that some times you don't want to dance at all. On rough days, remind yourself it's not any one moment, but your overall dance— the pattern of all your moments together—that determines how your baby will grow.

If dancing smoothly with your baby influences his overall growth, shouldn't you at least focus on *dancing* perfectly? Shouldn't you concentrate, for instance, on trying to achieve a perfect fit? No. In fact, amazingly, messing up is an intrinsic—and important—part of your natural dance. There's no way you can be an ideal dancer, exquisitely sensitive to your baby's every need, because your baby's needs change not only from day to day but from one minute to the next.

In the important dialogue dance, for example, you and your baby are constantly adjusting your behaviors to each other, thereby providing your baby with ever-changing levels and kinds of stimulation. There is an "optimum" interactional level, if you will.

When you and your baby are dancing at this level, you're providing just the right amount of stimulation your baby wants and needs. But as a natural part of your dance, you're constantly rising slightly above this level (giving your baby more exciting stimulation than he can handle) and then dropping below it (at which times your baby loses interest in the dialogue dance and gets bored).

In other words, as a Dancingparent playing with your baby, you're constantly undershooting and overshooting your baby's tolerance for stimulation. At times you may ignore his signals when he eagerly wants to play. Other times, you may elevate your dialogue dance to such a peak of excitement that your baby feels unhappily overwhelmed. As you make these subtle mistakes, your baby learns to adjust. He may learn to smile more broadly and add a "coo" to capture your attention. Or he may learn to pout more deeply to tell you that you've hurt his feelings by going too far. Subtly giving your baby more stimulation than he can handle (and you needn't strain to do this; you usually just do it naturally) helps your baby stretch and expand his repertoire so he can cope with greater stimulation in the future.

A tiny baby can't stand much intense stimulation; even a loud laugh may scare him. Yet by one year of age, your baby will delight in crowing loudly and gleefully himself. It's not clear how much of this change you encourage. Much of your baby's growing tolerance for stimulation obviously occurs simply because he's older. Yet it seems likely you also spur your baby in this growth by at times "messing up" your dialogue dance.

Daniel Stern has written cogently on the virtues of messing up while dancing.

> The virtues of "messing up" are simple. . . . First of all, only when a boundary is exceeded is the infant forced to execute some coping or adaptive maneuver to correct or avoid the situation or to signal to the mother to alter the immediate stimulus environment. The infant behaviors, like any others, require constant practice, constant opportunities under slightly different conditions to become fully adaptive behaviors. Second, unless the mother frequently risks exceeding a boundary, whether by design or miscalculation, she will be unable to help stretch and expand the infant's growing range of tolerance for stimulation.
>
> From this point of view, the mixture of off days, good days, bad moods, high moods, overcompensating is all part of the nec-

essary panorama of real events that help the infant acquire the interpersonal skills of coping with social interactions.[9]

While dancing, then, making mistakes is not only acceptable but helpful. The Dancingparent is one who blunders at times and yet trusts that even in the process of being less than perfect she's helping her baby grow.

Embrace the Joy of Uncertainty

Finally, to be a Dancingparent, it helps if you can embrace the joy of uncertainty and resist needing absolute security about every step you take. *Wanting* security is understandable. It would be comforting and require less creativity if you could follow a set formula and turn out a confident, bright, independent adult. Unfortunately, in the real world, you have to live on the uncertain edge of growth, accepting the fact that you won't always have all the answers and possessing the courage to act, anyway. Sir Isaac Newton once said, "No great discovery is ever made without a bold guess." You could easily rewrite this statement to apply to parenting: No healthy, happy child was ever raised without a parent taking bold chances.

If you resist this idea, perhaps you've succumbed to the popular myth that having children is one of the *easy* choices we make in life. People who crave safety supposedly stay home and have babies, whereas exciting folks are out becoming executives and skydiving and scaling Mount Everest. We all know humans crave both comfort and adventure. What we usually fail to recognize is that parenting (which has been advertised as "boring" and "dull") is on the adventures list, much higher than anything so simple as mountain climbing or white-water canoeing. In fact, it's precisely because parenting *is* so dicey that as a good parent you may find yourself craving the certainty of expert formulas, blueprints, and rules. Confused or afraid of failure, you may even be tempted to treat pronouncements in some child-rearing manuals as almost biblical; the experts sound so confident, you can find at least temporary relief from anxiety in following their advice and hoping things will work out. As I've said before, but it's worth repeating, expert advice *is* handy if you need to know how to burp your baby or give him a bath. But if you need to solve a more complex problem—like what to do right here in Lord & Taylor this minute about little Lauren's temper tantrum—trying to recall what some expert advised is like trying to phone your old canoeing instructor for an extra lesson when you're caught in a white-water rapids and are about to plunge over a waterfall. It's too late—and there's too much at stake—to seek professional help now. You have to depend on your own best judgment.

In the end, after reading all the formulas, you'll realize specific hard-and-fast rules offer no security, anyway. True security isn't having a nifty list of rigid rules (which don't work). The only genuine security as a parent comes from knowing that you—on your own, without experts—can handle most any problem that crops up.

But doesn't this make parenting less a science and more like a game of Russian roulette? Not at all. There are many solid, *flexible* guidelines you can follow. Yet I can't deny that some of your toughest parental decisions may have to be made in the parenting equivalent of the Twilight Zone. Babies are so unpredictable I'd sincerely advise anyone who cringes before uncertainty to think twice about having one. Babies tend to be curious, creative, messy, into everything, contrary, agreeable, noisy, quiet, spontaneous, aggravating, funny, playful—and nearly always unpredictable. There is no one right step for all babies because each baby is delightfully unique. And when you think about it, you'll realize you wouldn't want your baby any other way.

If in your less adventuresome moods you find yourself wishing parenthood were more certain, it might help to remind yourself how dull absolute certainty would be. Certainty is when everything is settled, when nothing can happen to you, when there is no excitement, no risk, no change. Worst of all, absolute security is a denial of healthy growth, the very antithesis of all the Dancing-parent is trying to achieve.

When I consider how dreary life would be if everything were certain, I'm often reminded of X. J. Kennedy's poem "Nothing in Heaven Functions as It Ought." It goes like this:

> Nothing in Heaven functions as it ought:
> Peter's bifocals, blindly sat on, crack:
> His gates lurch wide with the cackle of a cock,
> Not with a hush of gold as Milton had thought;
> Gangs of the martyred innocents keep whoofing

The nimbus off the Venerable Bede
Like that of an old dandelion gone to seed;
The beatific choir keep breaking up, coughing.

But Hell, sweet Hell, hath no uncertain part:
Nothing forgets nor rusts nor loses place.
Ask anyone, "Poor soul, how come you here?"—
And he will slot a penny through his face.
There'll be a little click, and wheels will whir
And out will creep a neat brief of his case.

The poet is right: Unrelenting certainty *would* be Hadean. Parental certainty was a myth perpetuated by old child-rearing experts who saw your baby as a predictable machine. But if you're to cope in today's complex parenting world, it's dangerous to believe you can find easy answers in one or two formulas or expert rules. You'll only have to discard the rules later anyway, perhaps after experiencing great pain or self-doubts because you believed a self-styled expert who insisted the answers were simple. Veteran parents know (though we often must learn the hard way) that there are no pat formulas. As George Leonard, a contributing editor of *Esquire*, writes:

> What I have learned in the process of raising [four] daughters—and perhaps it applies to other human affairs as well—is that there is no single answer, no magic formula, no rigid set of guidelines, no simple blueprint, no book of easy instructions, no sure way of sidestepping difficulties, no easy way out. There is love.[10]

This is the wisdom that dawns on veteran parents one day, often when all their children have grown. This is the wisdom dancing with your baby can teach you now, even while your child is small. But to know it means embracing the joy of uncertainty and leaving behind the need for simple answers.

THE TRADITIONAL WAY OF LOOKING AT PARENTING VERSUS THE NEW VISION

You and I have come a long way so far. We've discarded many "shoulds" left over from the traditional ways of looking at babies. We've introduced the approach I call Danceparenting, based not on linear causes and effects but on the New Vision of systems and of the nature of your baby. The rest of this book will describe in detail how you can enhance your parenting skills. But first you may find it helpful to see the traditional and new child-rearing approaches side by side. The first column (the traditional way of looking at babies) lists the ideas we discussed in Part I of this book. It's where we've been. The second column (the Dancingparent philosophy) delineates the ideas we have talked about in the last two chapters and will focus on in the rest of this book. It's where we're going.

THE TRADITIONAL PHILOSOPHY	THE DANCINGPARENT PHILOSOPHY
Describes the baby as a moldable blob or like a programmable machine over which the parent has nearly total *control*.	Sees the baby as a whole being with unique perceptions and feelings. Knows the parent has a strong *influence* over the baby, but allows the baby to freely explore, grow, and develop in his own special way.
Claims babies should develop according to a set timetable.	Sees each baby developing in different ways at different rates.
Provides rigid "learning experiences," such as formal lessons, baby-controlling educational toys, fast-track baby schools.	Offers a menu of experiences and lets the baby choose which ones he wants and needs most.
Emphasizes IQ. Sees academic learning such as reading, math, and rote memorization as the highest (perhaps only) form of intelligence.	Emphasizes the whole baby, especially his feelings. Knows there are many kinds of intelligence (IQ being only one aspect) and values development of the baby as a whole person.

THE TRADITIONAL PHILOSOPHY	THE DANCINGPARENT PHILOSOPHY
Talks of the baby's brain as though it were a rigid structure that must be hooked up precisely on cue. Believes in now-or-never "critical learning periods." Sees infancy as a make-or-break time.	Thinks of the baby's brain as plastic and knows we learn not just during infancy but all our lives. Knows it's never too late to learn, adapt, or change.
Sees the parent as teacher, the baby as student. Believes learning takes place in a linear, one-directional way—from parent to baby.	Sees both parent and baby as teacher and student. Knows learning is circular, with parent and baby teaching and learning from each other.
Talks about parents and babies as though they were either "good" or "bad."	Sees parents and babies as neither good nor bad, only delightfully different.
Leads the parent to fret anxiously about the baby's *future* and feels guilty over *past* mistakes.	Suggests the parent live in the *here* and *now*, plan wisely for the future, but not fret about it, realize guilt over past mistakes is useless, accept mistakes, make corrections when necessary, and go on.
Crucializes. Sees every small step as all-important to a baby's development.	Urges parents to relax, to try to do the best job possible, but know that little "mistakes" help a baby grow and there's plenty of time to overcome difficulties or to correct problems that crop up.
Parent is prone to burnout.	Parent is resistant to burnout.

THE TRADITIONAL PHILOSOPHY	THE DANCINGPARENT PHILOSOPHY
Believes that without strong, controlling parents, a child will go astray.	Trusts the baby to reach out toward his own growth.
Believes if parents make one wrong move, a baby will wind up neurotic.	Believes a baby has a strong, built-in biological urge to grow as healthy as he can be and trusts that with love and support he will reach toward his own emotional health.
Believes the infant's goal is to "grow up" and become adult-like as quickly as possible. Thinks, in acquiring any skill, "the earlier the better."	Knows the baby has no particular urge to become like adults. Appreciates the baby for his many child-like traits (honesty, curiosity, spontaneity, joy, etc.).
Emphasizes doing and goals. Is cause-effect oriented.	Emphasizes being and process. Is dance oriented.

Now that you understand this new philosophy and where it comes from, let's see why I keep saying dancing with your baby is the best thing you can do to help him grow.

6 Why Your Dance Matters

. . . dancing is the loftiest, the most moving, the most beautiful of the arts, because it is no mere translation or abstraction from life; it is life itself.

—HAVELOCK ELLIS
The Dance of Life

When you dance with your baby, you help him grow in many ways. You can't predict precisely *how* he'll develop. He may become an artist, a mathematician, scientist, politician, musician, or football player. But you *can* know that however he develops, he'll become the best person he can be.

When parents and babies dance synchronously together, many wonderful kinds of growth take place. The dance doesn't *cause* a baby to have a high IQ or to become a concert violinist or anything else, because causes always have to work 100 percent of the time. In the dance, nothing is inevitable, but anything is possible.

Here, for example, are just some of the many good outcomes that have been shown to go hand in hand with a synchronous parent-baby dance:

• *A higher IQ.* In a long-term study, the late Dr. Leon Yarrow and his colleagues at the National Institute of Mental Health did find that a child's IQ at age ten correlated with how sensitively mothers responded to their babies' signals during the first year. (Parental sensitivity to a baby's signals is one part of the dance.) Mothers who responded sensitively had ten-year-olds with higher IQs than mothers who tended to ignore their babies' signals during the first year.[1]

• *A more curious, less irritable baby.* In 1972, two studies looked at how smoothly mothers and babies were dancing—then observed how happy the babies were later. Both studies found that babies who had their signals read and their needs appropriately met were more interested in exploring. Babies who'd been interacting synchronously with their mothers also cried less.[2]

• *Emotional health in adulthood.* In 1957, Stella Chess, M.D., and Alexander Thomas, M.D., at New York University began studying 133 babies and their mothers. In the late '70s, the kids had become adults. Drs. Chess and Thomas found a synchronous dance (they called it a "good fit") during infancy was related to a child's emotional health when he was nineteen or twenty.[3]

• *Trust in adults at ages two and three.* New York infant psychiatrist Sirgay Sanger watched parents playing with their babies in their early months and then studied the same children when they were two and three years old. He found babies who danced (interacted) joyously with their parents during their first year were the ones most comfortable later about asking other adults for advice. They were also likeliest to trust and use the advice they'd received.[4]

• *Alertness.* Drs. Michael Lewis and Susan Goldberg at the Infant Laboratory in Princeton found that mothers who read and responded to their babies' signals had more alert babies than those who often ignored their babies' signals.[5] A study in *Child Development* also linked a baby's alertness with a synchronous dance.[6]

• *Resilience.* In 1985, E. Virginia Demos, Ed.D., at Cambridge Hospital in Massachusetts took a new look at the findings of a study that began in Boston more than thirty years ago. She wanted to see what parent-baby interactions are connected with a baby's resiliency (which she defines as "the capacity to bounce back or recover from a disappointment, obstacle or setback"). She found a synchronous dance (the "good fit") was related to a child's ability to bounce back from defeat.[7]

These plus dozens of other studies during the past twenty years lead to one overwhelming conclusion: It's not special lessons or fast-track baby schools, but dancing synchronously with you, that helps your baby become the best he can be. Some quite distinguished experts will even tell you that dancing with your baby *causes* him to be bright, happy, emotionally healthy, alert, and resilient. But now that you know about systems, you can see this explanation is far too simple. All we can say for certain is that you and your baby are involved in a system that's growing toward higher and higher planes of complexity. An optimal family system goes hand in hand with an optimally developing baby. And the smoothly flowing dance is how your strong family system expresses itself.

WHAT ARE THE QUALITIES OF AN OPTIMAL FAMILY SYSTEM?

You can't say any family system is either "good" or "bad," because (like many ways we've been taught to think about babies and parents) these terms are too simple. To answer whether a family is "good," you'd have to ask: Good according to whose definition? On what day? At what hour? Since each family system is unique, there is no "typical" family. It's also impossible to compare one family with another and say one is "better," the other "worse."

We can, however, look at family systems to see whether they *work*. So while we can't use judgmental terms like "good" and "bad," we can talk about a family in terms of optimal, midrange, and dysfunctional. An optimal family is working at its highest potential much of the time. A midrange family is doing okay, but could use some help. And a dysfunctional family is dancing unharmoniously and having problems. Optimal (working brilliantly) and dysfunctional (working poorly) aren't separate *types* of families. Rather, all families lie somewhere on a continuum between optimal and dysfunctional. Under extreme stress, an optimal family can become dysfunctional for a while (although the stronger the system the more stress-proof it is). Nearly every family has some growth-inspiring qualities, because in a *totally* dysfunctional system a baby would die from lack of food the first few days. Your goal as a Dancingparent isn't to change your parent-baby system to make it "better" but to focus on and enhance the positive qualities you already have.

What qualities does an optimal family system possess? As Dr. Irene Goldenberg at the U.C.L.A. Neuropsychiatric Institute and Dr. Herbert Goldenberg at California State University in Los Angeles note, the most authoritative word so far on how "healthy" families function comes from the research of clinicians J. M. Lewis, W. R. Beavers, J. T. Gossett, and V. A. Phillips.[8] These clinicians looked beyond the strengths and weaknesses of each person in the system to try to find what kinds of interactions help a family work best. Comparing thirty-three healthy families with seventy families that had a teenager with serious emotional problems, they found no one single quality that distinguishes optimal families from those that aren't working. But they did find a "tapestry" of differences that seem to make a family work or not work. Among the qualities common in family systems that work best:

• *Clear communication.* In an optimal system, a parent and child "talk" to each other with a minimum of hidden messages. Whether you want to or not, you and your baby are always communicating—on two levels. The surface level involves what you're actually saying and doing. The second level (which scientists call metacommunication) qualifies what you've said or done and gives the *emotional* content of the message. Problems (and muddled communication) erupt when the first message ("Ooooooh, pretty baby") is contradicted by a facial expression or voice tone (for example, a tone that says, "I'm really bored with all this playing. How soon can I get this baby to sleep so I can finally get the dishes done?"). The message a baby gets from this interaction is: "My mother/father says, 'Let's play,' but *means* 'I'd rather not.' " You can see why a baby exposed to such mixed signals all the time would have a hard time learning to trust his parents. How can you trust anyone who's always saying one thing and meaning another?

The fact that communication takes place on *two* levels illustrates clearly why you can't force yourself to dance, or constantly try to follow rules you don't really believe in. You can only consciously control your surface messages. Your secondary messages—the way you *really* feel—will leak through, anyway, especially when you're with someone (like your baby) who knows you extremely well.

In extreme cases, dysfunctional families in which a child is continually getting conflicting double messages like "I love you (hate you)" or "Come closer (get away)" can even produce pathology in children. As Goldenberg and Goldenberg write:

> It is as though the parent is saying, "I order you to disobey me" to a confused child who cannot escape, to whom the relationship is important, and who must develop a response to the incongruent messages occurring at two different levels. In that situation, he or she may develop an incongruent way of communicating back . . .[9]

In an optimal family, in contrast, parents say what they mean . . . and babies learn to say what they mean too. (In Chapter 10, I'll talk a lot more about how your baby communicates with you before he can talk, so you can read his signals even more clearly.)

• *Respect for feelings.* In less happy families, emotional censorship reigns. There are certain feelings (anger, frustration, or fear, for example) that you just "shouldn't" have. Psychologist Robert B. Hampson of Southern Methodist University and Dallas psychiatrist W. Robert Beavers recently did a study of three hundred families and found that in some less happy families, even a small glance or hand movement from a controlling parent can stop a family squabble or disagreement. The "total harmony" these families often display is actually a sign they're unwilling to talk about problems and that all negative feelings are being squashed and suppressed. Happy (optimal) families air differences openly, but anger focuses on what the other person *did,* not on how "bad" the person is.[10]

Since the system you and your baby establish during your first year tends to persist the rest of your lives, respecting your baby's feelings in your first year together is important to getting your system off on the right track. (We'll talk more about respecting your baby's feelings in Chapter 8.)

• *Flexibility.* In an optimal family system, people can adapt quickly to changes around them. That's why it's important to set your own rules and not to rely on too many unyielding "shoulds." When someone tells you that you should treat your baby any one specific way, they're limiting your ability to shift quickly and change.

• *Respect for each person as an individual.* In less effective families, babies quickly acquire labels. Sara is lazy, Marie is spoiled, Stevie is "like Grandpa." Labeling a baby, as we saw in the last chapter, is one way not to react to him or her as a real, unique human being. In some dysfunctional families, one child becomes the scapegoat: Johnny is considered the "naughty" one, the troublemaker. Creating a scapegoat is an unhealthy way for a family to cope with its own weaknesses. Rather than the whole family system needing to change, it's all blamed on poor little Johnny. A very common way to avoid respecting a baby's individuality is to turn him or her into the family "pet." The baby is then considered the model, carefree, happy, affectionate person in the family—the one whose main purpose is to make the family laugh. But as Goldenberg and Goldenberg point out:

> Unfortunately, "pets" are rarely taken seriously: it is as if they existed merely to bring laughter and lightness to the family. Yet there may be considerable sadness and depression underneath the surface playfulness and good citizenship. One reason is that the family pet, frequently the baby or youngest child, is treated in a sense as a nonperson, without position or status in the family, with a resulting loss of self-esteem. The cute, adorable, "darling" facade may hide inner feelings of emptiness.[11]

This is still another reason why the traditional views of a baby as a moldable blob or nonperson didn't work very well. Knowing that your baby *is* a real person from the moment he's born, you're highly unlikely to turn him into the family pet.

• *Allowance for individuality yet connectedness.* This is a careful balance and no one can tell you exactly how to achieve it. As in any intimate relationship, you're continually adjusting this balance as you and your baby grow. On one hand, you don't want the relationship to absorb you totally (you and your baby want to remain individuals). Yet on the other hand, you want still to feel "linked" together. Fortunately, when you're dancing, as you'll see throughout the rest of this book, a feeling of connectedness is inherent. When you and your baby are truly dancing, you *can't* feel disconnected: It's impossible.

• *Freedom yet discipline.* It's in this area where the idea of dancing with your baby could likeliest be misinterpreted. Since your baby is born dancing, you may think he should be allowed total freedom to dance any way he pleases. Not so. A strong family system still keeps the parents in charge. An optimal family system involves democracy, not anarchy. All optimal families have rules for children to follow and those rules are often laid out concretely by the parents. From the time your baby is born, you'll notice that many subtle, *unspoken* rules are also evolving. How often you or your mate holds the baby, how frequently each of you feeds him, when you play with the baby, and so forth, all reflect your value system and priorities.

The above are a reasonable list of prime ingredients in a healthy family. How do you create such an optimal family system? Obviously, you can't "create" a system in the same way you can whip up a chocolate cake. But by dancing with your baby, you're expressing your system. A happy dance (which you *can* focus on) reflects a strong system (which is more elusive to define). Paradoxically, as you dance, you're also bringing your system into being.

HOW DOES YOUR DANCE RELATE TO YOUR SYSTEM?

To understand more clearly how your dance relates to your system, you might think in terms of *fractals*.[12] A fractal is a small design or pattern that reflects the much larger pattern it's part of. A snowflake exemplifies the idea of fractals: It's made up of designs within designs within designs . . . yet even the smallest design in the snowflake mirrors the larger pattern. Likewise, one of the qualities that makes music sound so beautiful to us is that all the little trills, couplets, and themes echo in some way the entire piece. In the same way the tiny patterns in a snowflake reflect the flake's overall pattern and the small trills in Mozart's Rondo in D Major echo the overall sound of the piece, all the little dances you do reflect your overall dance. A happy dance reflects a happy system. It's as simple—and complex—as that.

As you dance with your baby, you, he, and your system will reach higher and higher levels of complexity. And the more complex you are, the higher on the developmental ladder you've climbed. In short, the more complex you are, the more you've grown. Einstein's thoughts were much more complex than those of the physicists before him. Martin W. Hoffman at the University of Michigan theorizes that as we grow we develop a more complex empathy with others. Likewise, it's self-evident that Vladimir Horowitz is a more complex pianist than the local high school music teacher, just as Shakespeare was a more complex writer than Judith Krantz is.

No one can predict where your baby's talents and potentials will lead him. You can't dance to *get* a higher IQ because, quite frankly, IQ is only one very crude measure of a highly complex intelligence. But I do know from my knowledge of how systems work that your dancing with your baby leads him to higher levels of complexity so he can develop in many ways as a whole person. And that, in a nutshell, is why the dance matters.

A BRIEF CAUTION BEFORE WE GO ON

In the following chapters (in fact, for the rest of this book), I'm going to talk about dancing with your baby. But before I do, I have to add a warning. The findings about the dance can be misused to throw blame right back on parents like you. What if parents and babies *aren't* dancing an optimal dance? Isn't this, after all, the parent's fault?

No.

It turns out that when talking about how well your system works, it's naive to blame anyone. Just as, when two people divorce, if you're being honest you can't necessarily blame just one or the other or even both of them (sometimes divorce just happens because outside or past pressures become too much to bear), when you and your baby dance, you *both* play a role in how the dance is going.

Some babies are hard for some parents to dance with. If you've always wanted a cuddly baby and get one who hates to cuddle, your dance could become disrupted (although that's much less likely to happen now that you know the dance exists and that each baby is special). If a parent and a baby are too disharmonious, they may have what scientists call a "poor match" or a "poor fit" . . . and growth may not be as optimal as it could be. But a poor fit isn't anyone's fault, and scientists see many more good fits than poor ones. The vast majority of warm, caring mothers and fathers (like you) dance beautifully with their babies—without lessons and without straining.

Experts (many of them well-meaning) will come along in the future and try to tell you precisely how to dance. Don't listen to them. Anytime you try to narrow the dance down to a few simple "right" steps, you lose the spontaneity that's essential to helping your baby grow. "How-tos" inevitably wind up making the dance sound robotic and mechanical. If you were to dance according to the "rules" in any program, chances are you'd wind up looking and feeling more like a marionette than like Mikhail Baryshnikov.

Remember, dancing with the free, flowing spontaneity of Baryshnikov is your aim. And though that sounds like a tall order to fill, you can do it—just by tuning in to your baby, relaxing, and being yourself.

In the rest of this book, I'll talk about the many ways you can dance joyously with your baby. You'll discover that you can dance beautifully together even when your baby is asleep or you're at work. Since spontaneity is one key to a good dance, it's highly important to take these ideas only as *suggestions* offered to help you understand your dance better. If on any page in the following chapters you read something that makes you feel anxious or fret that you're dancing "all wrong," forget that section and trust yourself. Understanding your dance helps you realize it's *okay* to be out of step some days, and no great harm will come to your baby or your system because of it.

In the rest of this book, I'll talk about what you can (but not *must*) do to help the dance flow smoothly. In the next three chapters, I'll reveal three things you can do to get ready to dance: understand your baby's capabilities (Chapter 7); respect your baby's feelings (Chapter 8); and appreciate rhythms (the music for the dance) (Chapter 9).

After that I'll reveal how your baby "talks" to you from the moment he's born (Chapter 10) and how you "talk" back, using your biological wisdom (Chapter 11). I'll also give you tips on dancing with a crying baby (Chapter 12), making your baby smart—with love (Chapter 13), and choosing a dance partner for your baby while you're away (Chapter 14).

Now let's get ready to dance.

PART III

GETTING READY
TO DANCE

*My style is a dance. . . . Every day I
count wasted in which there has been no
dancing.*

—FRIEDRICH NIETZSCHE

7 Understanding Your Baby's Nature

Nature is already as good as it can be.
It cannot be improved upon.
He who tries to redesign it, spoils it.
He who tries to redirect it, misleads it.

—LAO-TZU

The first thing you can do when getting ready to dance is to understand how much your baby can do. If your baby can see only about eight inches in front of his face (which is the case for newborns) and you're dancing three feet from him by making funny faces, you obviously won't get much response.

We hear much today about how smart babies are. Yet there's also a contrary feeling that a baby's quite helpless. So let's see what your baby can—and can't—do.

EXACTLY HOW COMPETENT IS YOUR BABY?

William James saw the baby's world as just a "buzzing, blooming confusion."[1] And even though we know today that a baby is highly adept at perceiving his world, old myths die hard. Many people today continue to see your baby as quite helpless. A baby *is* dependent, there's no doubt about that. But any new parent who has been summoned at 2 A.M. by the siren-like cry of a hungry baby knows that even a newborn is quite able to get attention and what he needs—promptly!

Not only is your baby quite capable of calling you to get his needs met, but he has built-in qualities that encourage adults to love meeting those needs. One of your baby's most potent qualities is aptly called *babyness*. Babyness is simply looking cute, a quality nearly all mammal babies (including kittens, rats, and rabbits) share. The oversized head, the big eyes, the button nose, the tiny, perfectly formed hands and feet—all have been designed by evolution to attract grownups. Cynics who insist they dislike babies or find them ugly are denying their own basic biology. When a baby is in a room, as many a disgruntled actor knows, he quickly upstages everyone and becomes the center of attention. Whenever they see a baby, most adults have an overwhelming, built-in urge to look at him (a fact that hasn't been lost on Madison Avenue, where advertisers use adorable, attention-getting babies to sell everything from Pampers to Michelin tires).

But your baby has a lot more than just his babyness going for him. At birth, he's already extremely competent and complex. To give you an idea *how* complex, let's just look at his brain.

YOUR BABY'S INCREDIBLE BRAIN

During the last four months in the womb, your baby grows brain cells at the blitzkrieg speed of over 250,000 cells a minute.[2] By the time he's born, he has a mind-boggling 100 *billion* brain cells, a number so incredibly huge we can barely begin to comprehend it even with our sophisticated adult brains. To give you some idea what a humongous number 100 billion is, suppose a rich aunt died and left you $100 billion. If in the year A.D. 1 you had started spending this $100 billion fortune at the rate of $100,000 a day, you'd still have about $28 billion left—enough to buy half the state of New Hampshire at about $10,000 an acre.

In addition, these 100 billion cells in your baby's brain are interconnected with fibers so densely packed there are 10,000 miles of fibers in one cubic inch. If you took all these connecting fibers and stretched them end to end, they'd reach from here to the moon and back four times.

Even before your baby is born, the billions of fibers in his brain begin interconnecting and cross-connecting at lightning speeds until by the end of the baby's first year, as many as 70 percent of his brain cells will be on the job. You'll often hear that in your baby's brain, his "circuits" are "hooked up." This unfortunate metaphor, which likens your baby's brain to a fancy computer, is misleading. It implies that once "hooked," your baby's brain is rigidly wired and can never be unhooked. Not so.

Some parts of your baby's brain (those that control his digestive tract and heartbeat, for example) are more or less set. But most of his brain is extremely flexible. Connections are being made, broken, and re-formed all the time as your baby busily explores his world. This is the underlying biological reason why you needn't worry about making a few parenting "mistakes." During a baby's first year, his brain is so irrepressibly active and ever-changing he'll hardly notice a parent's minor slips, let alone remember them the rest of his life.

What can your baby do with his marvelous great brain? More than scientists of the past ever dreamed. Contrary to past myth, a healthy baby isn't born deaf and blind. A newborn can see, smell, taste, hear, and feel in very special ways. Not all of a baby's senses are the same as an adult's. This fact that *differences* exist between adults and babies has led many scientists (all of them *adults,* of course) to conclude the baby is somehow inferior. Just as individuals suffer from narrow-minded egocentrism and groups from ethnocentrism, adults (alas, even scientists) often succumb to what I call "adult-centrism": They truly believe the "goal" of every baby is to be a Great Big Wonderful Adult—just like themselves. In fact, babies have their own quite interesting baby lives to lead. And a baby's highly developed senses, while different from an adult's, are elegantly designed to serve his special baby needs. In his own way, your baby is every bit as competent and complex as you are. He's *different.* But these differences don't make him inferior. They just make him an interesting (baby) person.

A BABY'S-EYE VIEW OF THE NURSERY

Your baby has undeveloped control over his body movements at birth. But one system he can control well is his eyes. Shortly after birth, your baby will probably be extremely alert, his eyes darting curiously back and forth as he gets his first look at this strange, marvelous new world.

You may have heard all babies are born "legally blind." Not so. Your newborn can't see a great distance. Any object more than eight to fifteen inches or so from his eyes may be unfocused and fuzzy. But far from being a handicap, this inability to focus on all the objects in the room may be a handy advantage. Being able to see everything suddenly in a flash can be a horrendous ordeal. Blind adults who've had miracle operations to restore their sight often find the sudden ability to see so disorienting they become severely depressed. Regaining their sight, some of them say, was the most traumatic experience of their lives.[3] Since a tiny baby can be easily overwhelmed by too many exciting sights, nature has given your baby a special protection: He can only see those objects closest to him. The objects your baby *can* focus on, however, he sees quite well.

At birth, for example, your baby can see you waggle your finger if you're standing within nine feet of his crib. He can spot the iris of your eye from four and a half feet away. And he can zero in on the pupil in your eye from a distance of about sixteen inches. A medium-sized freckle on your face doesn't come into focus until you're about eleven inches away . . . but then who needs to see freckles across a crowded room? Amazingly, when you hold your baby to feed him, your face is almost always eight to fifteen inches from his eyes—the perfect distance for him to explore every delicious detail of you, from your earlobes to your eyes.

What do babies love to see most? Of course, you have to watch your baby to discover what he prefers. (More about this in Chapter 10: How Your Baby "Talks" To You.) But as a rule, babies share similar tastes. Years ago, Case Western Reserve psychologist Robert Fantz found that babies would rather look at a checkerboard than at a plain colored surface, at a bull's-eye target rather than stripes and at complex patterns rather than simple ones.[4] Other researchers have found that newborns can see and distinguish colors, enjoy dramatic contrasts, and are more excited by curved patterns than by straight lines.[5]

Having observed that babies love bull's-eye targets, some misguided experts have come up with the notion that you should fill your baby's nursery with striking, bold black-and-white checkerboards and colorful targets to capture your baby's attention and stimulate his mind. Contriving to create the "perfect" visual environment for your baby isn't necessary and may even do him some harm. If you bombard your baby constantly with such dramatic sights, one of two things may happen. Either he may become what scientists call habituated (in other words, bored), and so he won't find the patterns "fascinating" anymore, or he may feel overwhelmed and overstimulated (in which case, you may have an irritable or a withdrawn baby on your hands). One of the hardest things for many people in our society to grasp is that if a *little* stimulation is good for a baby, *more* of that same stimulation isn't necessarily *better*. We all know the saying "too much of a good thing." Well, when getting ready to dance with your baby, it's handy to remember that too much "good" stimulation may be not so good. As you'll learn by watching your baby, it's a *variety* of intriguing sights offered in a stimulating but not overwhelming way that most attracts your baby's curiosity and encourages him to reach out and explore his world.

A mother once said to me, "Wouldn't it be great if scientists would combine all the latest findings about what babies love to see and design the perfect toy to capture a baby's attention?" Remarkably, one object *has* been created which contains all the elements that fascinate your baby most. If we were to design the perfect toy for your baby to look at, we'd wind up with *you*.

Babies only one minute old will turn their heads 180 degrees to look at a picture of a human face, even if they've never seen a real person before.[6] The face can be real or sketched, in the flesh or on film, two- or three-dimensional, even a mask with two eye-like dots. No matter. The baby will be mesmerized by it. Watch your baby closely, and you'll discover he's literally in love with your beautiful face.

WHAT CAN YOUR BABY HEAR?

Your baby's hearing is especially fascinating because he can hear even before he's born. The snail-shaped cochlea, an organ in the inner ear which is the real center of hearing, was fully formed about four months before birth. By two months before birth, some babies startle in the womb to a loud clash of pans or even dance energetically to music.[7] To find out what a fetus can hear, a French obstetrician inserted a hydrophone into one mother's uterus as she was about to give birth. He heard a virtual orchestra of sounds: the mother's loud, thumping heartbeat, all sorts of whooshing and gurgling, the faint voices of the mother and her doctor talking, and in the background, the unmistakable strains of Beethoven's Fifth Symphony.[8]

The fact that babies can hear in the womb has led some wrongheaded experts to suggest you should start reading your baby stories before birth or even playing Mozart and Grieg to him. The logic of this advice escapes me. A baby can't understand stories and he'll hear you talking throughout the day anyway, without your having to make an extraordinary effort.

At birth, many sounds your baby hears may be muffled. That's because a newborn's middle ear contains extra fluid, most of which disappears after several days. Again, this fluid may be wise nature's defense against too many sudden sounds at birth. Yet though a newborn may not hear with crystal clarity, he can still hear in a wide range from 16 to 30,000 cycles (vibrations) per second. If he could hear much below 16, he'd be able to hear the vibrations of his own body. Much above 30,000, he could detect a dog whistle. In fact, your baby is the most sensitive to high-pitched tones that he'll ever be in his life. By the time he reaches his teens, his upper level of hearing will drop to 20,000 cycles. By his late forties, he'll be unable to hear sounds over 8,000.

What does your baby love to listen to most? As with sight, it's the most *natural* sounds that excite him. He may or may not adore Bach and Beethoven. But he *loves* the human voice. When alert and ready to play, a baby generally prefers high-pitched voices. When upset or drowsy, he'll likelier be soothed by lower tones. As for music, a study by Gary N. Siperstein and Earl C. Butterfield at the University of Kansas found that babies prefer vocal music over instrumental pieces. The twenty babies in one of their studies were especially fond of folk songs by the Clancy Brothers![9]

Not only does your baby love voices; he loves *your* voice best. In one study by Dr. Margaret Mills at the University of London, babies only twenty to thirty days old were given nipples to suck and were rewarded whenever they sucked by getting to listen to a tape recording of a human voice. Babies sucked much more vigorously to hear tapes of their own mothers' voices than they did to hear a stranger talk.[10] Your baby also likes knowing your voice belongs to *you*. In several studies,[11] infants only one and two months old cried when they saw their mothers in one part of the room yet heard their mothers' voices coming from a speaker across the room. Of course, by a few months of age, your baby's preference for you will be obvious from the happy smiles he greets you with.

WHAT ABOUT YOUR BABY'S SENSES OF SMELL, TASTE, AND TOUCH?

Your baby can also smell, taste, and touch . . . and he has distinct preferences in all these. Israeli neurophysiologist Jacob Steiner reports a baby only twelve hours old will gurgle with delight when he tastes a drop of sugar water and grimace at a drop of lemon juice. A newborn will also smile beatifically when he smells bananas or vanilla and spit with disgust at the odor of rotten eggs.[12]

Not only does your baby have more taste buds than you, but (as you'll discover when you introduce him to solid foods) his tastes are unique. Whereas some babies adore peas, others will spit them back at you . . . and the baby who refuses to eat his peas isn't just being "picky" or spoiled. Scientists have now shown that people actually *do* differ dramatically in taste sensitivity. To you, carrots may taste pleasingly sweet, but to your baby they may honestly be sour and disgusting. Studies with various pure chemicals have clearly shown how we differ in the ways we taste foods. Sodium benzoate, for instance, is tasteless to some; but to others, it tastes sweet, sour, salty, or bitter. So if your baby hates green beans, you can try making him eat them if you want to. But you may want to save your energy for more important efforts.

Your baby's sense of smell, of course, is virtually inseparable from his sense of taste. In a well-known study done at the Radcliffe Infirmary in Oxford, England, pediatrician Aiden Macfarlane let babies choose the odor of either a breast pad saturated with their mothers' milk or one soaked with a stranger's milk. By only ten days of age, babies rapidly turned their heads toward their own mothers' breast pads, showing that even at this young age they could smell—and preferred—their mothers' milk.[13]

As for touch, it goes without saying that your baby is quite sensitive to stroking, cuddling, and holding. Some babies (known as non-cuddlers) are so sensitive to touch they actually find it unpleasant.

One subtlety you may overlook at first is that not all touches are equal. Though your baby has hundreds of thousands of exteroceptors all over his skin, these sensitive receivers are most concentrated on his lips, the tip of his tongue, and the pads of his fingers. When getting ready to dance, it's handy to know that if you want to excite your young baby with a touch, your best bet is to hold his hand. (If you just pat his knee or tap his shoulder, he may hardly notice.)

Your baby's hands, by the way, are intriguing because they're both highly sensitive to touch and quite insensitive to pain. This useful combination makes your baby's fingertips the perfect gadgets for exploring his world. If he gets a finger pinched, it may hurt; but as you kiss the pain away, you can take comfort in knowing that your baby's fingers are twenty times less sensitive to pain than his abdomen.

AND FINALLY—HOW MUCH CAN YOUR BABY LEARN?

When distinguished scientists begin discussing what a baby can learn, their tales often sound like anecdotes you'd read in Ripley's *Believe It or Not.* T. G. R. Bower, professor of psychology at the University of Edinburgh, tells of one blind baby who at only sixteen weeks of age made a variety of puzzling, strange, sharp clicking sounds with his tongue and lips. A baby researcher for twenty years, Dr. Bower had never heard a baby make such peculiar sounds before. To test a theory, he dangled a large ball in front of the baby, moving it silently back and forth. Soon the baby began making clicking noises, then turning his head to follow the ball. Dr. Bower's conclusion: This little blind baby, who because he'd been born ten weeks prematurely was actually about as mature as a normal six-week-old, was using *echoes* to explore his world. The baby's parents later took advantage of this skill by hanging over the baby's crib toys that made sounds when they were touched or pulled. In *The Perceptual World of the Child,* edited by (among others) the well-known child-development expert Jerome Bruner, Dr. Bower writes, ''The baby quickly learned that when he was put in his crib there would be a toy somewhere for him to play with. However, the only way he could find it would be to use echoes. By the age of 16 weeks he could reliably find any largish object.''[14] Believe it—or not!

In another ingenious experiment, Dr. Bower fitted babies with

3-D goggles. These goggles, of course, create the illusion that solid objects are floating in midair. Young babies, Dr. Bower reports, will keep reaching for the phantom objects until they get frustrated and cry. But an eight- or nine-month-old can't be so easily fooled. At first an older baby will reach for the object. But when he grasps only thin air, he'll often do a curious thing. He'll often stare at his hand or bang it on a nearby surface, as if to make sure his hand is still "working." Then he'll slowly inspect the object visually. By tilting and moving his head, the baby learns that unreal objects "behave" differently than real ones do. From then on, whenever the baby is presented with an object during the experiment, he'll inspect it closely. If the object is real, the baby will reach for it. If it's an illusion, he'll often look at Dr. Bower and giggle. In short, by eight months of age, some babies are mastering their first lessons in distinguishing appearance from reality.[15]

In some ways, your baby may be even more accurate than you are in seeing the world as it truly is. If shown a miniature Rolls-Royce a hundred feet away, most adults will distrust their senses, do some mental acrobatics, and *perceive* the Rolls-Royce as full-size but farther away—say, 150 feet from them. Up until age six or so, your child won't do that. Because a child doesn't know yet how big a Rolls is supposed to be, he'll actually see the Rolls as a miniature car only a hundred feet from him.[16]

If your baby can learn so much, under what conditions does he learn *best*? Ah, that's most interesting of all. Studies consistently show that a baby learns most and fastest—and will likelier remember what he learns—when *he* can control what's happening.

In an ingenious experiment at the Planck-Institut für Psychiatrie in Munich, Hanus Papousek showed three- and four-month-olds a board of electric lights. When lit, the lights created several distinct patterns. Could the babies learn and remember these patterns? When Dr. Papousek first showed the babies the lights, he concluded they were too young to master the task. Not only couldn't the babies remember, but they found the lights a colossal bore. Then Dr. Papousek had a brainstorm: He rigged up a lever the babies could push. Every time a baby pushed the lever, Dr. Papousek flicked on the lights. Suddenly, when *they* were in control, the babies' interest skyrocketed. Delighted with their wonderful new skill, the babies began happily pushing the lever and gazing intently at the lights. The babies also began learning rapidly. Once they were able to control their own learning, their ability to remember the patterns soared.[17]

In short—and this is crucial to remember when getting ready to dance—your baby isn't sitting passively in his infant seat waiting for you to switch on his brain with lessons. He's constantly choosing what he wants to learn about. And it's those experiences *he* chooses (not necessarily those chosen *for* him) that help him learn fastest and most completely. In other words, those experiences your baby *feels best* about are the ones likeliest to help him grow. How your baby feels will greatly determine what he'll explore and therefore what he'll learn about. So let's talk about your baby's feelings next.

8 Respecting Your Baby's Feelings

Children are most like us in their feelings and least like us in their thoughts.

—DR. DAVID ELKIND
Tufts University child psychologist

The second step you can take when getting ready to dance is to gain respect for your baby's feelings. The latest findings about how competent your baby is have led some self-styled experts to focus almost exclusively on what your baby can learn. Thus the rush is on to make babies even "smarter" by giving them lessons, in an attempt to raise their IQs and make them all geniuses. What would-be Superbaby creators fail to understand is that what your baby seems to "think" in his first months of life is actually more what he feels. Your baby is both a thinking (or what scientists call a cognitive) and a feeling (or affective) being. And though some scientists disagree with me, I have strong reasons for believing that feelings come first.

To understand why I say your baby is born dancing (and not doing arithmetic), you need to know something about the inner structure and workings of a baby's brain.

YOUR BABY'S BRAIN (OR WHY I SAY FEELINGS COME FIRST)

You could say your baby's brain is three brains in one, or what Dr. Paul MacLean, chief of the Laboratory of Brain Evolution and Behavior at the National Institute of Mental Health, calls a triune brain.[1] Though constantly interacting, these three brain systems all have their own memories and special kinds of intelligence. While it's important to remember your baby's brain can't *really* be split into three parts, it helps when trying to understand how your baby's brain works to talk about these three brain systems separately.

First there's the "reptilian" brain, located at the very center of the forebrain. This is the oldest of a baby's brain systems and governs such unlearned and relatively primitive tasks as flinching from pain, breathing, blinking, and swallowing. This part of the brain is well developed at birth, although some activities this brain system oversees (most notably fighting and submission) won't be evident in your baby's behavior for several years. Man's baser feelings or urges—lust and rage—also lurk here.

The second of your baby's brain systems—the one we're most interested in when talking about the dance—is what Dr. MacLean calls the "old mammalian" brain, or limbic system. Highly developed at birth, the limbic system plays a key role in governing emotions. This part of your baby's brain is the seat of man's highest drives; curiosity, joy, spontaneity, playfulness, a sense of wonder, a drive to explore, optimism, a sense of humor, and the feelings that cause laughter and tears are here.

Nestled in your baby's limbic system is a vital group of cells about the size of a small prune, the hypothalamus. Sometimes called the body's "master clock," the hypothalamus helps regulate body temperature, sleep-and-wake rhythms, appetite, pulse, and other rhythmic functions. Though only one three-hundredth of your baby's brain weight, the hypothalamus acts as a sort of CEO for much of the baby's nervous system and for his powerful pituitary gland (which, in turn, discharges the hormones that regulate growth, metabolism, and many other bodily functions). Not only do your baby's pleasure centers lie deep in the hypothalamus, but most of the ways a baby behaves in his early months spring from this highly complex emotional brain.

It's the limbic system, working with other parts of your baby's brain, that makes it possible for him to pick up on the tone and emotional inflections in your voice. Just as, even if you can't hear a friend's exact words, you can often catch the gist of her meaning from her tone of voice, your baby can grasp the emotional meanings of what you're telling him long before he understands your exact words. When you feel your baby "knows" what you're saying, you're right. But there are two ways to know the world: through logic and reason and through emotional, intuitive understanding. When you talk to your baby, he does "know" what you're saying . . . but he's picking up on the emotional quality of your words, not the logic.

To demonstrate this yourself, wait one day until your baby is content and bright-eyed. Then stand where your baby can clearly see your face, and say gently, but cheerily (in a slightly raised voice with drawn-out vowel sounds), "Aaaaaaaaah, pretty baby!" Open your eyes wide and smile. With your whole body and tone of voice, try telling your baby how much you love him. Watch his eyes light up in response. Wait quietly for a minute or so until your baby has time to calm down. Then repeat the same words, this time keeping your tone and expression as emotionally flat as you can. When you eliminate all emotional communication from your words, chances are your baby (if he's a newborn) won't even look in your direction, or (if he's older) may look away, puzzled or surprised. When you and your baby are dancing, you're communicating mostly on an emotional level.

The importance of the limbic system may also hold the key to a puzzle scientists have only begun to explore. Adults often talk of feelings that well up for no apparent reason and seem unrelated to the logical realities at hand. For example, highly successful people admit they suffer from the "impostor phenomenon." The complaint "I've done so well—why do I feel so bad?" has become the lament of many a high-wattage baby-boomer. Why? Though we can only speculate at this point, the answer may lie in the preverbal, prelogical limbic system, which has its own intelligence and memory. Though, as you saw in Chapter 2, a fleeting emotion certainly won't register in the brain forever, *persistently* anxious, sad, or insecure feelings experienced in childhood may lurk in our emotional brains, giving some of us a vague, illogical, ineffable feeling of being disjoint with the world.

Can experiencing many good feelings during his first year, before he can talk, help your baby avoid later such pervasive contemporary maladies as the impostor phenomenon? Adult emotional problems are highly complex, so we can't answer this question with an unequivocal yes. But clearly much evidence points in this direction.

Leaving your baby's fascinating limbic system, let's talk just a minute about his third brain system—the neocortex. It's this incredible brain that masters such complex logical processes as planning, subtracting, talking, writing, and creating designs that send an astronaut to the moon. Unlike your baby's limbic system, his neocortex is only partially developed at birth. That's why it seems clear to psychobiologists like myself that your baby experiences feelings at birth but is much less likely to come up with concrete ideas.

One driving force that helps your baby's neocortex learn faster and better is feeling happy and content (feelings that originate in his limbic system). When your baby feels lousy, chances are he'll learn very little. (Or he'll learn mainly about what makes him feel lousy!) When he feels cheerful and cherished, your baby will be much likelier to explore and pay attention to whatever you'd like to show him. As the famed Swiss psychologist Jean Piaget pointed out, without such feelings as interest, curiosity, self-esteem, and confidence, your baby won't learn as much as he otherwise could. Piaget likened your child's thoughts to a car and his feelings to the gasoline that runs the car.[2] In short, without the "fuel" of feeling loved, a baby can emotionally and mentally languish.

How can you help your baby feel loved? By dancing in step with him. And the first step in dancing with him is to respect and respond to his feelings.

RESPECTING YOUR BABY'S FEELINGS: A FEW TIPS (OR REMINDERS) TO GET YOU STARTED

Much of the following advice you may already know and understand. If so, congratulations. This just shows that your biological wisdom is actively at work, and you and your baby are probably already dancing beautifully. Still, in this busy world, when we're constantly being torn in ten directions, it never hurts to remind yourself of the wisdom you already possess. So let's look at four major things you can (but not *should*) do to respect your baby's feelings.

Accept Your Baby's Feelings at Face Value

One of the many refreshing things about a baby person is that he hasn't yet learned to hide his feelings. Legend has it that the cynical Greek Diogenes went about Athens in broad daylight with a lighted lantern, searching in vain for an honest man. Alas, Diogenes' error was in looking for a *man*. He would have found his honest person easily had he only headed straight for a nursery.

Too often, new parents are warned, "Don't pick up your baby whenever he cries. He's just trying to manipulate you." Nonsense. Your baby never thinks, "I'm happy, but I'll cry anyway to control you," or "I hate you, but I'll pretend to like you anyway because you give me food." Among babies, there are no connivers, con artists, or hypocrites. Happily, babies haven't yet learned the deceit some adults have mastered or the social pretenses we've all learned. When your baby laughs, cries, coos contentedly, looks puzzled, or frowns, he's expressing his real feelings.

Actually, you probably already take your baby's feelings more at face value than some scientists do. Mothers and fathers have always felt that when a baby smiles he's happy or when he looks sad he is sad. Scientists have been less willing to accept this. Take smiling. For years, whenever parents insisted their newborns smiled at them, a nearby doctor or nurse would reply, "Babies can't truly smile until they're two months old. It's just gas." But Peter Wolff, a well-known Harvard pediatrician, reports he's been able to get babies only a few hours old to smile by talking to them or playing them tape recordings of their own mothers' voices. Most of the newborns Dr. Wolff watched smiled in their sleep, but two were able to manage smiles when awake if Dr. Wolff passed objects before their eyes.[3] A newborn's smile is more subtle than a four-month-old's wide, beaming grin. But newborns do smile. And their smiles say, "Hey, this makes me feel good." Babies are honest: What you see is what you get.

Let Your Baby Know You Take His Feelings Seriously

As an adult, with a wider perspective on the world, you may have trouble at times taking your baby's feelings seriously. After all, you're about to feed him in five minutes, anyway, so why is he screaming so hard? Viewed objectively, a baby has such relatively minor problems that his crying often seems quite out of proportion. He's crying not for world peace but only over a wet diaper or hunger pangs.

Unfortunately, a baby can't see things as adults do. He has no idea he'll be fed in five minutes. Unable to understand "wait," he only "knows" what he feels: He has hunger pangs and feels un-happy. When his feelings are seldom taken seriously and responded to, he may feel helpless and abandoned.

Some loving mothers or fathers so hate to see their baby un-happy they try to deny any negative emotions the baby feels. When a baby cries, rather than cuddling him gently and handling him quietly in a way that matches his mood, this type of good parent begins shaking a rattle enthusiastically in the baby's face or bouncing him vigorously. Sometimes a baby can be jostled, teased, or smiled out of an unhappy mood, and in your growing wisdom you'll come to sense when these times are. But often when a baby is sad, he may feel best when you respond to his sadness by holding him close, rocking him gently, and communicating through the many special ways you touch and talk to him that you understand his unhappiness—that you're there and you care.

Learn and Respond to Your Baby's Facial Expressions

Since your baby's feelings are internal, however can you read them? You'll learn a lot more about this in Chapter 10: How Your Baby "Talks" to You, but one good way is to study your baby's face. Scientists have recently discovered that all babies share uni-versal facial expressions when they feel such emotions as anger, surprise, fear, joy, or sadness. In short, your baby's face is his emotional mirror.

Psychologist Carroll Izard and his colleagues at the University of Delaware's Human Emotions Laboratory have found that when a baby is angry, he invariably uses one set expression: His brows are sharply drawn together and lowered; his eyes are narrowed and stare fixedly ahead; and his mouth is wide and squarish as he cries. A baby who's distressed or in pain looks almost the same as an angry one, except for one difference: His eyes are squeezed tightly *shut*. Since babies the world over use similar faces to express the same feelings, Dr. Izard concludes that some basic facial expressions are universal and inborn.[4]

Dr. Izard's and other scientists' research into emotions grew out of observations by Charles Darwin, which had been ignored for nearly half a century. In his 1872 landmark volume, *The Expression of Emotions in Man and Animals*,[5] Darwin noted that people everywhere displayed the same facial expressions when they felt a specific emotion, like anger or fear. He concluded that some human facial expressions must be inborn and part of our biological tool kit. As an evolutionary tool, Darwin reasoned, universal facial expressions in babies make sense. A baby is totally unable to fend for himself. If he's to survive, he somehow has to let any adult caring for him know what he needs. Imagine a chaotic world in which each human baby had to learn from scratch how to signal his delight and discomfort. If a baby got it wrong for a few days and looked surprised rather than distressed when he was hungry, he might starve before he got his emotional signals on target.

If you observe your baby closely when he's hungry, you'll see he almost always looks much the same way. Of course, babies have far more complex emotions than the few scientists have been able to isolate in the lab so far. But aside from anger and distress, just mentioned, here are six other facial expressions Dr. Izard has been able to define:

• *Joy.* You can recognize this one without a description. The mouth smiles, the cheeks lift, and your baby's eyes twinkle.

• *Interest.* Your baby raises or knits his brows and holds his mouth softly rounded, with pursed lips.

• *Disgust.* Another easy one. Your baby's nose wrinkles, his upper lip rises, and his tongue pushes out as if he's saying, "Get that awful stuff away from me." (An especially common expression when eating mashed peas.)

• *Surprise.* Your baby's eyes widen and his brows rise as his mouth rounds into an oval.

• *Sadness.* This is the classic pout. The inner corners of your baby's eyebrows are raised as his lower lip pushes out and turns down.

• *Fear.* Often a difficult expression to decode, fear is shown by keeping the brows level and drawn in and up, the eyelids lifted, and the mouth retracted and open.

These aren't the *only* expressions your baby uses, of course. Nor does every baby display his feelings in precisely these ways. (Some babies, for example, use blends of these expressions, which makes things more complex.) Still, once you know that your baby's facial expressions are part of his emotional dance, you can watch the expressions more closely and monitor them to see how he's feeling. And you can come to learn a great deal about his inner emotional life by doing this.

Suppose one day your baby gets frightened when a neighbor's Lhasa apso barks in his face. It doesn't take any great insight in this situation to know your baby is scared. But later, in a more ambiguous situation, when you're not quite certain whether your baby is frightened (perhaps one day when Aunt Mabel appears at the front door in her huge flowered hat), you may recall your baby's earlier expression of fear and better understand what he's feeling about Aunt Mabel.

How to respond to your baby's facial expressions? You probably already do so naturally. But one thing you can do is mirror him. When he looks happy, you can try a happy face too. When he frowns, you can frown. When he seems proud of himself for mastering a new task, you can praise him warmly and show by the look in your eyes how proud you are too. Scientists now believe that by accurately mirroring your baby's feelings, you'll help him develop a sense of self. When he sees his own emotions happily reflected in your face, your baby may conclude, "Yes, that's how I feel. I feel glad!"

Respect Your Own Feelings

In the end, respecting your baby's feelings involves respecting your own. Often we can only give to others what we're willing to give ourselves. Responding to your baby's feelings, even when you don't want to, *does* often show adult maturity. After all, though you may dislike feeding your baby at 2 A.M., you do it anyway, because he needs food. But artificially trying to respond to your baby's fleeting feelings every second of the day because you think you should will only disrupt your dance. With your baby, you don't always have to be "on." Sometimes you're too worn out or distracted to be understanding. Such feelings are part of the emotional fabric of your life. Thus, if your baby wants to play after his 2 A.M. feeding and you want to go back to bed, there's nothing wrong with ignoring his jubilant invitations to play and letting him know with your own tired, blank expression that you'd rather sleep. Remember, it's not any one interaction that makes a difference in your baby's life. Rather, it's an overall *pattern* of relaxed, mutual caring that you and your baby are trying to establish through your dance. Missing or ignoring a few of your baby's emotions—if you are *usually* sympathetic and responsive—can be healthy for both of you.

By respecting your own feelings, you're giving your baby a clear message: "*My* feelings count too." This is a lesson even a newborn can begin to understand. Though it seems as if you're having to make all the effort to adjust to your baby and he's doing nothing to adjust to you or your schedule, your baby is already doing his part to groove into your feelings and mesh with the rhythms of your life.

9 Appreciating Rhythms (The Music for the Dance)

The closer you move in rhythm with someone, the closer you become to that person.

—DR. WILLIAM S. CONDON
Boston University

The third step you can take to get ready to dance is to understand the importance of rhythms. Somewhere, underlying all the ways you talk to, play with, feed, and otherwise interact with your baby, there beats a continual music.

When holding your baby in your arms, you can feel his rhythms. Feel him breathing against your chest. Notice the way he nurses in rhythm—suck-suck-suck-*pause*, suck-suck-suck-*pause*. Your baby sleeps and wakes in rhythm. His body temperature rises and falls, his brain thinks, his glands release hormones—all in predictable rhythm.

Like the air we breathe, rhythms are so ubiquitous we hardly notice them. Yet rhythms are the stuff life is made of. If you're a film buff, you may recall an old movie called *Fantastic Voyage*, in which Raquel Welch and Stephen Boyd were shrunk to the size of germs and took a perilous journey through the bloodstream of a human body. In one scene, we hear in the background a continual throbbing *thump-thump, thump-thump,* the beating of the human heart.

If Welch and Boyd had been reduced even smaller, so they could have strolled inside an atom, they would have found more rhythms. Though it sounds more like a Hollywood fantasy than science, modern physics teaches us that at the very heart of all reality, subatomic particles are dancing rhythmically in and out of existence. When poet T. S. Eliot wrote, "There is only the dance," he was right.

As a basic building block of reality, rhythms permeate our lives. Your patterns of hunger-and-eating, sleeping-and-waking, energy-and-quiet, ebb and flow in daily rhythms. Your blood pressure and body temperature are also circadian (that is, they rise and fall over more or less a twenty-four-hour day). Once ignored, biological rhythms are becoming increasingly respected in the treatment of diseases. Doctors now know, for example, that in many diseases—from epilepsy to cancer—our rhythms become disorganized, and that this fragmentation may be not just a symptom but part of the disease itself. They've also found that many medicines and treatments work best when a patient's body temperature reaches its daily peak.

Whereas nature is on a twenty-four-hour day, our bodies seem to operate on closer to a twenty-five-hour cycle. No one knows why. Usually, you reset your biological clock each day with the help of various outside cues (meals, bedtime, alarm clocks, etc.). But if you go on vacation and start living on a more freewheeling schedule, you may begin staying up later and later. That's because your body's natural twenty-five-hour cycle is being allowed to set its own pace.

Though we may not notice it, being out of touch with the rhythms around us gets on our nerves. Factory workers forced to switch frequently from night to day shifts often find the continual disruption of their daily rhythms makes them groggy, restless, irritable, and unable to sleep. You may have felt a slight touch of this when crossing several time zones in a plane; the malaise and lack of well-being we call jet lag is actually the feeling of our rhythms' being out of whack.

Conversely, being in sync with our own rhythms and those around us makes us feel good. Think of what you like most to do for relaxation. Not just to kill time but to really relax. Whatever your favorite method of unwinding—playing tennis, swimming, watching waves crash on the beach, reading poetry, yoga, walking, jogging, making love—chances are it involves rhythm. Music lovers find just listening to their favorite composer for a few minutes can revitalize them after a hectic day. Music—which is basically *all* rhythm—seems to take our jangled nerves and help them flow smoothly again. It may be no accident that among professions, concert musicians and orchestra conductors live the longest.[1]

It's *certainly* no accident that babies love lullabies, rocking, patting, and rhythmic games like Gotcha and Peek-a-boo. No matter how old we are or who we are, we humans are rhythmic. Rhythms just feel good.

THE RHYTHMS OF RELATIONSHIPS

In a very real sense, *you* are a rhythm. And the rhythm of you is as unique as a snowflake. Anyone with a bit of musical training can distinguish a piece Mozart wrote from one Beethoven wrote just by listening to the rhythms. Likewise, when you read poetry, the rhythms of Shakespeare (all of which, put together, reflect *the* rhythm of Shakespeare) differ distinctly from the rhythms of e.e. cummings (all of which, put together, reflect *the* rhythm of e.e. cummings).

Just as you have internal body rhythms and a rhythm of individuality, you have rhythms to your relationships. When your unique rhythm meshes with another person's rhythm, you feel good. The "vibes" are right. When, no matter how hard you try, you're late, out of step, unable to get your point across, the unrhythmic interaction is not just psychologically but *biologically* disturbing. Too great a mismatch for too long may even make your stomach queasy or your head hurt.

Similarly, whether or not you and your baby are in rhythm can affect how you feel about each other. In a major study, Drs. Stella Chess and Alexander Thomas at New York University followed 133 children from infancy to adulthood. They found that a mother who perceived her baby as unrhythmic (in other words, as out of step with her) was apt to see her child as "difficult," whereas a mother with a rhythmic baby was likelier to call her baby easy.[2]

Just being aware that out-of-sync rhythms can make you and your baby uncomfortable with each other and throw off your dance can be extremely helpful. If you're unaware of rhythms, you may feel, "I can never understand what this baby will do next. He's just downright difficult!" Or (if you're the type who tends to blame yourself) you may conclude, "I can't seem to satisfy my baby. I guess I'm just a rotten mother." Once you understand how rhythms affect your moods, you can say (more realistically), "Well, this baby and I are quite different. Our rhythms seem out of step. So let's see what we can do to get our rhythms flowing more smoothly."

Once you sense your baby's rhythms, you're much more able to understand how he's feeling. Dr. Paul Byers, a nonverbal-communications expert at Columbia University, suggests that when we know other people well, we detect changes in their feelings (whether they've become tired, angry, scared, or restless, for example) by unconsciously "reading" the subtle changes in their rhythms.[3] You may have a hard time reading a stranger's moods because you don't know his natural rhythms to start with. You don't know "where he's coming from." But changes in the rhythms of people you love tell you a great deal about their emotional stages. (We'll talk more about your baby's very special rhythmic states in the next chapter.)

When your baby is peacefully tired, for example, you'll notice his rhythmic movements become quieter and slower. He just begins to "run down." On the other hand, if your baby is *overly* tired (this is especially obvious in a toddler), his rhythms often quicken and become highly erratic; at such times, the child is much likelier to crash into a chair, slam his finger in a drawer, or fall down and hurt himself. His rhythms have gone beyond tired and he's out of control. At times like these, I've often seen a sensitive mother quietly and gently take over and do even simple tasks the child normally does for himself. It's as if she's saying, "I know you can do these things, but I also know you're too tired to do much of anything. Let me help you get back in control so you can get some much-needed sleep." (This is certainly a form of helpful "let be," which we discussed on pages 74–75.)

Once you recognize the importance of rhythms, you can see that there are no "good" babies or "bad" babies, no babies who are always hungry too soon or who sleep too long. There are only *different* babies. A so-called difficult baby may be merely one who's a bit out of step with the people around him. Often this same baby becomes much "easier" when his and his parents' rhythms begin to mesh. Some babies have more erratic rhythms than others and this makes their behaviors more difficult for you to predict. But even less rhythmic babies become easier over time as you begin to get into sync.

THE MAGIC OF ENTRAINMENT: HOW RHYTHMS MESH NATURALLY

Since being in sync with your baby makes you both happier, is it possible to synchronize your rhythms? To a large extent, that's what dancing is all about. But much synchronization occurs naturally—through a process scientists call entrainment.

To understand this complex process, let's start with a simple example. Picture two pendulum clocks side by side on a wall. Imagine you've set the two clocks so they're running at about the same time and the pendulums are therefore swinging back and forth in almost the same arc. If you leave the clocks on the wall a few days, then come back, you'll discover an amazing thing has happened: The pendulums will now be swinging in *exactly* the same time. It appears almost as if they "want" to keep the same beat. The same thing will happen with a dozen pendulum clocks on a wall. Even if the clocks are out of sync and none keeps very good time, if you leave the clocks on the wall long enough, they'll all start swinging in synchrony. Not only that, but every clock will start keeping perfect time!

This phenomenon (first observed in 1665 by Dutch scientist Christiaan Huyghens, who happened to have a couple of pendulum clocks on his wall) is, in fact, universal. When two or more oscillators are close to each other and are pulsing in *almost* the same rhythm, they'll tend to "lock in" until they're pulsing in *exactly* the same rhythm.

Why? Because nature tends to move toward a state requiring the least energy to maintain. And it requires less energy to pulse together than in opposition. In short, it takes less energy to dance than to fight. (An interesting corollary is that it also takes less energy—and fewer facial muscles—to smile than to frown.)

Similar entrainment occurs among humans. As Dr. Byers has pointed out, rhythmic activities such as rowing, singing, and sometimes marching will synchronize breathing. And sometimes when a psychiatrist and a patient are really "grooving," their hearts beat in unison.[4]

As I've indicated many times, you and your baby aren't clocks.

So your rhythms aren't mechanically perfect. In fact, biological systems such as you and your baby make up are strengthened by slight variations.

I've had a chance to observe an example of biological entrainment firsthand during my research with prematurely born babies, using the Breathing Blue Bear. One of a baby's first major tasks in life is to get his own rhythms in sync. Premature babies, because their central nervous systems are immature, have a tough time doing this. So I've developed a little companion for them in the form of a soft, blue teddy bear* to help them.

The teddy, which has simply become known as the "Breathing Bear," uses principles of entrainment to help tiny premature babies breathe more rhythmically. The bear is attached by tubing to a specially designed pump outside the baby's hospital crib. When the baby is quietly asleep, we set the pump so that the bear's "breathing" matches the baby's natural breathing rate. We then place the bear in the crib, so the baby can cuddle up to it or move away from it whenever he chooses. Preemies are extremely sensitive to being overstimulated; that's why we've been extra careful to let the *baby* control the amount of stimulation he receives.

At first, of course, the baby has no idea the bear is there. But after a few days, he discovers the bear and gradually begins cuddling up to it more often. Over time, as the baby comes more in contact with the bear's rhythmic breathing, the baby also starts breathing more rhythmically.[5] In short, his breathing becomes entrained with the bear's. By helping these babies get their *own* rhythms in sync in the hospital, we expect it will be easier for these babies to relate synchronously to their parents when they get home.

As I said before, parents and babies have rhythms of relating— from short rhythms that last only a minute or two to longer ones that stretch over days and weeks. Since you and your baby aren't clocks or toy bears, of course, your rhythms aren't mechanically perfect. In fact, biological systems like that you and your baby make up are made stronger by slight variations.

An example: One day you may feed your six-month-old dinner at 5:30 P.M., another day at 6 P.M. And through such variations,

* Patent number 4606328.

your baby comes to accept and understand, "Hey, dinnertime varies slightly around here from one day to the next, but I always get fed." You're dancing with your baby in the sense that you're giving him an expectation (dinner will be served sometime around five-thirty or six) and then fulfilling that expectation. And he's dancing with you by not whining for dinner at 3 P.M. (although at three o'clock he may ask for a cracker). Slight variations in your dance help keep it flexible, happy, and stress-proof.

Too *great* a swing in your rhythms, however, can throw you, your baby, or both of you into turmoil. If you normally eat dinner between five and six and one evening dinner gets delayed until nine-thirty, odds are everyone will get edgy and irritated. Your dance is thrown off for a while. But even this isn't disastrous. In a warm, loving relationship, both you and your baby will adjust and soon everyone feels fine again.

How do you and your baby establish your first expectations so you can dance in rhythm together? What exactly can you do to get your daily rhythms entrained? Amazingly, you usually don't have to *do* anything. Just by paying attention to your baby and responding to his needs, you'll naturally fall into step.

Years ago, University of Oklahoma sleep researcher Boyd Lester reported a fascinating instance of entrainment. He observed that as mothers and their babies slept in a medical school sleep lab, some mothers and babies slipped into REM sleep simultaneously—a synchrony that Dr. Lester speculated may have begun while the baby was still in the womb. With no conscious effort by either baby or mother, their REM cycles had become beautifully entrained.[6]

In what other ways can you and your baby be entrained? Do your body temperatures rise and fall on the same cues? Do your hearts beat in unison? Unfortunately, scientists don't have the answers to these questions yet. But certainly you and your baby groove into each other's rhythms in many subtle ways. Two of the most important ways you become entrained are in your communication rhythms and your sleep-wake rhythms.

YOUR UNSEEN RHYTHMS OF COMMUNICATION

As the late Boston University researcher William S. Condon found, your baby moves synchronously in rhythm with your speech as early as the first day of life. Though the process is so subtle it can only be measured in microseconds and observed in slow-motion films, when you talk your baby's body dances—not *in response to* your words, as if you were causing him to dance, but *in unison with* your words, as if your baby already knew what you were about to say. Human beings, it turns out, may be a lot less isolated from each other than we've ever believed.

The idea that your baby dances to the music of your voice from the day he's born requires a little background. It turns out nearly all speakers and listeners dance when they talk. When you talk, you emphasize your words by gesturing with your hands, arms, eyes, and just about every other movable part of your body. Whoever's listening to you also uses his or her body to listen. Sometimes you can clearly see listening movements (such as when the other person nods her head, raises her brows, or rolls her eyes). But most listening dialogue is so subtle it can only be detected by careful slow-motion film studies such as those Dr. Condon did. When Dr. Condon first began studying micromovements of human communication in the early 1960s, he spent one and a half years going over just one four-and-one-half-second dialogue between two people. In the process, he told one reporter, he wore out 130 copies of the film and estimated that before wearing out, a film would have to be played about 100,000 times.[7]

What came out of Dr. Condon's painstaking studies were findings so astonishing they helped give us a whole fresh way of looking at human relationships. In a paper published in the *Journal of Autism and Childhood Schizophrenia* in 1975, Dr. Condon wrote:

> *Listeners* were observed to move in precise shared synchrony with the speaker's speech. This appears to be a form of entrainment since there is no discernible lag even at $\frac{1}{48}$ second . . . it also appears to be a universal characteristic of human communication and perhaps characterizes much of animal behavior in general. Communication is thus like a dance, with everyone engaged in intricate and shared movements across many subtle dimensions,

yet all strangely oblivious that they are doing so. Even total strangers will display this synchronization. Such synchronization appears to occur continuously *if the interactants remain attentive and involved* [italics added].[8]

Writer George Leonard, who describes the Condon findings beautifully in his book *The Silent Pulse: A Search for the Perfect Rhythm That Exists in Each of Us,* observes quite accurately:

> At the most fundamental level, the listener is not *reacting* or *responding* to the speaker. The listener is in a sense *part of, one with* the speaker. This becomes startlingly clear when there is a silence in one of the conversations filmed by Dr. Condon. *At the precise $^1/_{48}$ second the speaker resumes talking, the listener begins his or her series of synchronized movements.*[9]

The rhythms between a listener and a speaker are so exquisitely entrained that a listener will shift position even when the sound changes at a rate of a few *hundredths* of a second! And the reason the speaker and the listener are dancing in unison, of course, is that they're relating to each other as a *system* and not as a cause-effect chain.

So much for human communication in general. Now back to you and your baby.

After discovering that adults move in rhythm, Dr. Condon and his colleague Dr. Louis Sander wondered, How early in life does this amazing synchronization begin? So they videotaped babies twelve hours to two weeks old as the infants listened to adult speech. Astonishingly, they found that babies only a few hours old also move in synchrony with the human voice, whether that voice is speaking English, Swahili, or Chinese.

When the babies listened, their movements were amazingly matched to each sound. In the 0.07 second it took an adult to utter the *kk* sound in the first word of the sentence "Come over and see who's over here," Sander and Condon wrote of one baby:

> the infant's head moves [to the] right very slightly, the left elbow extends slightly, the right shoulder rotates upward, the left shoulder rotates outward slightly, the right hip rotates outward fast, the left hip extends slightly, and the big toe (yes, the big toe!) of

the left foot [curls]. These body parts sustain these directions and speeds of movement together for this 0.07-second interval.[10]

This was the "unit" or "package" of movement—the dance step, if you will—that went with the sound *kk*. To other sounds, the baby danced with very different motions. With the *mm* in *come* (which lasted one-tenth of a second), for example, the baby danced by moving his left elbow faster, extending the right hip more, rotating the left hip more inward, and stopping the movement of his big toe.[11]

Equally mind-boggling, tiny babies seem able to tell real language from nonsense. When eight- and nine-day-old babies listened to tapes of disconnected vowel sounds, they stopped dancing, as if to say, "Why are you talking gibberish?"

Somehow your baby is born dancing in a split-second world to the rhythms of your words. Your baby's ability to move not *in reaction to* but precisely *with* your words is a form of entrainment. What's equally remarkable, this incredibly complex form of communication just happens. When I consider the wonder of entrainment, I'm often reminded of a passage in *The Lives of a Cell*, in which physician Lewis Thomas marvels at the wisdom of his own liver.

> If I were informed tomorrow that I was in direct communication with my liver, and could now take over, I would become deeply depressed. I'd sooner be told, forty thousand feet over Denver, that the 747 jet in which I had a coach seat was now mine to operate as I pleased; at least I would have the hope of bailing out, if I could find a parachute and discover quickly how to open a door. Nothing would save me and my liver, if I were in charge. For I am, to face the facts squarely, considerably less intelligent than my liver. I am, moreover, constitutionally unable to make hepatic decisions, and I prefer not to be obliged to, ever. I would not be able to think of the first thing to do.[12]

Just as nature has provided us with a liver that knows what to do, it has given our bodies the wisdom of entrainment. If we had to think *consciously* about how to respond to one another in precise, split-second movements, we'd probably trip over our own words, nod too quickly or too slowly, and wind up tongue-tied.

Yet without consciously focusing on what we're up to, we become the most highly complex, capable communicators on this planet. The most stunning part about entrainment is that when you and your baby relax and pay attention to one another, it just happens.

YOUR RHYTHMS OF SLEEPING AND WAKING

If your unseen rhythms of communication sound almost mystical, your and your baby's opposing sleep-and-wake rhythms will snap you back to a more worldly realm. Nothing is more nerve-jangling than being awakened out of a peaceful sleep at 2 A.M. by a screaming, hungry baby.

How soon can you get a decent night's sleep again? How soon can you get *this* rhythm in sync?

Though it's not readily obvious, at only ten days of age your baby is already attuned to your sleep-and-wake cycle. To test how soon babies groove into their caregivers' daily rhythms, Dr. Sander studied three groups of babies. Group A roomed in with their mothers from birth. Group B, awaiting adoption, spent ten days in a brightly lit, bustling nursery and were cared for by many nurses. Group C spent ten days with one foster mother, then were moved to another foster home on day 11. Then all the babies' rhythms were charted. The babies in Group B, who had no single person to entrain to, hadn't settled into any kind of routine. But the babies who were cared for by their mothers or foster mothers had already begun to shift their crying and activity levels more to daytime hours and were sleeping longer at night.

The effects of rhythm disruption were made obvious by the babies in Group C, who had to switch to a "new" mother on day 11. These babies fussed more during feedings and cried a lot more on the eleventh day than the babies in the other groups.[13]

How can you best help your baby become entrained to your day-night cycle? Paradoxically, by first getting your rhythms in step with his (by responding to him fairly promptly when he cries, for example). Once you get in step with your baby so you're matching his rhythms, your baby will (hopefully) gradually adjust his nighttime wakings to accommodate your rhythms until he's sleeping through the night.

Your next thought may very well be: "Yes, *hopefully* he will.

But what if my baby doesn't start sleeping through the night? Is there anything I can do to help him adjust his rhythms more closely to mine?" Possibly so. There are limits to how soon a baby can sleep through the night and babies vary considerably on this score. Whereas babies on *average* start sleeping all night at sixteen weeks, some babies sleep all night much earlier, while others are still waking several times a night at two or three years of age (a rarity, but if the whole family is being exhausted and you feel in need of help, sleep centers across the country now deal with such problems).* If your baby does sleep poorly, Richard Ferber, M.D., director of the Center for Pediatric Sleep Disorders at Children's Hospital in Boston, observes that this does *not* mean you've been a rotten parent or that your child is ill. He adds that by six months of age, nearly every baby (but note: he doesn't say *all* babies) should be able to sleep all night.[14]

As I said before, most babies start sleeping through the night naturally once they become entrained to your rhythms. But to help your baby sleep all night, here are some ideas and techniques that may help.

• *Think of your baby's nighttime sleeping as part of his overall daily rhythms.* Though it's not readily apparent, how well a baby sleeps at night is often hooked to how rhythmic the rest of his day is. To establish a predictable circadian rhythm, a baby needs a fairly consistent routine surrounding his resting, waking, and feeding times. Reasonable variations, such as those we just talked about (serving dinner at six instead of five-thirty), are of course fine and make your baby more flexible and less subject to stress. But extremely *wide* swings in your rhythms (where lunch might be served anytime from 10:30 A.M. to 3 P.M.) can make the day quite unpredictable from a baby's point of view.

On an irregular schedule, where there's no particular time for waking in the morning, going to bed at night, napping, or eating meals, a child's daily rhythms can become so disorganized that his body temperature may be rising as he goes to bed at night and falling in the morning (the exact opposite of what occurs in people who stay up during the day and sleep at night). In such a case, a

---

* For a list of sleep disorder centers in the U.S., write the Association of Sleep Disorders Centers, P.O. Box 2604, Del Mar, CA 92014, or phone (619) 755-6556.

baby literally *cannot* go to sleep; it's almost physically impossible, no matter how tired he may be. So when you're thinking about your baby's sleep patterns, examine them in terms of his whole day. Is he napping at 5 P.M., so he can't fall asleep at seven-thirty? Is he taking too many naps? Are his meals fairly regular? Some babies are quite rhythmic throughout the day, others less so. If you don't know what your baby's rhythms are normally, you might want to chart them for a week or so and see if you can spot an emerging pattern.

• *Try gradually adjusting your baby's rhythms.* If your baby is six months or older and still isn't sleeping on your schedule, you may be able to shift his rhythms gradually until they're more in sync with yours. Some babies will just be a few hours off your cycle (for example, they'll be sleeping eleven hours a night, but those hours will be between 5 P.M. and 4 A.M., so you're still having to get up much earlier than you'd like). In a case like this, just keeping your baby up fifteen minutes later each day—until you've got him going to bed at 8 P.M. and getting up at 7 A.M.—will often work. Likewise, if your baby is going to bed at midnight and arising at 10 A.M., when you'd rather he go to bed at eight and get up at seven, you can often gradually shift his rhythms back by getting him up fifteen minutes *earlier* each day. The key when trying to shift your baby's rhythms to a later or earlier cycle is to do so gradually and *gently.* Trying a blitzkrieg approach, in which you just suddenly try putting your baby to bed three hours later, can be wrenching for both you and your baby. I hope your baby won't have more complicated sleep problems. But if he does, you may want to pick up a copy of Dr. Richard Ferber's book *Solve Your Child's Sleep Problems.* Now that you know the importance of rhythms, I think you'll be able to avoid many sleep problems from the start.

• *Don't expect too much too soon.* A baby does need time to get his daily rhythms flowing smoothly. So try to be patient. Also, don't expect your baby to sleep more than he actually needs to. In the first week, a baby typically sleeps about sixteen and a half hours a day—about eight hours during the night (with one feeding break in the middle of the night) and about eight hours during the day. By the age of one month, a baby typically needs only fifteen and a half hours of sleep in a twenty-four-hour day, and by a year of age he'll be down to about fourteen hours. Again, some babies need less sleep than this, some more. If you want to know how much sleep your baby needs, you can keep track of his sleep times for a week or so.

• *Be reluctant to play at 3 A.M.* A baby who always wakes up in the middle of the night to a bright-eyed, playful mommy or daddy may decide, "Hey, getting up at 3 A.M. is fun!" Certainly you don't want to be crabby with your baby. Warm cuddling is always in order. But being a bit boring at 3 A.M. isn't such a bad idea if you want to get back to sleep.

• *Recognize that your baby learns to put himself to sleep.* All people (even adults) wake spontaneously several times a night. Usually, as an adult, you simply fluff your pillow, roll over, and fall back asleep. The ease with which you do this is deceptive: Falling asleep after you've awakened in the middle of the night is a complicated task. (Insomniacs will vouch for this.) To sleep through the night, your baby has to *learn* how to soothe himself during these spontaneous wakings so he can fall back asleep. Some babies hum, suck on their fists, rock their bodies, or even fuss lightly for a few minutes. Since a baby has to master this task himself (nothing you can do will master it *for* him), you can help by paying special attention to your baby's bedtime ritual to try to make it as easy as possible for him to duplicate this process for himself in the middle of the night.

There are many wonderful rituals parents use to put their babies to bed. Some enjoy rocking the baby for ten minutes, then placing him in his crib with a favorite toy, turning out the lights, and leaving the nursery. Others like to sit by their baby's crib and pat his back gently to help him unwind. A few quiet minutes of rocking, patting, gentle massaging, or lullabies may help your baby calm down so he can drift asleep. Use whatever ritual you enjoy most, but remember that your baby may come to associate this ritual with falling asleep. Thus, when establishing bedtime habits, ask yourself, "Is this a ritual I'll be comfortable with at 2 A.M. as well as at 7 P.M.? Are my actions helping my baby gain control of himself so he can put himself back to sleep, or is he coming to rely on my external control?" These aren't easy questions to answer. For one thing, your bedtime ritual will change as your baby gets older. An appropriate ritual for a newborn, who often needs extra soothing to adjust to this new world, would be quite inappropriate for a four-year-old. Usually, a newborn does need *some* help in getting his rhythms organized, and often rhythmic stimulation like rocking, singing, walking, and rubbing help get his internal rhythms under control. Yet at the same time, if you find you're having to rock or walk your baby three hours straight before he goes to sleep, it is probable that this ritual will eventually get on your nerves!

No one bedtime ritual will work for all babies. This is where you can rely on yourself to be creative. If one strategy doesn't work, try another. I'll talk a lot more about how to soothe a crying baby in Chapter 12. But for now, let me give you just one example (from Sandy Jones's book *Crying Baby, Sleepless Nights*) of how a mother, using her biological wisdom, calmed her very unhappy, unrhythmic, screaming baby:

> She planted the tiny baby against her shoulder, holding it firmly by the buttocks in one hand and gently cupping its head in the other.
>
> Then she began a dance that looked like an ancient mothering minuet. She took eight or ten rhythmical paces forward, turned around and took eight or ten paces back to where she had started from: step . . . pause . . . step . . . pause. Her hand slipped down to the baby's back, patting with each pause, and his toes uncurled.
>
> Sensing that the baby was still wound up, she continued her walk, adding some sounds that I had never heard used with a baby before. She produced deep guttural groans; kind of like the groans that people make when they're having an orgasm. The groans welled forth each time she came to a pause in her rhythmical stepping. Groan-pat-pause-walk, groan-pat-pause-walk, the dance went on. The baby's hands uncurled and he let out a huge, chin-quivering sigh that racked his tiny body.
>
> Ellen continued the dance, firmly holding the baby in place, refusing to move him from her chest even to check on his expression. After another deep sigh from the baby, as if to say "Home at last!" his eyes fluttered to half-mast. Within ten minutes of her mothering performance the baby fell into a profound sleep that left his body limp.[15]

Sensitivity like this cannot be *taught*. It can only be *learned*. And you learn to be sensitive to your baby by getting to know his rhythms and learning how he "talks" to you from the minute he's born.

Now that you understand your baby's capabilities, have perhaps an even deeper respect for his feelings than you did before, and appreciate the importance of his rhythms, let the dance begin!

PART IV

LET THE DANCE BEGIN

. . . whatever age one may be, one should dance, and dance frequently, for there are few activities so wholly and deeply gratifying.

—ASHLEY MONTAGU
Growing Young

10 How Your Baby "Talks" to You

"I've hundreds of things to say to you. I've never loved anyone so much before. I have dozens of things to say, but my tongue just can't manage them. So I'll dance them for you."

—ZORBA
Talking to "Boss" in Nikos Kazantzakis'
Zorba the Greek

By the time we've grown up, we think we need words to communicate. But often words only get in our way. At the deepest, most essential levels of communication, words no longer matter.

Psychiatrist Melanie Klein once wrote, "However gratifying it is in later life to express thoughts and feelings to a congenial person, there remains an unsatisfied longing for an understanding without words."[1] Al Huang, a Chinese sage, expressed something of the same idea when he said that "sooner or later we reach a dead end when we talk."[2] And an ancient Chinese aphorism goes, "A bait is used to catch fish. When you have gotten the fish, you can forget about the bait. A rabbit trap is used to catch rabbits. When the rabbits are caught, you can forget about the trap. Words are used to express meaning. When you understand the meaning, you can forget about the words. Where can I find a man who forgets about words to talk with him?"[3]

The answer to this riddle: Find a baby.

Your baby talks without words in myriad ways: by the way he looks at you, the way he holds his head, even by the way he sleeps. And how readily and smoothly you respond to his conversational dance helps him learn a lot about the world. Not only does he come to trust *you* (because when he's in pain or happy, you respond), but he comes to trust *himself* and his own ability to handle the world. When your baby cries and you come and comfort him, or when he coos and gurgles and you laugh with delight, you're telling him, "This world is a pretty wonderful, responsive place—and *you*, little as you are, can have some effect here."

Perhaps the idea that your baby communicates with you from the moment he's born doesn't surprise you. Parents have nearly always believed that how a baby looks, moves, gestures, and even holds his body have special meanings. But experts have only just discovered how right parents were all along. Slow-motion video-tapes made in the lab have shown that when your baby is only a few hours old he's already quite capable of telling you what he needs in order to grow (and of course, each day of his life, your baby gets better at communicating with you). If you start "listen-ing" to your baby from the moment he's born and responding to his signals, a rich, strong communicative bond will form between you that can, quite literally, last a lifetime. Many experts have written books telling you how to talk to your child, and even more elaborate techniques have been worked out on how to talk to a rebellious teenager. Few until now have told you how to talk to your *baby;* and yet it's this very communicative system that you and your baby form in your first year—even in your first weeks together—that is the prelude to the way you'll dance together the rest of your lives.

I'm not saying your dance can't or won't change. Of course it changes, in thousands of ways (some quite subtle), as you and your baby grow. But if you establish synchrony in your dance in your early months together, when the steps are simplest and easiest to learn, chances are you'll find it easier to dance with your child later, when the steps get more complex.

How to dance smoothly with your baby? The first thing you can do is learn the incredibly sophisticated ways your baby tells you what he needs. The signals a baby sends are often (but not always) quite easy to decipher—once you realize your baby *is* communicating. When adults miss these clues, it's usually because they think a newborn is just a blob of putty or an empty slate, so they don't bother to look for and pay attention to the baby's in-tricate language.

The following conversational steps are common to most babies. It's important to remember as you read them that though we've had to break down these signals into basic steps like gaze, head turning, and such, a *real* baby seldom uses just one cue at a time to tell you what he likes or needs. The fact that we have to talk about these cues separately rather than being able to talk about all of them at once reflects one of the limitations of our linear language. Babies "talk" in what scientists call a *gestalt*, in which the whole baby talks with his whole body.

We also have to take care not to assume too simplistically that these are the *only* messages a baby sends or that every baby dances in precisely these ways. Still, knowing the basic steps in your baby's communicative dance (even if he does add his own idiosyncratic dips, spins, and twirls) can give you a strong idea of what to look for when you want to know how your baby feels.

So let's see some of the dance steps your baby uses to tell you how he's feeling and what he needs.

GAZE

Your baby has little control over some of his movements at birth. But he *can* control his eyes fairly well. The message your baby sends when he gazes intently at any object or person within his visual field is simple: "I like this. It makes me feel good."

Knowing your baby uses gaze to tell you what he likes is incredibly important. Just by showing your baby a variety of objects and watching to see what he looks at most, you can find out which objects he prefers. (And it's those objects *he* prefers, not those you choose arbitrarily for him, that will most stimulate him and help him grow.)

The *look* in your baby's eyes is also a tip-off to how he's feeling and what he likes. Is he bright-eyed and perky? (Then he's probably ready to play.) Or does he have a dull, glazed look to his eyes? (Then he's probably in what we call a daze and may be either bored or ready to drop off to sleep.) I'll talk more about the alert and dazed looks in a few pages, when we discuss your baby's states.

HEAD BEHAVIORS

How you hold and move your head tells other adults how you feel. Tilting your head slightly to one side, for example, often signals that you're interested in what a speaker is saying and you're listening intently, whereas if you've been listening for some time and suddenly hold your head erect, you may be signaling, "This is getting boring. I've had enough."

Your baby's head postures also tell you much about him. If your baby turns toward a sight, sound, touch, or smell and looks bright and alert, he's saying, "Gee, I like that." If he turns consistently away and perhaps even shuts his eyes, he's sending the message: "Get that away from me," or "I'm feeling too overwhelmed to play right this second." Often when you're playing face to face with your baby, he'll turn away or avert his eyes to avoid overstimulation and regain control of himself. He's not rejecting you or your attempts to play when he does this; he's usually just regrouping after all the excitement.

Very important is whether your baby is looking directly into your eyes (a totally positive "let's play" look) or at you out of the corner of his eyes, with his head turned slightly away. This "sideways" gaze suggests ambivalence: Your baby may be uncertain whether or not he wants to interact just now. The sideways gaze is usually resolved quickly: Either your baby will look directly into your eyes (an open invitation to begin a dialogue dance) or he'll turn his head and lose eye contact totally (meaning "I don't like what's happening," or maybe "Let's stop playing for a while"). Another way your baby may tell you he's had enough stimulation is by lowering his head. I've often seen babies lower their heads and go limp with resignation after they've tried to fight off overstimulation and have been unable to make themselves understood. As a more drastic sign of discomfort, your baby may even go into a *stress sleep* (more about this shortly).

HICCUPING, YAWNING, ETC.

Many other baby gestures have special meaning. Take the tongue thrust, for example. When a six- or eight-year-old sticks out his tongue, he means "I hate you" or "Yuk!" When a newborn sticks out his tongue, he may mean, "I like you. Come a little closer." A baby has very little control over his body, but one thing other than his eyes he can control quite well is his tongue. The tongue thrust has been interpreted by some child-development specialists as an imitative gesture. In the lab, a research scientist will stick out his tongue and the baby will stick out his tongue too, and the scientist will conclude, "Isn't that interesting. He's imitating me." In fact, the tongue thrust is also an *approach* signal. (If you doubt this, cup your baby's head in your hand. As he sticks out his tongue, you can feel his neck muscles tense and untense as he tries to move his head toward you.[4])

Less positive signals include sighing, gagging, coughing, hiccuping, sneezing, and yawning. Although these cues have the same meaning for a baby that they have for you (babies *do* yawn when they're tired or sneeze if they get a whiff of pepper), they can also signal distress. If an exuberant neighbor sticks her face too eagerly into your baby's crib, thereby invading his personal space, your baby may yawn, sneeze, or hiccup to shut out the excessive stimulation. He's saying, "I wish you'd get away from me and leave me alone." Of course, if your baby's signals go unheeded for long or if the neighbor was just too scary or intrusive from the start, your baby may signal more severe distress by starting to cry.

FOUR WAYS A BABY CRIES

Only ten years ago, many pediatricians were telling parents that babies often cry just to "exercise their lungs" and that you shouldn't pick up a baby quickly when he cries or you'll spoil him. The old idea was that if you weren't careful, you'd give your baby reinforcement for crying and actually "train" him to cry. These old doctors' tales have, thankfully, gone by the wayside. We now know that a young baby cries not to be obnoxious or to "get his way" but because he feels unhappy or uncomfortable and needs help.

Parents have always believed their babies' cries had special meanings. Yet when a mother insisted she could tell whether her baby was hungry or wet just by the sound of his cry, doctors used to pooh-pooh this idea as merely Mother's wild imagination. Only recently, with careful studies of babies' cries, have scientists begun to find what mothers always knew: A baby's cries often do differ, depending on what the baby needs or wants.

Baby cries are sometimes extremely difficult to decipher and they are even more difficult to explain in black and white. To tell the differences in babies' cries, you need to hear them. Depending on how distinct your baby's cries are, you can come to learn which sound precedes a feeding (indicating, of course, "I'm hungry"), which type of cry occurs when your baby bumps his head or otherwise hurts himself (meaning "I'm in pain"), and which cries mean "I'm just winding down and about to fall asleep." Of course, some cries are inexplicable even to the most experienced parent, and a few babies will cry long periods for no apparent reason. (We'll talk in Chapter 13 about how you can handle an extremely fussy baby.) Before long, you'll come to know more about your baby's unique cries than I can ever presume to tell you. But when you're first starting out with your baby, here are a few ways you may be able to tell one cry from another.

The Common Healthy Cry

Of all cries, this one is most rhythmic. It often starts as a soft whimper but, if unanswered, can quickly build to an even, robust *wawa-wawa-wawa-wawa*, in which you can almost hear the "waves" of tears. Other cries can be high-pitched and wailing or thin and weak. But this loud, full-throated cry is guaranteed to bring you out of a sound sleep and running toward your baby's crib. A baby often cries this way when he's feeling his first hunger pangs or he wants to be picked up. In several studies, scientists found that babies most frequently stop this healthy cry when they're picked up. Of course, if your baby is hungry, such soothing may only work for a second or two, if at all, and the crying will stop only when the baby is fed.

Distress Cry

This is undoubtedly the most piercing, unpleasant, screeching cry you'll ever hear. University of Massachusetts developmental psychologist Edward Tronick calls this cry a "long and catlike wail," and that's as good a description as any. When a baby emits this unrhythmic, disconcerting *Waaaaaaaaa!* at the top of his lungs, you'll think he's been stuck by a pin (and of course he may have been). A longish pause will occur as your baby gathers his breath; then a second long, ear-shattering cry will split the air. A baby who's bumped his head or fallen down may emit this cry out of pain and of course deserves a warm, comforting cuddle. An unanswered hunger cry can also escalate to a distress cry. Some babies—especially those who are having trouble establishing rhythms—cry this way a lot. Or a baby who wakes up quite hungry may bypass the Common Healthy Cry and go straight into this howling wail. Sorry, but I'm afraid this is one cry you'll eventually hear.

The Out-of-Control or Angry Cry

This cry, which sounds as if your baby is angry, is as full and vigorous as the Common Healthy Cry. Yet there is a distinct difference. Listen closely, and you'll notice less rhythm and more agitation. It often sounds most like *wawa-wa-wa, wawa-wa-wa.* There's a definite rhythm, but it's less smooth and consistent.

A baby whose Common Healthy Cry hasn't been answered may also launch into this turbulent scream . . . and once that's happened, he may be hard to soothe. It may *seem* as if the baby is angrily saying, "See what you've done. Now you'll just have to listen until I feel like calming down." But actually the baby thinks no such thing. He only feels. That's why, even though this cry has been called angry, I prefer to think of it as "out of control." Once a baby's rhythms are thrown off and he's become disorganized by gasping and crying hard, he can't readily regain his emotional balance. An out-of-control baby requires extra patience and often plenty of relaxed, easy, rhythmic stimulation (or if he's hungry, the breast or bottle) before he can regroup and calm down.

Fussing

Some babies frequently fuss and fret for no apparent reason. A baby who is just lightly whimpering may be saying, "Hey, I'm feeling a little blue," in which case, once you pick him up, chances are he'll calm down. Or he may be saying, "I'm just using this fussy stuff to organize myself so I can drift off to sleep." As pediatrician T. Berry Brazelton points out, a baby who fusses also seems to be one who can sleep for long stretches at night.[5] It's as if some fussing before falling asleep helps your baby unwind and release the day's tension.

No aspect of your baby's communicative repertoire is likelier to disrupt your dance than his incessant crying. If you respond and your baby is soothed, you feel competent and appreciated. If you can't console your baby, no matter what you do, you may feel guilty, inept, annoyed, and even angry. Therefore, if you have a hard-to-soothe, sensitive baby, handling his crying in the early months—and notice I didn't say *stopping* his crying, but *handling* it—may be the biggest challenge of your life. But more about crying in Chapter 12.

FOUR WAYS YOUR BABY SLEEPS

Your baby's sleep may look to a casual observer like one continual process. But watch your baby closely and you'll notice he sleeps several different ways. Observing which stage of sleep your baby is in can tell you a lot more about him than you might at first think.

Quiet Sleep

In this stage of sleep, your baby looks very peaceful, yet his face and body retain their muscle tone. His breathing is slow, deep, and regular, his eyes are closed, and he moves very little (except for an occasional startle or jerk, or a rhythmic movement of his mouth or chin). This is the stage when your baby is sleeping so quietly that you may find yourself going in and gently poking him to get him to move—just to reassure yourself he's okay (which of course he is). When in quiet sleep, your baby will be so difficult to awaken that even if you drop a rattle on the floor in his room he may not hear it (although of course some babies awaken much more easily than others). Often when your baby's in this state, you can get him up, put on his sweater, and take him outside without his fluttering an eyelid.

Active Sleep

In this stage, your baby is really incredibly busy. His brain is as active as when he's awake and alert. When looking at EEG readings, which measure brain activity, scientists can't tell from the chart whether the baby was alert or in active sleep. Often, in active sleep, your baby lies quite limp. But then his eyelids will flutter, and these flutters range from brief, light flickers to (especially among newborns) prolonged, intense, rapid-eye-movement (or REM) storms in which your baby may raise his brows and even open his eyes.

Many other behaviors occur, including: smiles, frowns, grimaces, mouthing, sucking, sighs, sigh-sobs, twitching of arms and legs, and even high-pitched cries. Your baby may even strain, grunt, and stretch mightily. Meanwhile, the baby's breathing is irregular and faster than in quiet sleep.

Babies may even sleep with their eyes slightly open in this stage. So before picking up your baby when he's in this active state, you may want to watch a few seconds to make sure he's truly awake. I once saw a mother bathe her baby and try to feed him for twenty minutes, never realizing her infant was snoozing in active sleep the entire time!

Active-Quiet Transition Sleep

This type of sleep is often so subtle you can't readily observe it. I only mention it because at times you may watch your baby and be unable to decipher whether he's in active or quiet sleep . . . and that may be because hc's between the two. In this in-between state, which may last from a few seconds to several minutes, your baby's breathing is more regular than in active sleep, but less so than in quiet sleep. Your baby also displays other mixed active-quiet signals. For example, he may breathe fairly evenly, but his eyes may flutter.

Stress Sleep

We tend to think anything that puts a baby to sleep is a godsend. But some methods of making babies sleep may go too far. If a young baby is subjected to unrelenting stimulation over which he has no control (a constantly rocking mechanical swing, for example, or a loudly droning TV), he may have no escape except to "shut down" all his senses and fall into a stress sleep.

How to tell stress sleep from natural slumber? If your baby has just fallen asleep after being highly stimulated, observe his closed eyelids. A young baby (under one month old) usually drops directly into active (REM) sleep first and only later descends into his quiet sleep state. If your baby has gone *directly* into quiet sleep, he could be sending a powerful message: "I was overstimulated, so I turned off." (Note: There's no harm in a baby occasionally retreating into stress sleep. But this may be a signal to you to try to reduce stimulation for your baby before nap time.)

FIVE WAYS YOUR BABY LOOKS WHEN AWAKE (AND WHAT THEY MEAN)

When awake, your baby also has various states that tell you a great deal about what he's feeling. These states rise and drop in rhythm and are governed, in part, by what's going on inside him (when he last ate, for instance). But what you as a parent *do* can also change these states. By watching your baby and understanding which state he's in, you can then decide what you'd like to do (whether, for example, you'd like to help him drop off to sleep or bring him to an alert state so you can play). The first three states are those between wakefulness and sleep; the last two are the ways your baby "talks" to you when he's fully awake.

Sleep-Wake Transition

This is the way your baby usually looks when he's about to wake up. He acts in some ways as if he's awake (his eyes may open and close rapidly) and in some ways as if he's asleep. Often your baby stirs or frets and it's hard to tell whether he is awake or asleep. This is the time when, if you're feeling superorganized, you may want to get your newborn's bottle ready: He may soon awaken and will probably be hungry. (But don't be surprised if when you return with the bottle, he's slipped off to sleep again!)

Drowse

In this state, your baby is on the road to sleep. He's quiet and his eyes either are heavy-lidded or tend to open and close slowly. When your baby's in this state, you have an option: You can either handle him slowly and gently to help him go completely to sleep, or you can smile and look bright-eyed at him to see if you can stir him up and make him stay awake longer. You may want to try to keep your baby awake during this state if you're trying to adjust his rhythms and get him to nap a bit later. (Too *strong* a stimulation during this state, however, may make your baby cry.)

Daze

In this state, your baby's eyes are glassy or glazed, and he's bored, overstimulated, or about to drift into a drowse. This is another way your baby has of withdrawing from the world when he's been overwhelmed by too many sights or sounds. Sometimes just holding your baby upright and talking to him when he's dazed can make him alert and ready to play. Holding him quietly may (or may not) help him drift off to sleep.

Non-Alert

Though awake, with his eyes open, your baby isn't really paying attention at this time. His eyes are dull looking. Or his eyes may be closed, but he continues to be very active and obviously awake. Body movements will vary, but often your baby's arms and legs will be in motion and he may startle easily. Breathing is irregular and your baby may also vocalize, fuss, or fret. Even if your baby looks toward or focuses briefly on a sight or sound during this state, he's not really ready to play and learn.

Alert

This is the delightful "play stage," that wonderful time when your baby's ready to invite play and interact joyously with you. Often called "quiet alert," this special state tends to arise when a baby feels content, comfy, and well-fed. Your baby's eyes become bright and he'll tend to track moving objects with his eyes. He may also imitate your facial expressions. Breathing may be quite regular (but less so than in quiet sleep). Although during his first weeks your baby may be very inactive during this state (with his arms and legs peacefully quiet), at later ages your baby may be quite active when he is alert. All the fascinating dialogue dances you and your baby share take place during this fun-filled state. Your baby may coo, grunt, and make other contented sounds as he looks at you, tries to make eye contact, and invites you to play. Enjoy it!

As you can see from the above descriptions, some of the ways your baby dances are extremely easy to see. But other steps, especially during the first few weeks, may be quite subtle. By the time your baby's a few months old, his dancing will be so obvious to you that you'll find it amazing it's taken scientists all these years to notice it.

Does only your baby dance? Of course not. You dance too. In fact, *your* dance is what the next chapter is all about.

Your Biological Wisdom

Truth is within ourselves; it takes no rise
From outward things, whate'er you may believe . . .

—ROBERT BROWNING

Dancing with your baby comes easiest when you feel confident of your parenting skills. That way, instead of focusing on all the ways you could be "better," you can relax, knowing you *already* have special qualities that will help you become the best parent you can be.

Too much has been written about how rotten parents are at their jobs. In one child-rearing manual, you're told, "Some parents are so ignorant, indifferent, or incapable of meeting even the most basic needs of their children that permanent damage is almost inevitable."[1] In another, you'll read, "Researchers have discovered that even well-read, educated and intelligent parents have probably handicapped their children in the past because of child-rearing practices which ignored the needs of the developing brain."[2] And in still a third manual, a *mother* states, "I could . . . write a book-length report on the ways my mother fouled me up and the ways I did it to my son. To sum it up, you can't be good parents if you are still hung up on your past, which most of us are."[3]

It's been said that parents are too emotionally involved with their children to be consistent and logical. And it's even been proposed that psychologists should train and "license" parents so they'd be psychologically fit to raise their babies.[4] For some parents, this brave new world of parent licensing is already close at hand. At the Better Baby Institute in Philadelphia, you can take a course to learn how to teach your baby facts, after which you'll be awarded a certificate proclaiming you a "professional parent."[5]

What nonsense! Most parents have always known and research

over the past twenty years undeniably confirms that you—by yourself, without special training—are the best person in the world to raise your baby. Why? Mostly because you *are* emotionally involved.

In his book *The Farther Reaches of Human Nature*, humanistic psychologist Abraham Maslow spoke of a "love knowledge" that is more objective, more accurate, and more *real* than any more distant observations made by an uninvolved expert in a lab. Maslow wrote:

> The mother, fascinated with her baby, who examines every square inch of it again and again with the greatest absorption, is certainly going to know more about her baby in the most literal sense than someone who is not interested in that particular baby. . . . "Love knowledge," if I may call it that, has other advantages as well. Love for a person permits him to unfold, to open up, to drop his defenses, to let himself be naked not only physically but psychologically and spiritually as well. In a word, he lets himself be seen instead of hiding himself. In ordinary interpersonal relations, we are to some extent inscrutable to each other. In love relationships, we become "scrutable."[6]

To show you how much your baby needs emotionally involved *you*, let me tell you a couple of stories.

TALES OF THREE BABIES

Years ago, Stephen Bennett, M.D., told the story of two babies up for adoption who'd been left for a few weeks in a hospital nursery. Baby boy Smith (who quickly won the nickname Smitty) was by far all the nurses' favorite. A sturdy, handsome, friendly baby, Smitty captured everyone's heart. At only seventeen days of age, when tickled, rocked, or sung to, Smitty would open his eyes wide, purse his lips in greeting, and invite more play. Dr. Bennett recalls, "One comment made in the second week was, 'Oh, Smitty, you've been out with the girls all night, you bad boy, you naughty boy.' This talk was accompanied by hugging, kissing and comments that he loved to be loved."

Baby boy Jones was another story. Well built, but thin, he was much less alert and more irritable than Smitty. When tickled, Jones would writhe and flail his arms. Though he liked to be rocked, no one cared to hold him, and when he was only fifteen days old all the nurses agreed he was a disagreeable baby. Said one, "He's irritable and tightens up and gets purple so he doesn't get held as much. I think that in 20 years you'll find that he is brain-damaged." (A revealing comment, since a child who's ignored for twenty years very well *could* wind up appearing to be brain-damaged.) Dr. Bennett described how the two babies were cared for during one thirty-minute session.

> When I entered the nursery I was greeted with "Jones is waiting for you. I'm not going near that spastic kid." He was in the treatment room because of his crying and Smith was being played with in the nurses' room while a discussion was under way as to what solid foods to feed him. [One nurse said] "Look at Smitty, he's full of beans, he needs a steak. Do you hear that Jones in there, he should be dumped somewhere." After 15 minutes of play with Smith, the conversation again turned to Jones and someone went in and picked him up, and the crying stopped immediately. [The nurse said] "Now that's what I call a spoiled baby." He was put down after one minute, the crying resumed, and the comment was "Oh, come off it." . . . At the end of 30 minutes Smith had been played with the entire time, Jones had been picked up for one minute.[7]

A sensitive pediatrician, Dr. Bennett was worried. The Jones baby seemed unusually grim. When Jones was twenty-two days old, Dr. Bennett recalls, "After I held [him] for over an hour with gentle rocking, his face became less tense, several times there was truly a coo with an associated affect that was almost positive."[8]

In short, Jones wasn't a "difficult" or "disagreeable" baby. He was only a little guy having a tough time of it in the world, who needed some understanding and love. As Cornell child specialist Urie Bronfenbrenner has said, every child deserves to have at least one adult who's crazy about him. Jones didn't need a roomful of objective, professional people; he needed one emotionally involved person who didn't mind if he had to have a little extra cuddling or rocking to feel good. Parents make the best parents precisely because they *are* emotionally involved and willing to go the extra distance when a baby needs extra help.

A clear contrast to the Jones story is the story of Mark, a baby I observed in one of my home studies. Mark had a special problem:

He cried more than most infants and disliked being cuddled or held. When Mark was picked up, his eyes glazed over and he looked almost pained. Some parents might have seen Mark as a very rejecting baby (as indeed he was with respect to cuddling) and I believe he could have been in trouble. But luckily, Mark had a very perceptive Dancingmother. Recognizing that her baby was quite sensitive to touch, Mark's mother carried him around during the day on a cradle board. Clinicians who heard about the case were deeply concerned. Nearly all the professionals agreed: Mark would possibly grow up autistic.

But while they worried, a remarkable thing was happening.

Because of her sensitivity to Mark's special needs, Mark's mother didn't insist on giving him attention by cuddling him. She loved him enough to let him be as he really was. Gradually, Mark grew happier and more relaxed. By one year of age, he was crying less than any other baby in my study. He still disliked being held closely, but he and his mother had found fun ways to be together and touch each other (by holding hands, kissing, etc.) that didn't involve close cuddling. Mark had been literally loved into being able to love—by a Dancingmother who'd never taken a how-to-parent course in her life.

Why do you make the best parent for your baby even if you've never been "trained" for your job? Because you have something far better than formal lessons to guide you. You have what I call biological wisdom.

BIOLOGICAL WISDOM: FOUR OF THE MANY WAYS YOU HELP YOUR BABY GROW NATURALLY

If over two hundred million years of evolution has developed the human heart (the most efficient of all pumps), you'd think evolution would have developed an ability in a parent to raise a baby successfully to adulthood.

In fact, it has. Biological wisdom isn't an inherited, inevitable trait (or what's popularly called an instinct). As humans, we're much too far from our animal pasts to have any behavior that can't be changed or modified by experience or learning. You can override your biological wisdom by being too anxious or by listening to misguided experts rather than your own inner signals.

Conversely, you can *enhance* your wisdom by learning about babies—particularly about your unique baby and what he needs.

You've already seen the subtle ways your baby talks to you. What you may not yet realize is that you biologically talk back. Nearly every way you behave with your baby differs from how you act around older children and adults . . . and somehow these differences in your behavior (which are part of *your* dance) help your baby learn.

If you have special ways of behaving around your baby to help him grow, why don't you *know* about this biological wisdom—or "biowiz"? Probably because it's so much a part of you, you seldom think about it consciously. Biowiz is a lot like running: You have to learn it, but it comes so naturally there's hardly a person alive who can't do it.

Surprisingly few parents are consciously aware of their biowiz. Dr. Daniel Stern of Cornell videotaped mothers playing with their babies, then showed the mothers the tapes and asked if they'd been aware of the special steps they'd used to capture their babies' attention. Of the mothers, 24 percent had no idea they'd been behaving uniquely, 43 percent had been only slightly aware, and only 32 percent said they'd been fully conscious of their baby-pleasing dances. Even these last mothers, Dr. Stern notes, weren't actually noticing their own special behaviors so much as the effects they were having on their babies.[9] Somehow, the dance seems best when, rather than focusing on yourself and what you're *doing*, you just focus on your baby, let him initiate the play, and let your loving nature handle the rest.

When you relax and pay attention to your baby, here are just some of the steps you spontaneously use to help your baby grow:

Baby Talk

Experts in the past have often advised you to avoid baby talk, arguing it just looks silly and keeps your baby from learning to speak clearly. But in fact, parents the world over use baby talk (or what some scientists call motherese). And babies love it.

If someone had to teach you to speak motherese or you had to study it in a Berlitz guide, this special baby-pleasing language might take weeks, even months to master. Luckily, no one has to teach you. When relaxed and tuned in to your baby, you automatically speak in highly simplified, short sentences. You'll use many nonsense sounds like "oooooooh," "mmmmmmmmmm," and "aaaaaaaah" (probably also a few squeaks and squeals). And you'll even change the pronunciation of some words to make them easier for your baby to understand. In his intriguing paper "Baby Talk in Six Languages," C. A. Ferguson reports that mothers the world over use such "silly" talk—and babies learn a lot from it. At this moment, mothers from Tokyo to Des Moines are, in essence, translating the words "pretty rabbit" into their languages' versions of "pwitty wabbit." And babies are relishing every minute of it.[10] Your speech seems finely tuned to capture your baby's attention. In a study at the University of Oregon, Anne Fernald played a variety of tape-recorded voices to four-month-olds and found motherese caught the babies' attention much more than other forms of adult talking.[11]

It's not *what* you say but *how* you say it that makes motherese unlike any other language on this planet. When talking to your baby, you may often raise the pitch of your voice (babies like higher tones). And you may also find yourself shifting dramatically from louder to softer sounds, even whispering at times. Many mothers and fathers will talk in a high, falsetto voice (one mother calls this her "Mickey Mouse" voice) and then suddenly slide or switch to a deep-throated bass, a whimsical tactic that often makes a four-month-old smile with delight.

Exaggeration seems to be a major ingredient in motherese (which could just as well be called fatherese, because fathers talk this way to babies too). Not only do you exaggerate your vocal pitch as described above, but you'll also probably exaggerate your vowel sounds, as in "Ooooooooooh, what a sweeeeeeet baby." When you talk this way, it's almost as if you're purposefully showing your baby all the nifty things the human voice can do.

When you talk to your baby, even the *pauses* in your speaking are prolonged. Dr. Stern describes a typical mother-baby "conversation," which went like this:

Mother: "Aren't you my cutie?" (1.42 seconds)
Pause: (.60 second)
Imagined response from infant: "Yes" (.43 second)
Pause: (.60 second)
Mother: "You sure are."[12]

Researchers speculate that through these unique one-sided "dia-logues" you carry on with your baby, you're teaching the baby how people take turns when they talk.

Not only do you use a special language when addressing your newborn, but as your baby grows older your motherese changes. A mother addressing a two-year-old no longer uses baby talk but continues to limit her vocabulary and use short, simple sentences. Over months, as she sees her child catching on to what she's saying, she'll use longer words and more complex sentences, staying just one or two steps ahead of her child's abilities. It's as if she's "lead-ing" her child into more and more complex ways of speaking.[13]

I'm not saying you'll talk to your baby in *exactly* the above ways, of course. As a unique individual, you have your own special style. Nor am I suggesting that the above is an exhaustive descrip-tion of the many ways you talk to your baby. Motherese is a highly rich language, with many subtle nuances scientists are only be-ginning to detect. But, clearly, you already have in your parenting tool kit many special ways of talking to your baby that help him learn, feel good, and grow.

Caution: Already some misguided experts are using these star-tling new findings to write formulas telling you precisely how to talk to your baby. One child psychiatrist with impressive credentials suggests you should always start your dialogues with one short, quick, crisp word like "Hey!" or "Hi!" to get your baby's attention. Then you're supposed to direct your baby's gaze (by pointing your finger, for example) to, say, the book you'd like him to see.[14] While these and other tactics might "work" (the baby may, in fact, look at the book), straining to talk to your baby in any rigid way can undermine your spontaneity. Rather than helping you dance "bet-ter," such experts may be introducing self-conscious inhibitions that make your dance tense and mechanical. It's more important to talk naturally to your baby—even if you *never* use motherese—than to strain to follow some nonsensical (unproved) formula.

Mock Surprise (and Other Baby-Pleasing Expressions)

One of the commonest facial expressions you may use when talking to your baby is your "mock surprise" look. Amazingly, this expression (which nearly every parent uses) is most effective in capturing a baby's interest. Often, the minute your baby looks at you, your eyes may open wide, you'll raise your eyebrows as high as you can, you may tilt your head or move your head closer to your baby, and you'll open your mouth wide (often in a big, almost clown-like smile). Not only will you let this expression spread slowly over your face, but you'll probably hold the look longer than those facial expressions you use when talking to adults. It's almost as if you're performing in slow motion. Recalling from Chapter 7 what a baby likes to look at, you'll realize your mock surprise look contains nearly all the elements: angular dark-and-white patterns (made more obvious by the wide-eyed look that shows more of the whites of your eyes), circular patterns (enhanced by your open mouth), and of course the entire pattern of your fascinating human face.

The mock-surprise look, according to Dr. Stern, is the number-one expression parents use when they want to invite a baby to play. Often, you may find yourself using this expression every ten or fifteen seconds—almost as if you're greeting your baby anew each time he looks at you.

Another exaggerated expression you may find yourself using (especially when your baby looks away from you or seems sad) is your mock frown. Dr. Stern remarks that like many expressions you use when dancing with your baby, this frown "often looks like a caricature or very bad acting."[15] Your eyebrows slowly knit together and lower, your eyes narrow, your head moves to the side or down, and your mouth purses or makes a tiny "o." You may even go further, pouting, wrinkling your nose, and adding a sympathetic "aaaaaaaaawwwwww" sound, which starts high and moves smoothly to a lower pitch.

Other expressions parents commonly use to communicate with babies include: the smile (of course); the oh-you-poor-dear look (a knitted-brow, wide-eyed, mouth-open expression); and the neutral or expressionless face, which tells your baby, "I'd rather not play just now."

Eye Play

Among adults, eye contact is governed by many unspoken rules. Though there are exceptions, as a rule you and another adult won't look directly into one another's eyes for more than ten or so seconds unless you're ready to make love—or fight. Usually, you'll meet a stranger's eyes barely at all or for only a couple of seconds at most. In contrast, when you and your baby are playing, you may gaze fondly into each other's eyes for a whopping thirty seconds or more. Looking into your baby's eyes seems to be a key way you tell him you care. When playing happily with your baby, according to Dr. Stern, you'll look at him about 70 percent of the time.

You and your baby also have a special way of using eye contact. Though there are exceptions, when *adults* converse, the listener generally watches the speaker's face most of the time, whereas the speaker will look in the listener's eyes a few seconds and will then look away as he talks (with only brief glances back to see how the other person is responding). When about to stop talking, the speaker will then gaze back into his listener's eyes. This final glance into the other person's eyes signals, "Now it's your turn to talk." Between you and your baby, a quite different exchange occurs: Looking and speaking usually occur *together.* In his early months, of course, your baby's "speech" involves mostly coos, grunts, and other baby sounds, along with body wiggles and arm waving. But nevertheless you're definitely involved in a dialogue.

Though why you and your baby communicate with such special gaze signals remains unknown, eye contact seems to matter a lot. When a parent and a baby rarely or never look at each other, therapists take this as a clear sign their relationship is in trouble. The late psychiatrist Selma Fraiberg, who worked with mothers and blind babies, noted that lack of eye contact and other clear signals from their babies left these mothers distraught, even grieved. Dr. Fraiberg taught the mothers that even blind babies communicate in many delightful ways. When alert and ready to play, for instance, a baby who can see will look bright-eyed, whereas a blind baby will grow quite *still* (so he can listen intently). Once Dr. Fraiberg taught mothers how to read their blind babies' signals, both mothers and babies danced more happily.[16]

Head Behaviors

When a human face suddenly appears, a baby invariably perks up. The classic game Peek-a-boo *depends* on your baby's delight at watching your face vanish and reappear. When your baby is only two or three months old, you may already be playing a simple form of Peek-a-boo to catch his attention. In *The First Relationship,* Dr. Stern writes how one mother typically played this game:

> The mother lowers her head as if looking at the floor, revealing to the infant the top of her head, and says something like "eeeeee-yah" and sharply brings her head back up to the full-face position on the accented "yah." She then lowers her head again for the next round. In this situation, the head does not disappear and reappear as in more formal peek-a-boo, but the full presentation does.[17]

As with all the other marvelous ways you play with your baby, the dramatic ways you move your head seem a prelude to more complex communication later. Nearly all the exaggerated head behaviors you use (nodding, shaking your head, cocking your head to one side, etc.) will be used later by your baby in more complicated dialogues to signal "yes," "no," and "I'm interested."

Another unique way you play with your baby may involve encroaching on his personal space. A baby usually hates to have objects looming too close to his face. Even a baby only a few hours old will turn his head and hold up his hands in self-defense if a big box is shoved rapidly toward him. But when playing with a baby, adults often violate the baby's wishes in this regard. You may get annoyed (and rightly so) when Great-Aunt Matilda zooms in to give your baby an Eskimo kiss and winds up making him cry. But chances are, *you* may also often violate your baby's personal space (to his discomfort) by popping in at him to kiss him on the cheek or to give him a pretend bite on the nose.

When involved in such an encounter, your baby may avert his eyes and even turn his head in distress. In fact, this reaction is so common that many scientists who understand how babies talk will advise you *never* to poke your face rapidly into your baby's face. That seems wise advice—and it may well be. Yet the fact that good mothers often *do* encroach on their babies' personal space without warning has led more careful researchers to be extremely cautious about telling you never to do this. After all, mothers and fathers have been dancing with babies for millions of years, and there may be good reason for *everything* they naturally do. Dr. Stern says that "this constant disregard by mothers of their babies' comfort zone may be important in preparing the infant to tolerate, or even more, to engage socially within an intimate distance. Later affiliative behaviors such as kissing and snuggling may partially depend on the successful outcome of these first experiences."[18] In short, scientists have gained great respect for the ways you play with your baby naturally. If most parents and babies play this way—even if the behavior *looks* wrong to an expert—it may in fact be the best way to help a baby grow.

· PUTTING THE STEPS TOGETHER

When dancing with your baby, of course, you don't use *just* eye contact or *just* baby talk at any one time. You execute many dance steps simultaneously. Trying to explain in words the beautiful way you dance is tricky. Just as you have to watch Mikhail Baryshnikov's dancing to appreciate it fully (no one can give you the same feeling by telling you how he danced), you can only feel the rhythmic, flowing way you perform with your baby by dancing yourself. Still, there are many special ways you execute your steps. And here are the three main ones.

You Notice What Your Baby Does

When your baby smiles, coos, waves his hands, or otherwise tries to attract your attention, you probably just naturally respond by nodding, smiling, or talking to him. Scientists call noticing what your baby does *acknowledging.* And this simple, seemingly trivial behavior is far more essential to your baby's growth than you might imagine. It's easy to notice when your baby suddenly learns a new skill such as being able to stack blocks or read a book, but it also seems important to notice your baby's subtler behaviors— for example, the way he looks, smiles, or moves his body to get your attention. To help your baby grow, certainly you don't have to be keenly attentive to every tiny move he makes. But by paying attention to his subtle cues *much* of the time, you're helping him learn about the world. Anything you do to let your baby know you've noticed his bid for attention—laughing, talking, smiling, or looking at him with an animated facial expression—helps him feel important and loved.

You Mirror Your Baby's Feelings

Again, this is such a common way for parents to behave, there's certainly no need to tell you "how." When a baby coos, moves, or makes a face, parents frequently match the baby's behavior by repeating what the child did.

It's tempting to say you "imitate" your baby . . . but mirroring goes far beyond simple imitation. When playing with your baby during his first nine months, chances are when he makes a face you'll make a face, when he vocalizes you'll vocalize back. But I. C. Uzgiris and other researchers point out that you don't just echo your baby's *exact* expression or sound back to him. Rather, you offer a slightly *different* face or sound, as if you're saying, "That's cute, and here's *my* rendition of that theme." You can see how highly complex your dance becomes. But, as with baby talk and entrainment, fortunately you needn't strain to learn how to mirror your baby's feelings. When you're just paying attention to your baby, you learn this complex form of communication without special lessons.

You Attune to Your Baby's Feelings

"Attunement" was coined by Dr. Stern, and it's a good usage. The very term hints of the musical, rhythmic quality of your communicative dance. Mirroring is a simple form of attunement. But when your baby gets to be about nine months old, a new, special behavior enters your dance. Suddenly, you're truly in step with your baby's feelings. Remarkable as it sounds, if you've been paying attention all along (and most parents have), you can suddenly match and respond to your baby's voice with your body movements and respond to his body movements with your words (this appears to be a type of rhythmic entrainment).

In *The Interpersonal World of the Infant,* Dr. Stern cites several examples of this amazing attunement at work:

> • A nine-month-old girl becomes very excited about a toy and reaches for it. As she grabs for it, she lets out an exuberant "aaah!" and looks at her mother. Her mother looks back, scrunches up her shoulders, and performs a terrific shimmy with her upper body, like a go-go dancer. The shimmy lasts only about as long as her daughter's "aaaaah" but is equally excited, joyful, and intense.

• A nine-month-old boy bangs his hand on a soft toy, at first in some anger, but gradually with pleasure, exuberance and humor. He sets up a steady rhythm. Mother falls into his rhythm and says, "kaaaaa-*bam*, kaaaaa-*bam*," the *"bam"* falling on the stroke and the "kaaaaa" riding with the preparatory upswing and the suspenseful holding of his arm aloft before it falls. . . .

• A ten-month-old girl finally gets a piece in a jigsaw puzzle. She looks toward her mother, throws her head up in the air, and with a forceful arm flap raises herself partly off the ground in a flurry of exuberance. The mother says, "YES, thatta girl." The "YES" is intoned with much stress. It has an explosive rise that echoes the girl's fling of gesture and posture.[19]

Amazingly, such complex emotional dialogues occur unconsciously. Yet by attuning to your baby, you're telling him you love him and also offering him the solid emotional support he needs to reach out confidently to explore his world. A distant professional who'd rather not get emotionally involved with a baby would have difficulty providing this special kind of support babies need to grow. It takes someone who truly cares—someone like you—to attune to your baby's feelings and tell him he's loved.

BRINGING FATHER INTO THE DANCE TOO

You've probably noticed that throughout this book I've talked mostly about *mothers* and babies. That's *not* because fathers are less important to their babies than mothers are.[20] It's just that the beautiful dances between fathers and babies haven't been all that well studied.

Sadly, the wonderful—and special—role the father plays in his baby's growth was ignored for decades. During the 1960s, just two studies of note considered infant-father relationships—and in both, fathers weren't even interviewed. (The researchers asked mothers how their husbands behaved.)[21] In *The Competent Infant*, a book more than 1,300 pages long, published in 1973, fathers were referred to—and then only in passing—just three times.[22] *Some* of the ignoring of fathers may have been justified. In 1971, Freda Rebelsky, then at Boston Hospital, analyzed tape recordings of all the voices ten babies heard for six entire days their first twelve weeks of life. In an average twenty-four-hour period, fathers spoke to their infants less than *thirty-eight seconds!*[23] Was it any wonder that in 1975 psychologist Michael E. Lamb, then at Yale, called fathers "the forgotten contributors to child development"?[24]

Happily, times have changed. Fathers are now often highly involved in child rearing. Today's upwardly mobile father is likely to have a spouse on the fast track too, and children have become not just Mom's responsibility but also Dad's. Just as fathers have begun to take a more active role in child rearing than ever before, researchers are beginning to find how incredibly *important* fathers are to their babies' growth (a fact that fathers, of course, always knew).

Psychologist Ross Parke and his colleagues at the University of Illinois have shown that new fathers are just as actively involved with their newborns as mothers are. In Dr. Parke's studies, fathers smiled, talked to, touched, looked at, explored, and imitated their babies as much as mothers did—and fathers actually held and rocked their babies more.[25]

Psychologist Robert McCall, of Boys Town Center, observes that while mothers have an obvious edge in breast feeding, fathers can bottle feed their babies as adeptly as mothers can. They give them about the same amount of milk; and they know when their babies are signaling that they want to stop eating for a minute or be readjusted to a more comfy position. When watching TV films of crying babies, fathers are also as apt as mothers to respond with increased blood pressure and heart rates.[26] In short, fathers possess just as much biological wisdom as mothers do.

Fathers also do a special kind of dance. When watching eight-month-olds playing with their parents, Dr. Lamb, now at the University of Utah, found that mothers and fathers touch and play with their babies about equally . . . but fathers offer a different play *style*. Fathers tend to bounce, jiggle, and roughhouse their infants more and often stimulate them without using toys or objects and by inventing new games. Mothers, in contrast, are likelier to shake a rattle or bell to get a baby's attention or to play well-known, traditional baby games like Gotcha, Tickle Your Tummy, and Peek-a-boo. (For a list of baby-pleasing games, see Chapter 13.) A mother's play style tends to be more patient. Mothers, for example, will often sit long minutes, showing a baby how to stack blocks, whereas impatient fathers often get fed up after two or three tries and move on to another game. Mothers also smile, sing, and talk to their babies more than fathers do.[27]

In the time he spends with his baby, a father is likely to play more. When Dr. Milton Kotelchuk of the University of Massachusetts observed parents and their six-to-twenty-one-month-old babies interacting naturally at home, mothers spent nearly an hour a day cleaning and about two hours playing with the baby. Fathers averaged only nine minutes cleaning and nearly ninety minutes in play.[28] In an Oxford study, English fathers spent 90 percent of their time with their babies in active play.[29]

Why the difference? To some extent, fathers and mothers dance differently because it's their nature to do so. Considering that from the moment of fertilization, a baby boy's chromosome content differs from a baby girl's—not to mention the fact that mothers and fathers are socialized differently from the moment they're born (mothers talk to and smile more at girl babies than at boys, for example)—it would be startling if mothers and fathers *didn't* dance differently. As Anne Fausto-Serling, Ph.D., of Brown University points out in *Myths of Gender: Biological Theories About Women and Men,* human behavior such as the ways you and your spouse play with your baby isn't "caused" by biology or environment, but springs from a complex web of interactions between the two. The old nature-nurture debate is the result of false dichotomizing: We're all products of both nature *and* nurture.

Whatever the reason fathers play differently than mothers, fathers provide a unique play style which captures babies' attention and helps them grow in many ways. For example:

• Dr. Lamb believes a father's distinctive play style may help his boy establish a gender identity. Since fathers are twice as active with boys as with girls, Dr. Lamb suggests that a father may be drawing attention to himself so his little boy will say, "This is how a man behaves."

• In a review of dozens of father-child studies, entitled "Fatherhood: The Myth of the Second-Class Parent," Marsha Weinraub, a psychologist at Temple University, notes that a warm, nurturing father seems to have children (especially sons) who do better on IQ tests. In several studies, warm, accepting fathers who listened to their children and were involved in their education (yet not to the point where they tried to dominate or control their children's choices) had more intelligent, creative, flexible, and imaginative sons.

• According to Dr. Weinraub, nurturant fathers may also play a role in motivating boys and girls to achieve. She notes:

> Surprisingly, fathers may play an even more critical role in influencing daughters' than sons' achievement motivation. . . . Fathers who are attentive and encouraging of their daughters' achievements without being overwhelmingly affectionate have highly motivated daughters who are willing to take responsibility for their own successes and failures. In both males and females of college age, high achievement appears to be related to perceptions of the father as distant, autocratic and punitive.[30]

Compared to mothers, fathers aren't better with babies. But they are delightfully different. And when you and your mate work together, your distinctive ways of interacting and playing with your baby just naturally enhance each other to help your baby grow. One study that looked at this special *enhancement effect* was reported by Alison Clarke-Stewart at the University of California. Dr. Clarke-Stewart watched how mothers and fathers played with their babies, then measured the babies' intelligence. She concluded that the family structure likeliest to go hand in hand with an intelligent baby involved a warm, positive mother and a playful father.[31]

Not only do you and your mate have biological wisdom, but your combined wisdom seems to help make for an optimal family dance.

A SPECIAL NOTE TO THE SINGLE PARENT

If you're a single mother or father, you may now wonder, "What about me? Does this mean if my baby doesn't have both a mother *and* a father to dance with, he'll necessarily be less advantaged than a baby who has both parents?"

No.

As Dr. Lamb observes, "It is important neither to understate nor overstate the difficulties faced by single parents. Most aspects of personality development involve input from a variety of sources (mothers, fathers, siblings, teachers, the media) and there is no reason to believe that any one source is irreplaceable."[32]

So if you're a single parent, relax and enjoy the biological wisdom you possess. It's far better to spend your time playing happily with your baby than to disrupt your dance with worry over some elusive form of stimulation you're *not* providing. What's most important isn't the style of dance you do, but the fact that you are dancing.

12 Dancing with a Crying Baby

The dance doesn't always have to be happy to be good.

—A WISE MOTHER

Joelle,* a corporate attorney for a large Silicon Valley firm, has been up all night. She's exhausted. The house is a mess. A report she brought home to work on last night still lies untouched on the desk. Usually calm, levelheaded, and confident, Joelle is beginning to think she's losing her mind and just can't cope.

The source of her distress? Her three-month-old, Marissa, has been crying for two hours, and nothing Joelle or her husband, Larry, does seems to help.

At one time or another, most parents have acted out a version of this floor-pacing scenario. Joelle says, "When Marissa screams, my heart pounds and I feel a sharp pang in my chest"—and her reaction isn't just psychological. When a baby cries, studies show, you actually *do* have a physiological response. Your heartbeat quickens. Your blood pressure rises. And if you're nursing, you may even feel a sensation in your breasts.

A baby's cry can also stir up powerful emotions, including anger, anxiety, and guilt. Says one mother of a particularly irritable infant, "When Brandon cries for hours, I feel I must be the most horrible mother on earth. Other people's babies don't cry for no reason!"

I've got news for her—and you. Babies often do cry for no apparent reason. A classic study done at the Mayo Clinic found that when babies cried, 36 percent of the time they were hungry and 29 percent of the time they needed a diaper change. But some of the best medical minds in the world concluded that a whopping 35 percent of babies' cries stem from "unknown causes."[1]

Estimates on how *much* the "average" baby cries vary. Pedia-

---

* Names of parents and babies have been changed to protect their privacy.

trician T. Berry Brazelton reports babies typically cry two to three hours a day during the first six weeks, with crying tapering off until by twelve weeks of age the "average" baby cries only about one hour in a twenty-four-hour period.[2] That estimate seems high to me because in my studies at the University of Connecticut, babies cried an average of only *thirteen minutes* between 9 A.M. and 5 P.M. The seemingly wide discrepancy between the two findings may be due to the fact that, as Dr. Brazelton says, babies cry *most* toward the end of the day, when everyone in the family is tired.

What to do when a baby cries? First, it helps if you can stay calm. When your baby's crying, you may be tempted to quicken your pace, pat him harder, and handle him more briskly than you otherwise would. But this is a time your baby needs *gentle* handling. Second, it helps to remember that each baby is unique, so what works for one won't necessarily work for another. Some easily soothed babies will settle down readily after being patted, walked, rocked, fed, or having their diaper changed. Others are more sensitive. They jump or startle at the slightest sound, wince at bright lights, are often keyed up, and are much more difficult to soothe. Since babies differ, no one can give you one or two quick "fixes" that works with them all. But here are some options to try.

SIX THINGS YOU CAN DO WHEN YOUR BABY CRIES

When seeking to soothe a baby, it's best not to try too many tactics too quickly. If you pat three minutes, walk two minutes, sing three minutes, you may not be giving any of these techniques time to work. So proceed slowly from one calming strategy to another, but don't be afraid to try a new tack if your current method isn't working. The following ways of soothing a baby are hardly new. But I hope some of the latest findings about these tried-and-true tactics will help.

Pick Up Your Baby Fairly Quickly

If you pick up your baby the minute he cries, aren't you training him to cry more and possibly spoiling him? No. That's a myth left over from the days when doctors thought a baby was robot-like and easily programmed.

A study by Susan Crockenberg, associate professor of human

development at the University of California at Davis, reveals that mothers who take longer to go to their crying babies for fear of spoiling them have babies who cry more often at three months than do mothers who answer their babies' cries quickly.[3] These findings echo a well-known 1972 study by Mary Ainsworth and Silvia Bell of Johns Hopkins University, who concluded that babies whose cries were ignored early in life tended to cry more often and persistently at one year. After the first six months, an unhappy cycle had been set up between these mothers and babies, with the babies crying so much the mothers felt discouraged about responding at all! Conversely, mothers who responded most quickly to their infants' cries had babies who cried the least at one year and who used other means of communication (such as gestures and happy coos) to get their mothers' attention.[4]

That's not to say you should pick up your baby the second he whimpers. By letting your baby fuss a little, you're giving him some practice in learning to soothe himself (some babies will start sucking on their fists or fingers to calm themselves down). Allowing your baby to cry for a short time also gives him the sense, when you arrive, he's truly communicating with you. Intriguingly, in one of my studies in the home, my colleagues and I found that when a mother picked up her baby before he'd cried ninety seconds, the baby soothed quite readily. If she took longer than ninety seconds, it was much harder for the baby to calm down.[5] So when picking up your baby, the general rule of thumb is: Not too early, not too late.

Carry or Rock the Baby

I'm sure you know rocking your baby can often be soothing. What you may not have heard is that the latest studies show both *how* you rock and how *fast* you rock may determine how successful this tactic will be. A 1983 study, for example, found that rocking your baby from side to side may make him more alert, whereas rocking him up and down or back and forth (as you would in a rocking chair) seems most soothing. Rocking also seems to make a baby most drowsy when you rock *continuously* rather than starting and stopping (although you'll have to check these findings out with your own special baby to make sure he follows the pattern of those babies studied).[6]

Rocking and carrying your baby can be done in combination with many of the other anti-crying strategies listed here. You'll recall the mother on page 134 had best results with her baby when she used her own creative combination of rocking, walking, groaning, patting, rubbing, and holding her baby close.

Treat Your Baby to Rhythmic Sounds

You'll often hear that a baby will calm down if you put a ticking clock near his crib or buy him one of the new high-tech teddy bears (one is called the Rock-a-Bye Bear) that play rhythmic, whooshing noises recorded inside a mother's womb. Another modern gimmick is a record put out by Capitol called *Lullaby from the Womb*, which consists of recordings of the aorta, veins, and blood vessels, as well as natural womb sounds, mixed with light classical music. Try these if you wish, but you ought to know there's been little published research to support the touted claims for such devices. The notion behind these gimmicks is that the stimulation that was appropriate in the womb is *still* appropriate once your baby is born—a dubious assumption. Once born, a baby (even a premature one) is so physically different from a fetus that it would be amazing if he *did* enjoy the same sounds.

Though some studies suggest that continuous sound will calm a very young infant, be careful about taking these findings too seriously. The fact that sounds calm only very *young* babies (once a baby is four months old, continuous sound seems less effective) would indicate that exposing your newborn to *inescapable* sounds may be more stressful than adults have realized. When faced with too much unavoidable noise, some tiny babies go into a "stress sleep" (see page 147). They literally shut out the world.

Your best bets when trying to soothe your baby with sounds? Sing a lullaby or play your favorite folk singing or classical music tape and watch to see if your baby likes what he hears. If he does, continue as long as he's interested. If not, don't bombard him with sounds that may be overwhelming.

Try a Pacifier

A common myth holds that a pacifier just sets up "bad habits" and should be used only as a last resort. I disagree. Babies love to suck on their fingers, wrists, fists, toys, or whatever's handy. And if your baby finds a pacifier soothing, why not use one?

In recent studies of newborns, Gene Anderson and her colleagues in Florida found that prematurely born infants given pacifiers were ready to take a bottle sooner and were able to leave the hospital four days before preemies who weren't given any extra sucking. In short, extra sucking for these babies was clearly related to growth.[7]

Another revealing finding was that extra sucking helped colicky two-day-olds calm down—if the pacifier was offered when the *baby* asked for it. Signals your baby may use when he wants more sucking include putting his hands to his mouth, sucking on his tongue, fist, or fingers, whimpering, rooting, or yawning. (Every baby uses his own cues, so you have to watch your baby to know his special signals.) In Dr. Anderson's studies, if a baby was given a pacifier when he first began to "request" extra sucking (usually right after a feeding), he calmed down quickly, sucked for about thirty minutes, and fell fast asleep. Once the baby was already thrashing and crying, however, it was often too late for a pacifier to help. (If you do decide to try a pacifier, be as consistent as possible about letting your baby use it. Some parents don't mind if their baby sucks on a pacifier privately, but find it embarrassing when the baby wants his old standby in public or around relatives. Don't let pressures from disapproving others bother you. You're the best judge of what your baby needs.)

There is a major drawback to using a pacifier at bedtime. If at 2 A.M. your baby "loses" his pacifier in the corner of his crib (as he inevitably will), he may wake up crying until you get out of bed and find it for him. Again, you have to decide how serious a problem this is for you. Mothers who have used pacifiers successfully say they'd rather play find-the-pacifier ten times a day than listen to their baby's screaming.

As for the notion that pacifiers become habit forming, I've seldom known this to be true. In my experience, when a baby is ready to give up extra sucking he will. Some mothers have hurried along the pacifier-relinquishing process (especially in a baby a year or two old) by telling their child, "This is the last one we're buying," or by poking a tiny hole in the pacifier and enlarging the hole a bit each day until the beloved object loses its shape—and appeal. You can do this if you like. But it really isn't necessary to hurry the process.

Try Swaddling

To many Americans, swaddling a baby snugly in a blanket seems freedom inhibiting and almost undemocratic. Yet lab studies have shown swaddling may help a baby more than you might think. In a major study reported in the journal *Child Development,* one-month-olds who were swaddled cozily cried less, slept more, breathed more regularly, and had slower heart rates than unswaddled babies. In fact, swaddling was the number-one way to stop the babies' crying and help them sleep.[8]

Why did swaddling work so well? Possibly because newborn babies have incomplete control over their movements, and their own jerks and random motions may keep them awake. Swaddling can help your baby get his body under control so he can settle down.

If you still dislike the idea of swaddling, you might try holding a warm hand firmly on your baby's tummy, cuddling your baby snugly, or holding him securely with his back to your chest. One aspect about swaddling that a baby may find comforting is the handling he gets when you're wrapping the blanket around him. But the point is that just by gently limiting your baby's movements, you may produce soothing effects.

Drawbacks to swaddling are threefold. First, a newborn baby, who can't regulate his own body temperature very well, may become too hot and develop a rash. Second, *some* babies who lay at odd angles in the womb (bent over backward or with their legs up against their chins, for example) may find being forced into a traditional swaddling position uncomfortable. Third, babies with congenital hip dislocations should never be swaddled. (In case of doubt, ask your pediatrician.)

Try a Baby Massage

Once almost forgotten, the gentle art of baby massage has been rediscovered, and many mothers swear by it. Why? Because a baby can't feel both tense and relaxed at the same time. In short, a relaxed baby won't cry. Your special way of touching your baby as you massage him can also enhance intimacy and understanding between you. British pediatrician John Kirkland, author of *Crying and Babies: Helping Families Cope,* calls baby massage "the physical parallel of trust."[9]

Though massage may relax even a wailing infant, this strategy usually works best to *prevent* crying rather than stop it. So if your baby has a usual cry time, try a massage *before* he has a chance to get worked up. Another good time to massage is right after your baby has been fed, bathed, or rocked.

To massage your baby, place a bottle of baby oil in a pan of warm water until the oil feels warm but not hot to your touch. Then undress your baby in a warm room. Lay him on a flat, firm-but-not-hard surface, such as a bed or changing table. Moisten your hands with the oil and begin your massage. Rub very *gently,* but use enough pressure so you don't tickle. Let each stroke tell your baby how much you love him.

Frankly, I think the best massage techniques are those you and your baby work out together. As you massage, you'll begin to see how your baby responds to your touch and which ways of touching he seems to like best. If you'd like to know more about baby massage, however, two handy guides are *The Baby Massage Book* by Tina Heinl and *Baby Massage: The Magic of the Loving Touch* by A. Auckett.

How often to massage? That's up to you and your baby. Some babies love massages so much that you may want to do it every day. With others, you may want to massage only two or three times a week. A good massage usually lasts ten or fifteen minutes, but watch your baby to see if he's enjoying himself. If he becomes tired or restless, that's the time to stop.

Does massage relax *all* babies? No. Some babies have especially sensitive skin and may dislike massage. Certainly you don't want to force massage on a baby who hates it.

Still, the most aloof of babies will unwind at times . . . and when he does, even a non-cuddler may find massage soothing. One mother says her baby would relax only in a full bathtub. She explains, "When I'd take Alicia in the tub with me and fill the tub with really deep, warm water, it was as if all her tensions were washed away." Once an "uptight" baby like Alicia is drained of tension, even she may like being touched and rubbed, and you may find that after being massaged over time, she'll cry less.

COLIC: WAYS TO LIVE THROUGH IT

Eight in ten parents don't have this problem, so I hope you won't. But there *are* some perfectly healthy babies who bawl one to four hours nonstop daily for no explicable reason. Doctors call these babies colicky, a catchall term that simply means: "This baby cries a lot; no one knows why."

If your baby wails irritably for what seems like hours on end and none of the above tactics works, what to do? There are no easy answers. But here are nine options to try.

• *See your pediatrician.* Contrary to popular myth, colic is seldom caused by gas or other gastrointestinal ills. Colicky babies generally have no symptoms of intestinal disorders. They don't gain weight poorly, spit or vomit a lot, suffer from constipation or diarrhea, or need extra food. They just cry. In a classic study by Dr. R. S. Illingworth (the English equivalent of our Dr. Spock), colicky babies were given x-rays and other tests during the peak of their crying spells. No stomach or intestinal problems could be found.[10] Still, if for no other reason than to reassure yourself, check with your doctor.

• *Resist self-blame.* Another common myth holds that irritable crying is "caused" by a tense, anxious, or nervous mother. Studies have consistently shown this isn't so. In one study reported in the prestigious *Journal of the American Medical Association,* for instance, Dr. Jack L. Paradise gave 146 new mothers detailed personality tests, looking for such telltale signs as maternal role rejection, anxiety, lack of enthusiasm about motherhood, and psychological problems. He found mothers of colicky infants were no more anxious or psychologically disturbed than mothers of non-colicky babies. His conclusion: "This evidence . . . does not support the frequently stated view that colic results from an unfavorable emotional climate created by an inexperienced, anxious, hostile, or unmotherly mother."[11] Other studies[12] have shown that colic is also unrelated to: overfeeding, underfeeding, the mother's intelligence, family history of colic, the baby's sex or birth order, and the type of formula the baby is fed. In short, no one knows *why* these babies cry. They just do.

• *Chart your baby's crying.* Often when a baby cries for hours on end, you lose a sense of perspective. It may seem to you that he's *always* crying, which only makes you feel worse. So for about a week, jot down on a notepad exactly what time your baby started crying and exactly when he stopped. Keep track of every time your baby cried. Then see if you can spot an overall pattern. Does he usually cry most in the morning? In the evening? What exactly did you do to try to stop the crying? Did anything work? Can you think of any other strategy to try next time? If you like, you might even keep a cry diary, in which you record such details as: How did the cry sound? How did this crying spell make me feel? Do I feel the crying is becoming more manageable? Anything you can do to put an objective *distance* between you and the crying may help.

• *Find an understanding baby-sitter.* All new mothers need a break from round-the-clock baby care. But mothers of colicky babies need *extra* time to recoup. (Perhaps you and your mate can take turns with the baby so you can *both* get at least some sleep.) If you stay home with your baby full time, try to find a patient, friendly sitter who's willing to cuddle your colicky baby several afternoons to give you a break. One single mother whose eight-month-old had been wailing nonstop for four nights found a good friend to take the infant one afternoon so she could get some much-needed sleep. Tactics like this don't mean you're rejecting your baby. They only mean you're wise and mature enough to problem-solve.

• *Keep your sense of humor.* Living with a colicky baby can be a nightmare if you allow it to be. So try to see the lighter side of all this. Find a friend (perhaps another new mother) you can phone for moral support. Read joke books. Go to funny movies. Laugh. Laughter, which has been likened to "internal jogging," has been found to stimulate your pituitary gland (which helps regulate all your hormones), enhance respiration, put more oxygen in your blood, raise your body temperature half a degree, and send brain chemicals called endorphins racing through your bloodstream. Annette Goodheart, a marital, family, and child therapist in Santa Barbara, California, who uses laughter therapy in her practice, advises, "Don't wait to laugh. Laughter *makes* you happy."

• *Give yourself healthy "self-talks."* When faced with a crying baby, we all have inner conversations: "Why didn't I feed him sooner? I guess my baby hates me. If only I hadn't . . ." Try to keep your self-talks positive. Rather than telling yourself, "This is torture.

I'll never recover," you can say, "Well, things seem bleak right now, but I'm doing the best I can. If I try patting, singing, *and* a pacifier next time, maybe that will help." The first attitude can lead to migraines, the second to more confidence in your abilities as a parent.

• *Focus on what you especially love about your baby.* Even the most irritable baby isn't always unhappy. Think about your baby's good traits. When your baby is cheerful and alert, relish every minute of it. Watch to see what sights, sounds, and ways of touching he adores most. Getting to know what your baby likes when he's content may give you clues to help him when he's upset.

• *Look for subtle signs of overstimulation.* A colicky baby is often only extremely sensitive. Is your baby being picked up too much by adoring relatives? Are the lights in his room too bright? Is the TV always blaring beside him? Sometimes keeping an irritable baby in a dark, quiet room and talking softly and gently to him can cut down on his crying.

• *Try to be patient.* Colicky babies generally outgrow their most severe crying spells by three or four months of age. So at times when your baby has been wailing so much you think you can't stand another minute, take a deep breath (Lamaze breathing works well), and relax. Remember the wise words of one veteran mother: "This, too, will pass."

13 Making Your Baby Smart—with Love

*The need for love . . . represents the evolutionary striving
of all living creatures, and is nowhere more intensely developed than in the child. From this central sun all virtues
flow, all potentialities are maximized. . . . Out of the learning of love grows the love of learning.*

—ASHLEY MONTAGU
Growing Young

A few months ago, I saw a great example of how parents
help their babies learn just by playing with them. A six-month-
old named Tina was fingering her brightly colored blanket. But
because she was only six months old, she couldn't do much more
with the blanket than touch it. Noticing his baby's signals, Tina's
sensitive father started playing some delightful variations of Peek-
a-boo: with the blanket between them, with the blanket over her
head and then over his head, with shorter and longer hiding periods. While Tina was learning how much fun her daddy was, she
was also learning about depth, light and darkness, object perma-
nence, timing, patience, and probably many other concepts.

By playing with your baby, you're making him a lot "smarter"
(in more ways than just raising his IQ) than you will by sending
him to a fast-track baby school or straining to teach him hundreds
of dry facts.

As I've pointed out repeatedly, the very latest research clearly
shows that by playing with your baby and making him feel good,
you're helping him develop not only his intellect but also his emotional health and his social abilities. Dr. Jean Carew, a child-
development researcher at Harvard, sums up the belief of nearly
all respected child-research scientists in this country today when
she says in a paper published in the book *Parenting in a Multicultural
Society*, "The more the mother (and I'd add the father) looks at,

talks to, and plays with the baby and the more age-appropriate, various and responsive her stimulating behavior, the better the infant's performance on standard perceptual and cognitive tests. The mother's interactive behavior with the infant also strongly affects the baby's social and emotional development—a truism that much research has established as scientific fact."[1] This doesn't mean by playing you make your baby smart in a simple cause-effect way. Rather, dancing is what you and your baby do *together* that helps your baby grow.

By playing happily with your baby, you're also doing more to lay the foundations for reading than any fast-track baby school or formal lesson plan could teach him. Child psychologist Dr. David Elkind, chairman of the Eliot-Pearson Department of Child Study at Tufts University, observes in *The Hurried Child: Growing Up Too Fast Too Soon* that his own and others' studies have found "what is crucial to beginning to read is the child's attachment to an adult who spends time reading to or with the child. *The motivation for reading, which is a difficult task, is social.*"[2] (Italics added.)

Playing with your baby also helps him develop what Dr. Dane Archer, a social psychologist at the University of California at Santa Cruz, calls a baby's Social Intelligence Quotient, or S.I.Q.[3] Social intelligence involves how well you can size up someone you've just met, understand other people's feelings, and predict how they'll behave. S.I.Q. involves what executives call "people skills." And as Dr. Elkind notes, in this service economy of ours, social intelligence is rapidly becoming more important to getting ahead than how high someone scores on just an IQ test.[4]

Most important of all, playing with your baby makes him happy. And as the late Pulitzer Prize–winning biologist René Dubos observed in his final work, happiness may be less trivial for the future of mankind than we've given it credit for. Dubos wrote:

> Happiness is contagious. For this reason its expression is a social service and almost a duty. The Buddhists have a saying about this commendable virtue: "Only happy people can make a happy world." Since optimism and cheerful spirits are indispensable to the mental health of technological societies, the most valuable people may turn out to be not those with the greatest ability to produce material goods but those who, through empathy and happiness, have the gift of spreading a spirit of good will.[5]

As you've seen throughout this book, your baby's good feelings are also the solid foundation he needs to reach out and explore his world.

In a minute, we're going to talk about many ways you can help make your baby smart with love. But first I want to point out that when playing with your baby, the golden rule is: *Try, but don't strain.* When you dance with your baby, there's a major temptation to slip back into old-fashioned cause-effect thinking. You may say to yourself, "Well, if dancing with my baby makes him smart, I'd better get *started*!" You may succumb to the trap of feeling you have to have jolly, joyous, carefree interactions with your baby every second of the day. Relax. An optimal dance is *not* a make-every-second-count dance. In fact, by trying *too hard* (which, frankly, I think is more of a pitfall for most good mothers in our society than not trying hard enough), you disrupt your dance.

Dancing without straining may be especially tricky if you've been working away from home all day and if you're normally a competent, hard-working, upward-striving achiever. The very skills that help you get ahead at work (being competitive, being in control, and never wasting a second) allow your baby few chances to make the first move. When Dr. Sarale Cohen of the University of California School of Medicine in Los Angeles studied working mothers who wanted the best for their babies and were trying *hard* to interact well, she found these mothers were so self-absorbed with giving their babies the most meaningful, enriching experience possible that they actually became *less* responsive to their babies' needs.[6] Straining hard to dance is just another version of straining hard to take the "right step." As you'll recall from Chapter 2, by pushing yourself to be the perfect parent, you can fall into the Superparent Trap. When that happens, you begin focusing more on what you're *doing* than on who your baby is and how good it feels just *being* together. By straining too hard to dance perfectly, Supermom (or increasingly Superdad) winds up dancing alone.

With these thoughts in mind, here are some things you can do with your baby to help make him smart—with love. You certainly don't *have* to try these techniques to make your baby grow . . . but I think you may find them a lot of fun.

THE WU WEI TECHNIQUE

Not unlike meditation or yoga, the *wu wei* technique involves letting yourself flow freely with your baby. In a quiet, pleasant room, place your baby upright in his infant seat or, if he can crawl, on the floor with plenty of toys he can explore freely. Breathe deeply and let yourself relax fully. Try to blank all worldly problems from your mind so you can really tune in to your baby. Then watch the baby closely and see what he does. The key word in this approach is *noninterference*. Whatever your baby does is okay, except, of course, sticking a button in his mouth or otherwise hurting himself.

Allow your baby to initiate the play. Then try to respond in a way you think will most please him. Observe how he responds to you in return. If your baby wants to crawl around on the floor and explore the toys, you can get down on the floor with him. If he "talks" to you, you can babble back. Try to really put yourself in your baby's place—to see what your baby is seeing, to feel what he's feeling, and to think what he's thinking. If your baby attempts a new skill and succeeds, you may want to clap and rejoice in his victory. If he falls and bumps his nose, you may want to mirror his unhappiness. Whatever you do, prize and reward your baby's and your own spontaneity. If you become bored or start feeling you have to ape exactly what your baby does, the quality of your interaction is lessened because spontaneity is lost. This *wu wei* technique is beautiful because it's extremely simple to use, you can do it for two minutes to a half hour, and you'll find that observing and responding to your baby this way gives you a wealth of information about him you probably didn't possess before. This technique is especially good to use when you're tired after working all day: You don't have to be actively in control anymore, but can just relax and let your baby take the lead.

THE FIVE-MINUTE CUDDLE

You can try this technique at the end of the day, right before your baby goes to sleep for the night. I call it the *five*-minute cuddle, but of course you can cuddle as long as you please.

Sit in a quiet, softly lit room and hold your baby gently in your arms. Sit in any position that feels comfortable. Breathe deeply. Feel all your muscles unwind. Use a technique of progressive muscle relaxation. Start at the tips of your fingers and feel them relax. Then feel your arms relax, your shoulders, the back of your neck. Begin the same process with your toes, until your whole body feels untensed and free.

Now tune in to your baby. Listen to his breathing. Feel his breathing against your chest. At first, try to match your breathing to your baby's breathing, so you're inhaling and exhaling in unison. Then slowly make your breathing deeper and see if your baby's breathing doesn't deepen too. Feel the rhythms of your breathing.

As you cuddle your baby closely, think back over the day. How did the dance go? When did you feel most in step with your baby? When did you feel out of step? What did you learn about your baby today that you didn't know before? What did you learn about yourself? The purpose of this inner reflection is to quietly contemplate your day, your baby, yourself, and your dance (*not* to fret over what you did right or wrong). You may find this technique so relaxing that before you know it, you've been sitting quietly half an hour and your baby has dropped off to sleep.

TWENTY-EIGHT WAYS TO MAKE A BABY LAUGH

Several years ago, University of Minnesota researchers L. Alan Sroufe and Jane Piccard Wunsch undertook what has to be the happiest scientific study of all time: Taking 150 babies, Drs. Sroufe and Wunsch did every silly thing they could think of to make the infants giggle with glee. Intriguingly, they found a baby's sense of humor changes dramatically during the first year.

A four-month-old, for instance, will laugh at only a few silly games (Gonna Get Ya is a special favorite at this age), whereas a year-old will laugh with delight at lots of games (yet not a single one-year-old liked being tickled under the chin or playing Coochy Coo). A kiss on the tummy was a great game for 77 percent of the seven-month-olds, but by ten months of age only 20 percent of the babies laughed at tummy kisses. Interestingly, by one year of age, the tummy kiss had again gained favor, with half the kids laughing when their bare tummies were kissed with four quick pecks.[7]

The first twenty-five games described below are among those Sroufe and Wunsch studied. Each game is numbered so you can find it readily on the chart on page 184, to see at what age babies liked that game most. When playing with your baby, of course spontaneity counts most. The *goal* of all such games isn't to make your baby smart (although that will be a happy by-product of your dance) but is simply to have fun. The procedures are described in great (almost silly) detail in order to relate the scientists' behavior in their study. However, I have added games 26–28.

1. Lip Popping

Start with your lips pursed and your cheeks full of air. Then pop your lips four times in a row. Pause. Then pop your lips four times again. As you can see from the chart, this wasn't a great favorite: Only one in ten of the five-, ten-, and twelve-month-olds laughed. Still, your baby may be among those who find lip popping a great joke. Variations: You can make a great many silly popping sounds with your lips. Which ones does your baby like best?

2. Aaaah

Start with your voice very low and quiet. Then, as you say "aaaah," raise your vocal pitch and loudness. Cut off your sound abruptly. Pause six seconds. Then repeat the "aaaah" again. When Drs. Sroufe and Wunsch tried this game, four- and nine-month-olds couldn't have cared less. But the other kids enjoyed it—especially eleven-month-olds (55 percent of whom laughed).

3. Boom, Boom, Boom

Among the two most popular games for five-month-olds (only Gonna Get Ya scored as high), this game is played by saying "boom, boom, boom" in a loud (but not *too* loud), deep, resonant voice. Drs. Sroufe and Wunsch paced their booms one second apart. But varying the pace and pitch of your voice can keep the game interesting.

PERCENTAGES OF BABIES WHO LAUGHED AT TWENTY-FIVE "JOKES"

		BABY'S AGE IN MONTHS							
	4	**5**	**6**	**7**	**8**	**9**	**10**	**11**	**12**
1. *Lip Popping*	0	10	0	0	0	0	10	0	10
2. *Aaaah*	0	20	33	33	13	0	40	55	40
3. *Boom, Boom, Boom*	0	40	11	22	25	0	20	0	20
4. *Robot*	0	20	0	0	0	0	0	0	10
5. *Whisper, Whisper*	0	0	11	0	0	0	0	0	10
6. *Squeaky*	0	0	0	0	25	0	0	11	40
7. *Tired Horse*	0	0	0	44	0	0	20	22	10
8. *Kissing Tummy*	33	30	44	77	50	43	20	33	50
9. *Coochy Coo*	0	20	22	44	25	14	30	0	0
10. *Bouncy Bouncy Baby*	0	20	11	22	25	29	20	22	30
11. *Jiggling Baby*	0	30	33	44	13	29	30	0	40
12. *Chin Chuck*	0	10	33	11	25	29	10	22	0
13. *Walking Fingers*	17	20	11	33	25	29	20	22	30
14. *Tug*	0	20	22	33	25	43	20	11	20
15. *Pull the Cloth*	0	10	11	33	50	14	30	44	50
16. *Gonna Get Ya*	50	30	44	77	63	43	30	33	70
17. *Where's the Baby?*	0	0	22	22	38	29	20	22	40
18. *Disappearing Tongue*	0	0	11	22	13	0	40	33	60
19. *Peek-a-boo*	0	10	11	55	38	0	10	11	30
20. *Mask*	0	10	33	55	38	14	30	11	50
21. *Hide and Seek*	0	10	11	11	25	0	30	0	30
22. *Yum! A Bottle!*	0	0	0	11	13	0	40	11	40
23. *Watch Me Crawl*	0	10	11	11	50	29	30	22	60
24. *Walk like a Penguin*	0	0	22	22	25	14	10	0	40
25. *Summer Breeze*	0	0	0	11	0	0	10	11	20

SOURCE: L. Alan Sroufe and Jane Piccard Wunsch, "The Development of Laughter in the First Year of Life," in *Child Development* 43 (1972); 1326–1344.

4. Robot

Make your voice as robotic as you can and then talk to your baby. You might say something like "Hi, [baby's name], I-am-a-robot-I-am-C3P0-do-you-like-me?" Variations: Walk around the room like a robot or lay your "robotic" head on your baby's tummy.

5. Whisper, Whisper

One of the least successful jokes, whispering tickled the funny bones of only 11 percent of the six-month-olds and 10 percent of the one-year-olds. With your mouth one foot or so from your baby's ear, whisper, "Hi, [baby's name], how are you?" Carefully avoid blowing in your baby's ear. Anything you can do to spice this game up might help. (Dr. Stern at Cornell has noted that babies like whispering when it's used in combination with louder mouth sounds; it seems to be the *variation* in sounds that captures a baby's interest.)

6. Squeaky

This game (a drag for tiny babies) became highly appealing to one-year-olds (40 percent of whom laughed). To play this game, just talk like Mickey Mouse.

7. Tired Horse

With your lips relaxed, blow through your lips as a horse does when tired. Seven-month-olds were especially fond of this one.

8. Kissing Tummy

You'll no doubt come up with many variations on this traditional favorite. Four quick pecks on a bare tummy sent 77 percent of the seven-month-olds into peals of laughter. A common variation is to combine Tired Horse with this game, shaking your head as you vibrate your baby's tummy with your lips.

9. Coochy Coo

Adults commonly play this game with babies of all ages. But it's most popular among seven-month-olds. By eleven months of age, not one baby laughed at this one. To play, simply stroke your baby's cheek gently with a piece of velvet, a stuffed animal, a feather, or another soft object.

10. Bouncy Bouncy Baby

Put your baby on your knee, either facing you or facing away. Bounce him happily up and down. A popular variation: Once your baby gets old enough to be rowdy, cross your right knee over your left, place your baby astraddle your right ankle, hold your baby's hands, and swing your leg to give your baby a "ride." Make a clicking sound as if you're urging a horse to trot.

11. Jiggling Baby

Hold your baby horizontally in front of you waist-high, with his tummy facing the floor. Jiggle him for three seconds. As with other games, variations in timing and jiggling style lend interest.

12. Chin Chuck

Gently tickle your baby under his chin. The Chin Chuck can, of course, quickly become the Neck Chuck, the Behind-the-Ear Chuck, the Cheek Chuck, etc.

13. Walking Fingers

Wriggle your hand to focus your baby's attention on your fingers. Then walk your fingers slowly toward your baby, ending by giving him a gentle poke in the ribs. If your baby laughs, repeat the game, this time *not* poking his ribs. Variations: Speed up or slow down the tempo, add silly sounds to the walking fingers, walk your fingers up your baby's leg or down his arm until you reach his tummy. Then tickle.

14. Tug

Give your baby a brightly colored piece of heavy yarn to grasp in his fist. Then gently tug the yarn three times. Tug just hard enough to give your baby a "contest," but try not to pull it away from him. Pause a beat. Then pull again.

15. Pull the Cloth

Place a clean, soft cloth in your mouth. Move your head close enough so your baby can pull out the cloth (and put it back in your mouth if he wishes). If your baby needs help in starting the game, place a corner of the cloth in his hand. (Especially popular among eight-month-olds and one-year-olds.)

16. Gonna Get Ya

Even the Eipos, a small tribe in the tropical rain forests of New Guinea, play a variation of this game, which suggests that Gonna Get Ya (also called Gotcha) may be part of your biological wisdom: Wiggle your finger in the air as you say musically, "IIIIIIIIIIIIIIIII'm gonna get ya." As you say "gonna get ya," gently poke your baby's tummy, allowing him to grab your finger if he wishes. If your baby laughs, try the game again, with variations (without poking, by grasping his tummy, etc.). Of all baby games, this is consistently the most hilarious to babies of all ages. In the Sroufe-Wunsch study, this game provoked laughter in 50 percent of the four-month-olds, 77 percent of the seven-month-olds, and 70 percent of the year-old babies.

17. Where's the Baby?

Standing beside your baby, lay a clean cloth or blanket gently over his face. If your baby pulls away the cloth, react with delight. If he doesn't uncover his face right away, do it for him. (The emphasis in this game is on getting your baby *out* from under the cloth.)

18. Disappearing Tongue

Stick out your tongue until your baby touches it. Then as soon as your baby touches your tongue, pull it back quickly into your mouth. Babies have to be about ten months old before they catch the humor in this game, but by one year of age, they find it delightful.

19. Peek-a-boo

Like Gotcha, Peek-a-boo is played around the world. I'm sure you'll come up with many more variations than I can describe here. Peek-a-boo can be played with a blanket, as the father at the start of this chapter did, with your two hands in front of your face, by popping out from behind a sofa, etc., etc. Many parents accompany the game with a musical "Wheeeeeeeeeere's Daddy?" followed by a suspenseful pause, then a sudden *"Here he is!"*

20. Mask

Make a face or a sound to attract your baby's attention. Hold up a white cloth or mask so your baby can see it. Then place the cloth or mask in front of your face and lean forward slowly until your head is about a foot from your baby's face. Lean back slowly and slowly uncover your face.

21. Hide and Seek

Place one of your baby's toys out of his reach and focus his attention on it. Then cover the toy with a cloth for two seconds. Uncover the toy quickly.

22. Yum! A Bottle!

When your baby *isn't* hungry, take his bottle, bring it to your lips, and pretend to suck on it noisily and happily. Babies under six months of age seldom get this joke, but older babies love it.

23. Watch Me Crawl

Place your baby in an infant seat or high chair where he can watch you. Then get down on the floor and crawl past him. Stand. Walk back to where you started, and crawl past your baby again. Interestingly, in the Sroufe-Wunsch study, babies first found a parent crawling on the floor funny between six and ten months of age— when the *baby* had just begun to crawl.

24. Walk like a Penguin

Lock your knees, hold your hands stiffly out from your sides, then walk in an exaggerated waddle in front of your baby. Walk normally back to where you began. Then walk like a penguin again.

25. Summer Breeze

Stand beside your baby and blow gently across the top of his head, ruffling his hair as you blow. Blow about three seconds. Pause. Then do it again.

Other games are designed not necessarily to provoke laughter (although they may) but to provide gentler fun. Among them:

26. Pat-a-cake

Place your baby in an infant seat. Take each of your baby's hands in each of your hands, and say rhythmically, as you clap your baby's hands together, "Pat-a-cake, pat-a-cake, baker's man. Bake me a cake as fast as you can. Roll it, and roll it, and throw it in a pan! Pat-a-cake, pat-a-cake, baker's man." On the "roll it and roll it," take your baby's hands and spin them around each other, then on "throw it in a pan," fling your baby's arms out wide. For the last pat-a-cakes, clap your baby's hands together gently again. Note: There are as many variations of this game as there are parents and babies. Studies by both Dr. Sroufe and Dr. Tiffany Field at the University of Miami show Pat-a-cake is *the* game of choice for babies three weeks to three months old.

27. Give 'n' Take

When your baby has a rattle or favorite toy in his hand, ask for it. Then hand it back. To accompany your back-and-forth pattern, you might say rhythmically, "May I have the [rattle or whatever the toy is]? . . . Thank you. Here's your [rattle] back," thereby teaching your baby the name of the object as you play. Especially popular among babies ten months and older, Give 'n' Take is another game played by parents around the world. German anthropologist Dr. Irenäus Eibl-Eibesfeldt found that Eipo mothers of New Guinea use pieces of tree bark instead of rattles . . . but the game is obviously the same.

28. Dance with Me

And finally, here's a great game to play when you and your baby are tired at the end of a long day. Put some soft, soothing music on the stereo, hold your baby close, and dance around the room as if you and your baby were partners. If you're feeling lively, you can put on more spirited music and do a polka. But if you're worn out, just flow with the musical rhythms. As this gentle game shows, your play needn't be rowdy to be fun.

What if you have a job and can't be around every minute of the day to play with your baby? Relax. Even if you were home, you wouldn't want to play all the time. (Your baby develops self-reliance and independence by spending time by himself.) Besides, your dance doesn't end when you go to work. Even when you and your baby are apart, your dance goes on.

14 Choosing a Dance Partner for Your Baby While You're Away

"Men work together," I told him from the heart,
"Whether they work together or apart."

—ROBERT FROST
"The Tuft of Flowers"

Patti,* one mother I've worked with, took a leave from her job as a commercial artist to give birth to her son, Corey. Now, two months after delivery, she's ready to return to work, but she's growing increasingly fearful, guilty, and ambivalent about leaving her baby at a day care center or with a sitter. Patti, who's heard me talk about the dance, says, "What will happen if I'm not around to play with Corey? Will his development suffer? Will he forget me while I'm gone? Will he come to love the sitter more than he does me? You hear so many different opinions—day care is bad, day care's okay. Oh, God, I don't know what to do."

Patti's hardly alone. More than half of all mothers with children under school age now work outside the home, and more are expected to do so in the future. By 1990, an estimated 75 percent of American mothers will have jobs. And nearly *all* working mothers struggle at one time or another with guilt, fear, anxiety, and confusion over leaving their babies with somebody else. Victoria, who has to work so she and her husband, Steve, can pay the mortgage on their $200,000 Victorian home, says, "I love my job, but I know no one can care for Ashley as well as I can. Every morning when I leave for work I just feel incredibly guilty."

Victoria's guilt is hardly relieved by the opinions of some experts she sees quoted in recent books and magazine articles and on TV talk shows. An outspoken opponent of day care, Dr. Burton White, director of Boston's Center for Parent Education, declared

* Parents' and babies' names have been changed to protect their privacy.

in a recent *Newsweek*, "A child needs large doses of custom-made love. You can't expect hired help to provide that. I see the trend toward increasing use of day care as a disaster." White has no patience with two-career couples like Victoria and Steve, who are working hard to provide a better life for themselves and their children. When told that many couples *need* two paychecks to get by these days, White replied, "That's a typical middle-class comment. Both parents don't *have* to work—they both *want* to work to maintain a house or a life-style. They are putting their desires above the welfare of the baby."[1]

Such statements (usually made by "experts" who have *their* houses paid for), of course, go a long way toward promoting the guilt-provoking myth that just by working, a mother shows she cares less about her baby than a stay-at-home mother does.

Is White right? Are you jeopardizing your baby by working? Or is Harvard developmental psychologist Dr. Jerome Kagan more right when he gives day care a "clean bill of health"?[2] And what of those experts who say children in day care turn out even smarter and more socially savvy than their stay-at-home peers?

As with nearly all questions about babies, simple words like "right" or "wrong," "good" or "bad" have little value. The two extremes ("day care never hurts" versus "day care always hurts") underestimate the complexity of the situation. How your baby will react to day care is a complex issue involving many factors we'll get to in a minute. Before we examine the latest findings about how you can leave your baby at a center or with a sitter and *not* do him harm, however, let's take a quick overall look at the day care research scientists have been doing for the past twenty years.

HOW WELL HAVE THE EFFECTS OF DAY CARE BEEN STUDIED?

If you were to pile all the studies on day care done during the past twenty years in the middle of your living room floor, the stack would probably reach to the ceiling. But notice I didn't ask how *much* day care effects have been studied. I asked how *well*.

The answer: Not as well as you may have been led to believe. There are three serious reasons why it's best not to take the findings from any of the current studies as the "last word" on day care.

First, as Harvard researcher Jean Carew points out in *Parenting in a Multicultural Society*[3] (and many other researchers have said the same), the vast majority of the studies examining pros and cons of day care have been done in high-quality, university-based centers at places like Harvard and the University of Chicago. It's highly unlikely that the findings drawn from these spiffy centers frequented by children of wealthier, better educated parents would apply to those much lower quality centers Ralph Nader has called "children's warehouses."[4]

Second, as University of Utah psychologist Michael E. Lamb points out, nearly all the studies on the effects of day care have been done in *centers* (where researchers can get a lot of kids together and study them cheaply). In fact, a whopping *90 percent* of children with working mothers don't go to centers: They're being cared for by grandmothers, elderly aunts, baby-sitters, or other mothers at home.[5] It's questionable whether the findings about day care centers apply to babies in these other, very different situations.

Third, as Dr. Alison Clarke-Stewart of the University of Chicago notes in her book *Daycare*,[6] to do a truly scientific study, a researcher would have to take a whole group of babies and families who were much alike in IQ, income, education, and attitudes, then send half the babies to day care and keep the other half home with their mothers. We can't do that, of course, because real families make their own decisions about such matters. Thus, the fact that babies in day care have been *self*-selected raises a serious question about the so-called effects of day care. Just because the day care children in this or that study have higher or lower IQs or better or worse social skills than babies staying at home does not mean day care *caused* these differences. It's possible the two groups differed to start with.

Besides, as I've explained throughout this book, trying to trace a certain "effect" on a baby back to one simple cause doesn't work. How a baby will respond to day care depends on myriad factors. Among them: the nature of the day care, how many hours your baby spends there, whether you take part in the day care program, what your baby's life is like at home, at what age your baby starts day care, etc. Until researchers examine all these factors together, our answers about how day care affects babies will remain primitive at best.

Keeping all these caveats in mind, what have scientists concluded so far about day care? Studies have shown children in day care do just fine.

THE REASSURING FINDINGS SO FAR

As psychologists Dr. Thomas J. Gamble of Erie, Pennsylvania, and Dr. Edward Zigler of Yale note in a recent issue of the *American Journal of Orthopsychiatry*, several extensive reviews of the day care research have overwhelmingly shown day care has "no strikingly negative psychological consequences" on babies.[7]

Take the effects of day care on a baby's intellectual growth, for example. Well over thirty studies over the past twenty years have asked, "Does day care hurt a baby's intellectual growth?" As Dr. Clarke-Stewart reports, "The good news from all these studies—in Canada, England, Sweden, Czechoslovakia, the United States—is that care in a decent daycare center has no apparent detrimental effects on children's intellectual development."[8] Only one study found babies in day care had lower IQs than those staying at home with their mothers—and the centers in this study were among the warehouses Ralph Nader mentions. In all these centers, there was only one adult to care for sixteen to twenty-four babies under age two. According to 1980 U.S. Government guidelines (which, unfortunately, Congress refused to make mandatory even for federally subsidized centers), an "adequate" center should have at least one adult for every *three* babies under age two!

A few studies have even found that children in day care have *higher* IQs than those kept at home. In some studies, children in day care averaged twenty to thirty points higher on IQ tests.[9] But lest we replace the myth that day care lowers IQs with a new myth that day care makes children brighter, let me remind you that your baby's IQ score is a limited measure of a child's abilities. Follow-up studies found that after a few years in school, the IQ differences between the two groups had vanished. Why? Because, as with the kids in Chapter 1 who weren't given early reading lessons, by age ten the kids who'd been staying at home had caught up.

By now, of course, I hope your baby's IQ isn't your major concern. Chances are your real worry will be: "What will leaving my baby do to our dance?" Now that you know how important dancing is, you may think you and your baby have to dance face to face all the time. Not so. The dance doesn't end when you drop your baby off at day care. You still love your baby, no matter where you are. Comings and goings can have rhythms too.

To understand why going to work won't necessarily disrupt your dance, let's talk for a minute about what scientists call attachment (a term for what you probably call love or affection). From the time of birth, a normal baby in a loving family develops a strong emotional feeling or attachment for the persons who play with, care for, and love him. If it is one person, and that person is Mother, he wants to be near her when he's scared, tired, or bored. He loves being held by her and prefers her company above everyone else's. In past decades, this person usually was Mother. But now that fathers are dancing with babies too, the baby grows equally attached to Dad.

Now, what happens to this bond if you're suddenly going off to work? Will your baby forget you while you're away? Will he start dancing more with the sitter than with you?

Naturally, if you leave your baby during the day, you'll want to set aside special times to play when you're home. But as for your baby becoming more attached to his sitter than to you, don't worry about it. If the day care dance is going well, your baby will feel affection toward his caregiver. And he may prefer this person to a stranger. But as for your baby loving this other person more than you, in normal, caring families it just doesn't happen. The many studies[9] done on this topic have repeatedly found that when both his mother and a substitute caregiver are in the room, a child goes to his mother for help. He stays closer to her, walks over to her more, and chooses to cuddle on *her* lap when he's tired, bored, or unhappy. Day care children also don't greet their teachers in the morning with the intense glee with which they greet their mothers at night.[10]

In short, research simply *hasn't* supported the claim that if you work, your baby will suffer dire consequences. So don't take the doomsayers seriously. By doing so, you may just feel anxious and guilty—negative feelings more disruptive to the dance than working all day.

The real question to ask isn't "*Should* mothers work?" but "How will we provide decent day care so working mothers can leave their babies in the best possible hands?" Incredibly, the

United States is the only advanced nation in the world that still has no federally set and enforced standards for day care. As Stella Chess, M.D., so aptly says in a recent essay:

> it is no longer the view of most mental health professionals that a mother of a young child who holds a job outside the home is necessarily doing harm to the child. All the serious research studies agree on this issue, as long as adequate substitute care is provided while the mother is at work. But that is the rub. Our local and federal governments have either abdicated their responsibilities to provide adequate day care facilities for those children who need them, or else have relegated this service to the bottom of the list of priorities. This is a battle still to be won.[11]

Despite these reassuring findings, you may still wonder how *soon* you can leave your baby and still not hurt your mutual "bond." There's currently a strong movement under way to pass a law requiring all employers to provide four months of leave to a mother (or father) who wants to stay home with a newborn. Those supporting the law argue you simply *must* stay home four months with your baby for your relationship to develop well.[12]

This bothers me. While I'm not against a four-month leave (it's great for parents who want and can get it), I worry about the load of guilt that may be placed on you if you *don't* want to stay housebound four months, or can't afford to. If you're a career woman, you may fear all you've worked for will be jeopardized by a four-month hiatus—and you may be right. Also, making four-month leaves *mandatory* for employers disturbs me: Will male chauvinists now have an even better excuse not to hire women for high-paying, high-responsibility positions? Will employers argue, "This job is too important to entrust to someone who may get pregnant and stay home four months"? Besides, there are absolutely no studies to support the notion that your *first four months* with your baby is an especially magical time. To adjust to a new baby, some parents need more time, others need much less. What's required is *not* better legislation to keep mothers home but legislation for better day care, so mothers who want or need to work *can,* knowing their babies are still being well cared for.

In the end, how day care will affect a baby depends on *what* day care and *which* baby. Dr. Sally Provence, a pediatrics professor at Yale, believes the *key* to making day care work is to collaborate with your day care center or sitter to create the best possible situation for your child.[13] In short, you need to find an appropriate dance partner for your baby.

HOW TO CHOOSE THE BEST DANCE PARTNER FOR YOUR BABY

Good day care *is* often pricey. You can easily shell out a hundred dollars or more a week at a good center, and I know one single executive mother who pays a nanny a thousand dollars a month to care for her two adopted daughters. Nevertheless, shop for the best day care you can afford. You might think of top-notch day care as an investment in your baby's future *before* he goes to Harvard or Yale.

How to find the best day care for your baby? Sometimes the best care is with a neighbor or a grandmother. But if you're shopping especially for a home care center (where a mother cares for several children in her home) or a more formal day care center, here's a checklist of things to look for during a visit.

• What's the ratio of babies to adults? The federal guidelines that *weren't* passed by Congress recommend that day care centers provide adult-child ratios of one to three for infants, one to four for two-year-olds, and one to eight for children aged three to six. For home care facilities, the recommended ratios are one to five for children under age two and one to six for kids aged two to six. In addition, the maximum number of children in any group should be:[14]

	AGE OF CHILD	MAXIMUM GROUP SIZE
For Day Care Centers	Birth–2 years	6
	2–3 years	12
	3–6 years	16
For Home Centers	Birth–2 years	10
	2–6 years	12

• How does the facility look and feel? Is it clean and well lit (but not so brightly lighted your baby will be overstimulated)? Is the temperature a comfortable 68 to 70 degrees? (Too much heat or air conditioning can be as uncomfortable as too little.) Are the floors carpeted or nonskid?

• How concerned is the staff or sitter about your child's safety? Look for such telltale signs as uncovered electrical outlets, detergents or medicines left where children can reach them, and dangerous toys (wooden toys with splinters, plastic ones with sharp edges, etc.). Ask if they have first-aid supplies handy. Does the person in charge ask for your child's medical information and request an emergency number to call in case your child gets hurt? Such requests reflect concern for your child's safety.

• How large is the facility? A recent Harvard day care study concludes a center should provide a minimum of 100 square feet of crawling and walking space per child.[15] To get this figure, of course, you can ask for the square footage of the center, then divide this figure by the number of children being cared for.

• How stable is the staff? Studies consistently show babies fare best when cared for by the same reassuring adult every day. Frequent staff changes can make some babies insecure and anxious. Also, having one person who knows your baby well so you can discuss subtle but important changes in the baby is vital if you and the caregiver are to work together as a team.

• Spend at least an hour in the center observing how the caregivers and children dance. Do the caregivers seem affectionate, patient, and enthusiastic over the children's achievements? Is there plenty of cheerful dialogue going on? If you're seeking care for a young baby, pay special attention to how the babies are handled during crying spells and feeding. Are the babies cuddled as they eat? When the babies see their substitute caregivers, do they try to establish eye contact? Or do they continually turn away?

• Are you invited to participate in your child's care? Do you feel welcome? Be wary of centers that won't allow you to drop in unannounced or refuse to give you names and phone numbers of other parents who have children enrolled there.

• Notice the number of playpens and rocking chairs. Plenty of rocking chairs suggests your baby will get cuddling and love. More playpens than rockers may imply he'll just be left to fend for himself much of the day.

• Observe the other babies and toddlers at the center. Are they bright-eyed and happily dancing? Or do they look glassy-eyed and dull? Children's honest reactions reveal more about the quality of care being offered than do a dozen recommendations from satisfied adults.

HELPING YOUR BABY ADJUST

Once you've chosen a day care arrangement, your job isn't over. It's important to watch your baby to see how well he's adjusting. One mother of a nine-month-old told me, "I worked hard to find Mitzi the best day care center I could. But still she clings to me and cries whenever I drop her off. Then I feel guilty the whole day. Are there some babies who just can't *ever* adjust?"

Many children display some "separation anxiety" between the ages of eight and twenty months. And though disengaging yourself from a screaming baby can provoke intense pangs of guilt, there are tactics you can try that may help.

• Before you even go back to work, you can prepare your baby months in advance by exposing him to other people. How quickly a baby adapts to day care may depend to a great extent on how many people he's had around him in the past. By letting your baby play with lots of aunts, uncles, grandparents, and cousins, you're showing him the world is full of friendly people, so it's okay for you to leave at times.

• Try to determine if your going away is really as "hard" on your baby as he's telling you it is. Working mothers are often stunned to find that the minute they pull out of the driveway, the baby stops bawling and runs happily to play with a favorite toy. Talk to the caregiver and ask how long and hard your baby cries after you've gone. Several studies have shown that the less anxious and guilty *you* feel about working, the easier your *baby* will adjust.[16]

• Show your baby that you like the new caregiver by talking to her, laughing, being friendly. Also, when in the day care situation, smile reassuringly at your baby. One study showed that when you direct positive attention toward your *baby* when you're in the center together, he's more likely to feel good about the situation than when you direct all your attention to others around you.[17]

• Show the other caregiver which games your baby loves and

encourage them to play the games together. Show your baby with your eyes and facial expressions how pleased you are that he's having a good time with this other person. To help your baby adjust to your leaving, you may have to give him *permission* to dance with someone else.

• A goodbye routine may also prove useful. If you go through the same ritual every day (hugging and kissing, playing a special goodbye game, asking your child to hand you your coat, waving at the window, etc.), your baby may more readily come to accept your leaving.

• If your baby is old enough to talk, help the other caregiver realize she can respond positively to your baby's feelings after you're gone by saying something like, "Yes, I know you feel angry or sad because your parents have left, and I understand."

• Your baby may adjust to the center more easily if he brings along a favorite toy or a picture of you. One mother had a silk scarf she let her fourteen-month-old take with him to day care. She recalls, "I'd say, 'Keep my scarf for me until I come to pick you up, okay?' It seemed to help."

• When your child is old enough, give him a note, a flower, or another "present" to give to the teacher for you. You're not only making your child feel important, but you're letting him know you and this other person are working *together*, as a team.

• Comings and goings can have rhythms too. So try to establish a fairly regular time when you leave for work and pick up your baby. Your baby will come to anticipate your return. Being predictable can help him adjust.

• Finally, once you've left your baby with a substitute caregiver, watch for signs that the dance is—or isn't—working. Though you can't tell *immediately* how the day care dance is going, over time your baby should adjust happily. If week after week your baby cries hard daily when you leave and return or if when you get home you find his rhythms continually disrupted, the dance with this particular caregiver clearly isn't working for your baby, however excellent the caregiver's credentials may be. Also be alert for signs your baby has outgrown the caregiver he currently has. A warm, easygoing, uneducated grandmotherly type may be great for a baby, but when your child gets older you may want a sitter with better grammar! If you're not sure how the dance is going, you might pop in at the center or the sitter's home unexpectedly to observe what's happening. If you feel your baby isn't dancing while you're away, by all means find another, better situation, in which he *can* dance.

15 And the Dance Goes On . . .

People should not consider so much what they are to do,
as what they are.

—MEISTER ECKHART

This hasn't been a traditional how-to book. I've offered
no ultimate answers. My aim has been to provide you, a thoughtful
parent, with information you can use in your own way to ask—
and answer—questions about your baby and yourself. In the end,
the only reason to read someone else's words is to enlarge your
vision of the world, not to narrow it down. So take this book in
that spirit. Use what you can, discard the rest. Child-rearing advice
is useful only when it leads you to ask meaningful questions and
thereby leads to greater discoveries about your baby and yourself.

Your dance with your baby is only beginning, but it will last
all your lives. Over the years, your dance will shift and change a
thousand-thousand different ways as you both grow along together.

For parenthood is a process of *self*-discovery and growth, whatever cynics may say. Once you've had a baby, you'll never quite
be the same person again. You'll see the world in a more cosmic
way than ever before. Suddenly, even if you were always an ecol-
ogist, the future of the whole earth matters more than it ever did.
Human values and what they mean and which ones are important
to pass on to the future become more than just abstract philo-
sophical questions. Your baby *is* the future. What will your legacy
to the twenty-first century be?

As a parent, you'll find yourself questioning and re-questioning
your motives and values. As one insightful father of three says,
"You start asking a lot more self-probing questions. Why am I so
intensely upset over the fact that Sammy can't catch a baseball?
Is it because *I* couldn't make the team when I was twelve? I've

also found myself becoming mellower over the years. When you're an adult among other adults, it's easy to fall into the trap of always believing the world's a rotten place and every man's out for himself. The old dog-eat-dog philosophy. But when you have a bright-eyed, innocent six-year-old looking up to you for guidance, do you really want to instill in him such blind, overwhelming pessimism? To raise my three sons, I've had to reexamine my youthful cynicism . . . and I've discovered the world is a pretty wonderful place, after all!"

Suzanne, a free-lance writer and mother of two, tells how her ten-year-old daughter stirred up a self-realization in her. "My free-lance career had finally taken off, and I was working literally night and day," Suzanne recalls. "When writing, I hated interruptions. So I hung a sign on my door that read in huge, bold, ominous letters: DO NOT DISTURB. My daughter Kimberly (who says she also wants to be a writer when she grows up) would often hide away in her bedroom, working on her 'book.' One day when I went to her room to borrow a pencil, I found Kim's door closed, and there was also a sign on her door." *Her* sign, written in delicate calligraphy, was a Shel Silverstein poem she'd copied, which read:

INVITATION
If you are a dreamer, come in,
If you are a dreamer, a wisher, a liar,
A hope-er, a pray-er, a magic bean buyer . . .
If you're a pretender, come sit by my fire
For we have some flax-golden tales to spin.
Come in!
Come in!

Suzanne continues, "Seeing that poem on Kim's door made me realize something very deeply about myself. I was becoming rigid, too eager to hide away in my study and shut out the world. In a very real way, I was locking out all the pretenders, wishers, and hope-ers—all the chances for *surprises* in my life. How sad for me, a woman so 'busy' that if a dreamer or a fanciful magic bean buyer came to my door, he'd find a sign that angrily read, DO NOT DISTURB! I took down the angry sign and put up one that read COME IN. And you know what? My writing didn't suffer. In fact, I'm writing even better."

Cynics say children only take from you and never give. I disagree. Once a parent, you'll grow in patience, wisdom, and myriad special ways those who never have children can never fully understand.

The dance of life, which of course includes the dance with your baby, is ever-changing, yet never-ending. You can search the world over and you'll find many cultures much different from ours. Some tribes have no clothing but loincloths. The herdsmen of Outer Mongolia move with their goats and have no permanent homes. Australian aborigines have no tools but a stone and a stick. A tribe in the Atlas Mountains of Africa has even been reported to have no names. But nowhere will you find a people without dance. From the waltzes in the courts of Europe to the peasant dances on the steppes of Russia to the wild, primitive dances in the dark jungles of Borneo and the break dances on the streets of Brooklyn, man expresses his deepest truths through the rhythmic music of his body. When you first started this book, you may have thought (as I once did) that the dance with your baby was just a pretty metaphor. By now I think you realize that all these *other* dances are the metaphors. At the heart of all meaningful human relationships, there is only the great dance of life.

NOTES

In these Notes, works are generally cited by the author's name and year of publication only; for full listings, see the Bibliography. The citation ET-SB refers to authors' interviews.

1. THE REAL TRUTH ABOUT SUPERBABIES

1. Oddly enough, researchers have only just discovered how competent babies are. As recently as 1964, one medical textbook reported not only that the average newborn couldn't fix its eyes or respond to sound, but that "consciousness, as we think of it, probably does not exist in the infant."

2. The *Time* cover (August 15, 1983) read "Babies: What Do They Know? When Do They Know It?" The same article was later picked up by *Reader's Digest*.

3. Doman and Doman (1985).

4. For the full story of William Sidis see Amy Wallace's book *Prodigy: A Biography of William Sidis* (Dutton, 1986). Wallace argues that Sidis wasn't "pushed" intellectually, that he just had great genes (which may be true). However, you'll notice if you ever read Sidis's story that there's much talk about his "genius" and very little about how good he felt.

5. Bloom (1985).

6. Doman (1984), p. 19.

7. Ibid., pp. 139–40.

8. Doman (1982), p. 37.

9. Piaget (1963).
10. Moore (1984), p. 7.
11. Elkind (1981), p. 109.
12. Greer and Wethered (1984).
13. Moore (1984), p. 4.
14. Bayley (1933). In 1970, Bayley pointed out that her early studies were still valid, writing: "The findings of these early studies of mental growth of infants have been repeated sufficiently often so that it is now well established that test scores earned in the first year or two have little predictive validity."
15. For a good review, see McCall (1972).
16. McCall (1972).
17. Published by Academic Press, 1970.
18. ET-SB, January 8, 1985.
19. Michael Lewis (1976), pp. 19–58.
20. Ibid.
21. ET-SB, December 12, 1984.
22. *Time,* August 15, 1983, p. 58.
23. Ibid.
24. Feldman (1982), p. 364.
25. Durkin (1961).
26. Beck (1975), pp. 7–8.
27. *New York Times,* February 1, 1985.
28. Durkin (1974–75).
29. Morphett and Washburn (1931).
30. Tufts University psychologist Dr. David Elkind (Elkind, 1981, p. 35) tells of meeting some children who had been pushed to read at four and five years of age. They read aloud beautifully—but in a whisper so low Elkind had to strain to hear them. Elkind writes:

> Although they had learned a skill, it had been at great cost, and I interpreted their low voices as a sign of embarrassment and fear. They experienced no pleasure in reading aloud or in my praise or approval of what they were doing. It almost seemed that reading had been foisted upon them, at great cost in time and effort, without their having any real understanding of the value of what they were learning. They showed the apathy and withdrawal that are frequent among children who are pushed too hard academically.

And these kids were four and five years old. What might such pressure do to a *baby*?

31. Feldman (1982), p. 364.
32. Lewis and McGurk (1972). They write (p. 1175):

> Despite . . . acknowledged limitations, infant intelligence scales are

widely used in clinical situations in the belief that, although lacking in predictive validity, these scales are valuable in assessing the overall health and developmental status of babies at the particular time of testing, relative to other babies of the same age. This use of infant intelligence scales is justified only if, in interpreting the resultant scores, the scores are regarded solely as measures of present performance and not as indices of future potential.

33. Wolff and Feinbloom (1969).

34. Dr. Spock appeared on the *Nightline* show, which aired at 11:30 P.M. EDT, June 7, 1984, in opposition to Glenn Doman. He's far from the only child-development specialist disputing Doman's approach. "The media, that's the problem," says Dr. Edward Zigler of Yale. "The media have made these people. There is scant research that what they're doing makes one whit of difference. So I don't have very much patience with them." (ET-SB, December 12, 1984.)

35. Bower and Wishart (1979).

36. *New York Times*, February 1, 1984.

37. *Time*, August 15, 1983, p. 53.

38. Bower and Wishart (1979).

39. Ibid., p. 87.

40. Pines (1979).

2. THE ALL-POWERFUL SUPERMOM TRAP

1. *U.S. News & World Report*, March 25, 1985, p. 63.

2. Caplan and Hall-McCorquodale (1985-A).

3. Caplan and Hall-McCorquodale (1985-B).

4. Thomas and Chess (1980), p. 87. As Drs. Thomas and Chess note, "Interestingly enough, Freud himself questioned the predictive adequacy of this psychoanalytic scheme in a rarely quoted statement: 'So long as we trace the development [of a mental process] backwards, the connection appears continuous, and we feel we have gained an insight which is completely satisfactory and even exhaustive. But if we proceed the reverse way, if we start from the premise inferred from the analysis and try to follow up the final result, then we no longer get the impression of an inevitable sequence of events, which could not have been otherwise determined. We notice at once that there might be another result, and that we might have been just as well able to understand and explain the latter.'" (Freud, 1950, p. 226.)

5. The author of this and many other mother-blaming statements wasn't actually Freud but Alfred Adler. A member of Freud's inner circle in Vienna, Adler believed it was up to you—the mother—to make or

break your baby for life. Freud disagreed with Adler's views and even called his theories "methodologically deplorable" (Ansbacher and Ansbacher, 1968). Nevertheless, Adler was a respected member of Freud's inner circle. He eventually became president of the Vienna Psychoanalytic Society and coeditor with Freud and Wilhelm Stekel of the *Zentralblatt für Psychoanalyse,* a special periodical devoted to the nonmedical uses of psychoanalysis. As Ansbacher and Ansbacher state (p. 56), "Thus, when Adler . . . became Freud's critic, he was well-qualified. His understanding of psychoanalysis was probably second only to Freud's." As J. A. C. Brown (1968) observes, far from Vienna (especially in the U.S.) Adler's ideas were so closely associated with Freud's that they took on Freudian authority. Even today, many child-rearing ideas we consider "Freudian" (particularly the more extreme aspects of mother-blaming) actually came from Adler.

6. Ansbacher and Ansbacher, pp. 388ff.

7. One of the most well known of these reviews was Caldwell (1964).

8. Schaffer (1977), p. 10.

9. Kagan (1976), p. 192.

10. For a review of plasticity research, see Gollin (1981).

11. Sperry (1971).

12. In the April 1, 1978, issue of *Saturday Review,* Albert Rosenfeld wrote a piece called "The 'Elastic Mind' Movement: Rationalizing Child Neglect?" in which he described—and attacked—the views of scientists who are apparently using plasticity research to argue that a baby is so sturdy and resistant to harm he's virtually invulnerable. Rosenfeld was right to be highly concerned over this nonsensical idea that a baby is invulnerable. Let there be no mistake about this: Plasticity does *not* mean a baby can't be hurt!

13. Sears, Maccoby, and Levin (1957).

14. Schaefer (1959).

15. Sears et al. (1957).

16. Yarrow, Campbell, and Burton (1968).

17. In *Human Development: A Transactional Perspective,* Ira J. Gordon of the Institute for Development of Human Resources at the University of Florida in Gainesville, observes (pp. 4–5) that

a concept of changing views of childhood was developed in which older views were classed as Newtonian and newer views as Einsteinian. These newer views, which reflect our current social system, technology, and sciences are:

1. Development is a process of transaction between organism and environment. Therefore, outputs (intelligence, socioemotional behavior, concepts, motor skills) are modifiable by experience.

2. The individual is a functioning whole. A person can be considered a self-organizing system, so that parts must be considered in relation to the whole and behavior understood in context.

3. The individual is an "open-energy" system. The child is characterized by activity. Instead of seeking tension-reduction, the organism seeks energy balance and information.

4. Development and organization are synonymous. From a systems approach, the system develops as it gets more complex and more integrated. Living systems follow this rule.

5. The individual is unique. Uniqueness is continuously evolving from organism-environment transactions. It is both *geno-* and *pheno-typical;* that is, behavior is made up of both a contribution from the genes and the impact of the world.

6. The individual develops as a self-system. This idea is not as generally accepted as some of those above. It represents a particular view in psychology and education. It is a basic postulate in the author's system of thought.

3. BANISHING TICS FROM YOUR PARENTING STYLE

1. Freud (1938), p. 182.
2. Leman (1984).
3. Schaffer (1971), p. 67.
4. Thoman (1970).
5. McCall (1979).
6. Ibid., p. 35.
7. Bell (1977).
8. This is so commonly known among scientists it's virtually a truism. But for a good review of the literature, see Caldwell (1964).
9. Verny (1981).
10. Spezzano (1981), p. 51.
11. Ibid., pp. 56–7.
12. Joan Beck (1975) is one of several early-learning advocates who use the "critical" or "sensitive" periods issue to try to support their contention that you should get busy and teach your child at home to raise his IQ.
13. Hinde (1966).
14. Thorpe (1961).
15. Wolff and Feinbloom (1969).
16. Wolff (1970).
17. Svejda, Campos, and Emde (1980).
18. Klaus and Kennell (1982).

19. McCall (1983), p. 80.

20. Ibid.

21. Type A and Type B distinctions have been discussed in K. A. Matthews (1979; 1981); and (for a popular discussion) *New York Times,* March 19, 1981, "Study Says Heart Ills Can Begin in Childhood." Well-known pediatrician T. Berry Brazelton in *Infants and Mothers* refers to babies as average, quiet, and active. And Sirgay Sanger, M.D., speaks of Alpha and Beta Infants in *You and Your Baby's First Year.*

22. Spock (1976), p. 139.

4. WHY AREN'T WE SAYING WHAT EVERYONE ELSE IS SAYING?

1. Source: U.S. Bureau of Census.

2. *Newsweek,* March 17, 1986, p. 63.

3. *Time,* December 9, 1985, p. 79.

4. Harman and Brim (1980), p. 162.

5. Hess (1980), p. 155.

6. Boulding (1968).

7. Personal communication, June 8, 1986.

8. Skolnick and Skolnick (1971), p. 306.

9. For those unfamiliar with the old clockwork views of man and the universe, a brief history of Western scientific thought might be in order. Some 2,500 years ago in Greece, there were philosophers who thought of the universe much as the new vision sees it today. At that time, a sage named Heraclitus of Ephesus was speculating on the real nature of things (the Greeks called this real nature *physis,* the word from which our word "physics" was derived). And he came up with a view of reality very similar to the view Eastern mystics have held for thousands of years (a view that sounds remarkably like that espoused by the new physics and the parallel new systems theory). Heraclitus saw the apparent struggles between such opposites as good versus bad and male versus female as an illusion that would be all cleared up if we just knew enough. He figured that if you could just strip away all the confusing stuff and look at the naked truth, you'd wisely see that all opposites aren't really opposites at all, but just part of the same overall, unified plan. He thought the law of the universe was *rhythmic change* (an important point to remember).

Heraclitus was rather gloomy, always pointing out the worst side of things, so some people called him the Weeping Philosopher. Because a lot of people couldn't understand what Heraclitus was getting at, he was also called Heraclitus the Obscure. Nevertheless, a lot of Greeks in his day thought Heraclitus was pretty smart and possibly onto something.

I won't go into all the Greek schools of thought about the nature of reality (some of which disagreed heartily with Heraclitus). For our purposes, you only need to know that as the centuries ticked by, Heraclitus's ideas fell out of favor. Then along came the Dark Ages, when the Greeks' ideas were pretty much forgotten.

Then in the 1600s a brilliant French philosopher, mathematician, and scientist came on the scene. He was René Descartes (1596–1650)—the man whose ideas formed the basis of modern science and most of Western thought. Descartes was born at a time when the upper classes, who loved elaborate gardens, were fascinated with machines, which they used in their gardens to drive fountains, make brooks babble over rocks, and generally duplicate nature as accurately as they could. At twenty-three years of age, while walking through one of these lifelike mechanized gardens, Descartes looked around him at all the machine-driven fountains, waterfalls, and rivulets and had what psychologists today call an "Aha! experience." In a sudden flash of insight, he "realized" that, like this garden, the whole universe was a machine, rather like a clock, governed by exact mathematical laws. The next night, Descartes had a dream of nature as a Great Machine and decided that his insight in the garden had been divinely inspired.

Descartes's vision led to a very fragmented view of nature, which he thought could be best understood by picking apart all the pieces and examining all the individual gears and wheels. He felt we could be absolutely *certain* of what we knew if we could only find the causes and effects.

Descartes later expanded his view of nature as the perfect machine to explain the nature of living organisms, including man. Animals, Descartes said, were like a "clock . . . composed . . . of wheels and springs." Viewing the human body as equally mechanistic, he said, "I consider the human body as a machine. . . . My thought . . . compares a sick man and an ill-made clock with my idea of a healthy man and a well-made clock." In short, according to Descartes, the human body was just a very fancy robot.

Humans, of course, also have a mystifying *mind*, which won't fit so neatly into this robotic framework. The as yet unfathomable human mind with its billions of cells simply can't be explained away easily as a few whirling, clicking gears. Descartes knew that. So he decided man must be divided into two separate parts: mind *and* body. Descartes's famous phrase "*Cogito ergo sum*" ("I think, therefore I exist") had such a profound effect that even today it has led most of us in the Western world to equate our identity with our minds, rather than with our whole being. (You still see Descartes's influence today in child-rearing advice that emphasizes what the baby knows or learns as all-crucial.) Descartes believed in careful, logical, step-by-step rational thought as the one path to all true knowledge. That is certainly necessary for any scientific approach, but it is not enough by itself. Thus, the dissection of complex events into more elemental parts (a process called reductionism in the philosophy of science) does not allow you to turn that process around and claim that the addition of all the parts together will allow you to construct the original event. This is one of the major points emphasized by Bertalanffy and Weiss in their arguments for the value of systems theory. As an example, Descartes's approach to science would not allow him to account for his own "Aha! experience" in the garden from which all his great insights sprang, because that experience is not simply the sum of other experiences but, instead, involves a reorganization of past events. The key idea here is in the word "reorganization." We can take the facts we know and configure (or organize) them into many different ideas and concepts. However, it is not possible to take the parts of a clock and assemble or organize them so that a *different* clock (or a different machine) results.

When Descartes died, at age fifty-four, there already lived a young English boy (only eight years old at the time) who would soon solidify Descartes's vision of reality by providing the mathematics and laws of physics that made Descartes's machine universe run. That boy was Isaac Newton, who at the age of only eighteen invented calculus and then went on to create "Newtonian" physics. Newton's world was basically one of actions and their opposite reactions. Newton saw the world in terms of linear causes and effects.

Thus Newton completed the view of the universe Descartes began, the view on which all science and Western thought until the early part of this century were based. The Newtonian-Cartesian view is that of a machine-like world that's best understood by breaking clock-like people and their surroundings down into their most basic elementary particles (cells and atoms), then studying these fragments to see how they work. Descartes's view of the clockwork human is so pervasive and such a "given" in our culture that we often don't even question it. Still, Cartesian thought even influences the way we talk about people. When we want to understand why a person acts in the peculiar way he does, for example, we often say, "I wonder what makes him tick?"

Descartes and Newton are important to you and your baby because it's their mechanistic view of the universe on which nearly all child-rearing advice in this century has been based. For example:

　• The fact that Descartes equated his entire identity with his rational mind has led many scientists to view your baby's *thoughts* as all-critical, his feelings as little or nothing.
　• Descartes's machine universe was fragmented and filled with many separate, disconnected wheels, springs, and gears. Likewise, the child-rearing theories that came from this worldview have seen parenting as a

fragmented task, best understood by looking at all the separate, disconnected "right" or "wrong" steps a parent might take.

• Descartes's view of fragmented people has led many child-rearing experts to talk about babies in a very piecemeal way, as if your baby were just a bundle of disconnected compartments (IQ, talents, creativity, feelings, etc.) that you can stimulate independently without influencing the whole baby.

• Newton's mechanistic world was best explained in terms of linear causes and effects. Thus, when child-development researchers began scientifically analyzing what it takes to be a "good" parent, they naturally began looking for ways parents *caused* their children to be smart, dull, happy, miserable, artistic, schizophrenic, etc. From this viewpoint, it was easy to assume that any problem in a child's life must have been directly *caused* by his parents (especially Mother).

In a way, the new physics and parallel systems theory have brought us full circle back to a view of the universe that's more as Heraclitus saw it.

10. Capra (1977), pp. 228–9.

11. For a full discussion of systems theory as it relates to the new physics, see Capra's *The Turning Point* (1982).

12. See Bertalanffy (1968) and Bertalanffy (1981).

13. For a brief discussion of systems theory in medicine, see "Behavioral Medicine: An Emergent Field," *Science* (July 25, 1980): 479ff. Many popular articles have also been done on the mind-body connection. See Cousins (1978); Pelletier (1977); Cherry (1980); Anderson (1982).

14. Two other books of possible interest: Zukav (1979) and Cole (1985).

15. For a systems view of family therapy, see Goldenberg and Goldenberg (1980).

16. For a thorough discussion of the new paradigm shift in both physics and systems theory, see Capra (1982).

17. Schuster and Ashburn (1980), p. 36.

18. See Thomas and Chess (1980) and Levine (1983).

19. For a good discussion, see Stern (1985).

20. Demos (1985).

5. DANCING WITH YOUR BABY: THE NEW PARENTING

1. Thoman (1974).
2. See Chapter 6.
3. Stern (1977).
4. Ibid.

5. Ibid.
6. Capra (1982), p. 37.
7. Maslow (1968), p. 54.
8. Montagu (1981).
9. Stern (1977).
10. Leonard (1984).

6. WHY YOUR DANCE MATTERS

1. Yarrow (1975). Many other studies have come to this same conclusion: that responsive parents and high infant IQ go together. Among them: Robertson (1962); Stern et al. (1969); Lewis and Goldberg (1969); and Gallas and Lewis (1977). As Eleanor Willemsen of the University of Santa Clara aptly says in *Understanding Infancy* (1979):

> Again and again, results of studies have indicated that the mother who is responsive to the baby's communications tends to have a more alert, cognitively mature and happy baby than does the less responsive mother. *Responsiveness* in this instance means reacting when the baby signals for attention. Going to a crying baby, smiling back at a smiling baby and looking with interest at a babbling baby are all responsive acts.

2. Lewis and Wilson (1972); Bell and Ainsworth (1972).
3. Thomas and Chess (1977).
4. Sanger (1985).
5. Lewis and Goldberg (1969).
6. Stern et al. (1969).
7. Demos (1985).
8. Lewis, Beavers, et al. (1976).
9. Goldenberg and Goldenberg (1980), p. 114.
10. Beavers, Hampson, Hulgus, and Beavers (1986).
11. Goldenberg and Goldenberg (1980), pp. 26–7.
12. For a discussion of this marvelous concept, see "Mathematical Games" by Martin Gardner, *Scientific American,* April 1978.

7. UNDERSTANDING YOUR BABY'S NATURE

1. James (1890).
2. Cowan (1979).
3. Restak (1979).

4. Fantz (1967).
5. Ibid.
6. Goren et al. (1975).
7. Tronick and Adamson (1980).
8. *Time,* August 15, 1983, p. 53.
9. Siperstein and Butterfield (1972).
10. McCall (1979).
11. Aronson and Rosenbloom (1971).
12. *Time,* August 15, 1983, p. 54.
13. Macfarlane (1975).
14. Bower (1977).
15. Ibid.
16. Ibid.
17. Papousck and Papousek (1977).

8. RESPECTING YOUR BABY'S FEELINGS

1. MacLean (1978).
2. Piaget (1981).
3. Wolff (1963).
4. For an easy-to-read discussion of Izard's work, see Trotter (1983).
5. Darwin (1872).

9. APPRECIATING RHYTHMS (THE MUSIC FOR THE DANCE)

1. Wassersug and Wassersug (1986).
2. Thomas and Chess (1977).
3. Byers (1976).
4. Byers (1977).
5. Thoman and Graham (1986), p. 8555.
6. Luce (1971), p. 103.
7. Leonard (1978), p. 17.
8. Condon (1975).
9. Leonard (1978), p. 18.
10. Condon and Sander (1974).
11. Ibid.
12. Thomas (1974), p. 66.
13. Sander (1975).
14. Ferber (1985).
15. Jones (1983).

10. HOW YOUR BABY "TALKS" TO YOU

1. Klein (1963).
2. Huang (1973).
3. Yutang (1948).
4. Bennett (1971).
5. Brazelton (1969).

11. YOUR BIOLOGICAL WISDOM

1. Lewis (1979), p. 7.
2. Beck (1975), p. 6.
3. Janov (1973).
4. Westin (1981), p. 41.
5. Moore (1984).
6. Maslow (1971), pp. 16–17.
7. Bennett (1971).
8. Ibid.
9. Stern (1985).
10. Ferguson (1964).
11. Fernald (1985).
12. Stern (1977), p. 17.
13. Ibid.
14. Sanger (1985).
15. Stern (1977), p. 12.
16. Fraiberg (1977).
17. Stern (1977), p. 19.
18. Ibid., p. 21.
19. Stern (1985).
20. For decades, experts *did* think fathers were much less important than mothers, and hints of this outmoded attitude still linger today. Even though fathers have consistently been shown to be incredibly important to their babies' growth, it's amazing that some misguided experts are still espousing the old doctrine that mother has some special "instinct" for raising babies that father lacks. On a recent *Phil Donahue Show*, for example, Otto Weininger, Ph.D., a clinical child psychologist and professor at the Ontario Institute for Study and Education at the University of Toronto, actually said of fathers raising babies, "They really can't do the job as well. I mean, they really are not the person that bears the baby, and that relationship from what we are finding out now is there is something about what happens in utero, and as it happens in utero the mother begins

to feel something and she also experiences the same kind of activity that goes on then, and then when the baby is born there is also a similarity in terms of continuity." Earlier, Weininger had said, "[The mother is] the only real person who can take care of that baby right from the start." And when Donahue replied, "Mother 1, Daddy nothing? I mean . . . ," Weininger's comment was, "Daddy's something but really Daddy doesn't come in to be nearly as important until the baby is around three or four months of age . . ." In short, the myth of the past (still espoused by some "experts") is that fathers don't count with their young babies as much as mothers do. And that's nonsense.

21. Lamb (1978).
22. Tronick (1980).
23. Rebelsky and Hanks (1971).
24. Lamb (1975).
25. Parke et al. (1972).
26. McCall (1985).
27. Lamb (1976; 1977).
28. Kotelchuk (1976).
29. Dunn and Richards (1977).
30. Weinraub (1978).
31. Clarke-Stewart (1982).
32. Lamb (1980).

12. DANCING WITH A CRYING BABY

1. Aldrich, Sing, and Knop (1945).
2. Brazelton (1962).
3. Crockenberg (1981).
4. Bell and Ainsworth (1972).
5. Korner, Kraemer, Haffner, and Thoman (1974).
6. Bryne and Horowitz (1981).
7. Anderson, Burroughs and Measel (1983).
8. Brackbill (1971).
9. Kirkland (1985).
10. Illingworth (1954).
11. Paradise (1966).
12. Weissbluth (1984).

13. MAKING YOUR BABY SMART—WITH LOVE

1. Carew (1980).
2. Elkind (1981).
3. Archer (1980).
4. ET-SB.
5. Dubos (1982).
6. Cohen (1982).
7. Sroufe and Wunsch (1972).

14. CHOOSING A DANCE PARTNER FOR YOUR BABY WHILE YOU'RE AWAY

1. *Newsweek,* September 10, 1984, p. 16.
2. Kagan (1977).
3. Carew (1980).
4. *Newsweek,* September 10, 1984, p. 14.
5. Lamb (1980).
6. Clarke-Stewart (1982), p. 64.
7. Gamble and Zigler (1986), p. 27.
8. Clarke-Stewart (1982), p. 67.
9. Numerous studies have shown that, intellectually, children in day care do as well as or better than those staying home. Among them: Doyle and Somers (1978); Ramey and Mills (1977); Robinson and Robinson (1971); Rubenstein, Howes, and Boyle (1981). Studies that have shown children who stay home soon catch up to their more precocious peers in day care include: Garber and Heber (1980); and Fowler (1978). As Clarke-Stewart (1982, p. 68) observes, "What daycare seems to do is to speed up children's intellectual development during the preschool period rather than to change it permanently."
10. Many studies have shown this. Among them: Kagan, Kearsley, and Zelazo (1978); Farran and Ramey (1977); and Blanchard and Main (1979).
11. Chess (1986), p. 23.
12. A leading proponent of this legislation is T. Berry Brazelton, author of *Working and Caring* (1985). I agree with Chess (1986), when she says of Brazelton's views:

This reviewer is in general agreement with Brazelton's opinions and advice, with one important exception. He states several times that there is something so special in an infant's first four months of life that maternity leave should be constructed so that separation need not take place earlier. Mothers who cannot do this without jeopardizing work or career are indeed in a dilemma. But Brazelton gives no hard evidence to support this view, and there are studies documenting that, on the contrary, a mother's return to work before her baby is four months old is not, as such, harmful. In an area where anxiety and guilt abound, it would be especially unfortunate to add to them unnecessarily.

13. Provence (1982).

14. These guidelines, known as the Federal Interagency Day Care Requirements, were developed in 1980 by a distinguished group of child-development specialists from several federal agencies. As Scarr (1984) notes, "Though not ideal standards of day care, the Federal Interagency Day Care Requirements . . . would improve many facilities in the nation if they were adopted." In addition to the staff-child ratios cited, other proposed requirements for adequate day care are: a planned program designed to enhance the intellectual, emotional, social, and physical development of the children; trained staff with training in child care, safety, health, and the type of program being used in the center or home; adequate, nutritious meals; immunization records required of every child in care (in conjunction with advice to parents on where to get their children immunized); and chances for parents to get actively involved in the day care, to watch their children in the center, and to take part in policy-making for the day care program.

15. Kagan, Kearsley, and Zelazo (1978).

16. Hock (1978, 1980) and Hock, Christman, and Hock (1980).

17. Lewis and Feiring (1981).

BIBLIOGRAPHY

Aldrich, C. A., C. Sing, and C. Knop. "The Crying of Newly Born Babies. I: The Community Phase." *Journal of Pediatrics* 26 (1945): 313–26.

———. "The Crying of Newly Born Babies. II: The Individual Phase." *Journal of Pediatrics* 27 (1945): 89–96.

———. "The Crying of Newly Born Babies. III: The Early Period at Home." *Journal of Pediatrics* 27 (1945): 428–35.

Anderson, Alan. "How the Mind Heals." *Psychology Today*, December 1982, 51–6.

Anderson, G. C., A. K. Burroughs, and C. P. Measel. "Nonnutritive Sucking Opportunities: A Safe and Effective Treatment for Preterm Infants." In *Infants Born at Risk: Physiological, Perceptual and Cognitive Processes*, edited by Tiffany Field and Anita Sostek. Orlando, Fla.: Grune and Stratton, 1983.

Ansbacher, Heinz L., and Rowena R. Ansbacher. *The Individual Psychology of Alfred Adler*. New York: Harper & Row, 1968.

Archer, Dane. *How to Expand Your S.I.Q.* New York: M. Evans, 1980.

Aronson, E., and S. Rosenbloom. "Space Perception in Early Infancy: Perception Within a Common Auditory-Visual Space." *Science* 172 (1971): 1161–63.

Bayley, Nancy. "Mental Growth During the First Three Years." *Genetic Psychology Monographs*, July 1933, 74–82.

Beavers, J., R. B. Hampson, Y. F. Hulgus, and W. R. Beavers. "Coping in Families with a Retarded Child." *Family Process* 50 (September 1986): 365–78.

Beck, Joan. *How to Raise a Brighter Child.* New York: Pocket Books, 1975.

Bell, Richard Q. *Child Effects on Adults.* Hillsdale, N.J.: Lawrence Erlbaum Associates, 1977.

Bell, S. M., and M. D. Ainsworth. "Infant Crying and Maternal Responsiveness." *Child Development* 43 (1972): 1171–90.

Bennett, Stephen. "Infant-Caretaker Interactions." *Journal of the American Academy of Child Psychiatry,* April 1971, 321–35.

Bertalanffy, Ludwig von. *General Systems Theory: Foundations, Development, Applications.* New York: Braziller, 1968; London: Penguin Press, 1971. Translated into French, German, Italian, Swedish, and Japanese.

———. *A Systems View of Man.* Edited by Paul A. LaViolette. Boulder, Colo.: Westview Press, 1981.

Bettelheim, Bruno. "Our Children Are Treated Like Idiots." *Psychology Today,* July 1981, 28–44.

Bloom, Benjamin. *Developing Talent in Young People.* New York: Ballantine Books, 1985.

Boulding, Kenneth. "General Systems Theory—The Skeleton of Science." In *Modern Systems Research for the Behavioral Scientist,* edited by W. F. Buckley. Chicago: Aldine, 1968.

Bower, T. G. R. *The Perceptual World of the Child.* Cambridge, Mass.: Harvard University Press, 1977.

———, and J. G. Wishart. "Towards a Unitary Theory of Development." In *Origins of the Infant's Social Responsiveness,* edited by Evelyn B. Thoman. Hillsdale, N.J.: Lawrence Erlbaum Associates, 1979.

Bowlby, John. *Maternal Care and Mental Health.* Geneva: WHO, 1951.

Brackbill, Yvonne. "Cumulative Effects of Continuous Stimulation on Arousal Level in Infants." *Child Development* 42 (1971): 17–26.

———. "Continuous Stimulation Reduces Arousal Level: Stability of the Effect Over Time." *Child Development* 44 (1973): 43–6.

Brazelton, T. B. "Crying in Infancy." *Pediatrics* 29 (1962): 579–88.

———. *Infants and Mothers.* New York: Delacorte Press, 1969.

———. *Working and Caring.* Reading, Mass.: Addison-Wesley, 1985.

Bridges, Katherine M. Banham. "Emotional Development in Early Infancy." *Child Development*, 1932, 324–41.

Broussard, E. "Maternal Perception of Neonates as Related to Development." *Child Psychiatry and Human Development* 1 (1970): 16–25.

Brown, J., and R. Bakeman. "Relationships of Human Mothers with Their Infants During the First Year of Life: Effects of Prematurity." In *Maternal Influences on Early Behavior*, edited by R. W. Bell and W. P. Smotherman. New York: Spectrum, 1979.

Brown, J. A. C. *Freud and the Post-Freudians*. London: Cassell, 1968.

Bryne, J. M., and F. D. Horowitz. "Rocking as a Soothing Intervention: The Influences of Direction and Type of Movement." *Infant Behavior and Development* 4 (1981): 207–18.

Byers, Paul. "Biological Rhythms as Information Channels in Interpersonal Communication Behavior." In *Perspectives in Ethology*, edited by P. P. G. Bateson and Peter H. Klopfer. New York: Plenum Press, 1976.

———. "A Personal View of Nonverbal Communication." *Theory into Practice: Journal of the School of Education* (Ohio State University), June 1977.

Caldwell, Bettye. "The Effects of Infant Care." In *Review of Child Development Research*, I, edited by M. L. and L. W. Hoffman. New York: Russell Sage Foundation, 1964.

Caplan, Paula J., and Ian Hall-McCorquodale. "The Scapegoating of Mothers: A Call for Change." *American Journal of Orthopsychiatry*, 1985, 610–14.

———. "Mother-Blaming in Major Clinical Journals." *American Journal of Orthopsychiatry*, 1985, 345–53.

Capra, Fritjof. *The Tao of Physics*. New York: Bantam Books, 1977.

———. *The Turning Point: Science, Society and the Rising Culture*. New York: Simon and Schuster, 1982.

Carew, Jean V. "Effective Care-Giving—The Child from Birth to Three." In *Parenting in a Multicultural Society*, edited by Mario D. Fantini and Rene Cardenas. New York: Longman, 1980.

Cherry, Laurence. "The Doctor Within Us All." *New York Times Magazine*, November 23, 1980.

Chess, Stella. "Woman's Work." *Readings: A Journal of Reviews*, 1986, 23–5.

Clarke-Stewart, Alison. *Daycare*. Cambridge, Mass.: Harvard University Press, 1982.

Crockenberg, Susan B. "Infant Irritability, Mother Responsiveness, and Social Support Influences on the Security of Infant-Mother Attachment." *Child Development* 52 (1981): 857–65.

Cohen, S. E. "Maternal Employment and Mother-Child." In *In The Beginning*, edited by J. Belsky. New York: Columbia University Press, 1982.

Cole, K. C. *Sympathetic Vibrations*. New York: Bantam Books, 1985.

Collins, Glenn. "Does Early Teaching of Infants Have Merit?" *New York Times*, February 1, 1984.

Condon, William S. "Multiple Response to Sound in Dysfunctional Children." *Journal of Autism and Childhood Schizophrenia* 5, no. 1 (1975): 43ff.

———, and Lou Sander. "Synchrony Demonstrated Between Movements of the Neonate and Adult Speech." *Child Development* 45 (1974): 456–62.

Cousins, Norman, with Susan Schiefelbein. "Medical Mystery of the Placebo." *Reader's Digest*, March 1978, 167–9.

Cowan, W. Maxwell. "The Development of the Brain." *Scientific American*, September 1979, 112ff.

Cummings, E. M. "Caregiver Stability and Day Care." *Developmental Psychology*, 1980, 31–7.

Darwin, Charles. *The Expression of Emotions in Man and Animals*. New York: D. Appleton, 1872. Reprint. University of Chicago Press, 1965.

Demos, E. Virginia. "Resiliency in Infancy." In *Resiliency*, edited by R. Coles and T. Dugan. New York: Brunner/Mazel, 1985.

Doman, Glenn. *Teach Your Baby Math*. New York: Pocket Books, 1982.

———. *How to Multiply Your Baby's Intelligence*. New York: Doubleday, 1984.

———, and Janet Doman. *How to Give Your Baby Encyclopedic Knowledge*. New York: Doubleday, 1985.

Doyle, A., and K. Somers. "The Effects of Group and Family Day Care on Infant Attachment Behaviors." *Canadian Journal of Behavioral Science* 10 (1978): 38–45.

Dubos, René. "Education for the Celebration of Life: Optimism Despite It All." *Teachers College Record*, Fall 1982, 266–76.

Dunn, Judy. *Distress and Comfort*. Cambridge, Mass.: Harvard University Press, 1976.

————, and M. P. M. Richards. "Observations on the Developing Relationship Between Mother and Baby in the Neonatal Period." In *Studies in Mother-Infant Interaction*, edited by H. R. Schaffer. New York: Academic Press, 1977.

Durkin, Dolores. "Children Who Learned to Read at Home." *Elementary School Journal*, October 1961.

————. "Children Who Read Before Grade 1: A Second Study." *Elementary School Journal*, December 1963.

————. "A Six-Year Study of Children Who Learned to Read in School at the Age of Four." *Reading Research Quarterly* (International Reading Association), 1974–75, 9ff.

Elkind, David. *The Hurried Child: Growing Up Too Fast Too Soon*. Reading, Mass.: Addison-Wesley, 1981.

Ellis, Havelock. *The Dance of Life*. New York: Houghton Mifflin, 1923. Reprint. Westport, Conn.: Greenwood Press, 1973.

Engelmann, Siegfried, and Therese Engelmann. *Give Your Child a Superior Mind*. New York: Cornerstone Library, 1981.

Epstein, H. T. "Learning to Learn: Matching Instruction to Cognitive Levels." *Principal*, May 1981, 25–30.

Fantz, R. L. "Visual Perception and Experience in Early Infancy: A Look at the Hidden Side of Behavior Development." In *Early Behavior: Comparative and Developmental Approaches*, edited by H. Stevenson, E. Hess, and H. Rheingold. New York: Wiley, 1967.

Farran, D. C., and C. T. Ramey. "Infant Day Care and Attachment Behaviors Toward Mothers and Teachers." *Child Development* 49 (1977): 1112–16.

Feldman, Ruth Duskin. *Whatever Happened to the Quiz Kids: Perils and Profits of Growing Up Gifted*. Chicago: Chicago Review Press, 1982.

Ferber, Richard. *Solve Your Child's Sleep Problems*. New York: Simon and Schuster, 1985.

Ferguson, C. A. "Baby Talk in Six Languages." *American Anthropology* 66 (1964): 103–14.

Fernald, Anne. "Four-Month-Old Infants Prefer to Listen to Motherese." *Infant Behavior & Development* 8 (1985): 181–95.

Fowler, W. *Day Care and Its Effects on Early Development: A Study of Group and Home Care in Multi-Ethnic, Working Class Families.* Toronto: Ontario Institute for Studies in Education, 1978.

Fraiberg, Selma. *Insights from the Blind.* New York: Basic Books, 1977.

Freud, Sigmund. *A General Introduction to Psycho-Analysis.* Garden City, N.Y.: Doubleday, 1938.

————. *An Outline of Psychoanalysis.* New York: Norton, 1949.

————. *Collected Papers.* Vol. II. London: Hogarth Press, 1950.

Friedrich, Otto. "What Do Babies Know?" *Time,* August 15, 1983, 52–9.

Gallas, H., and M. Lewis. "Mother-Infant Interaction and Cognitive Development in the 12-Week-Old Infant." Paper presented to the Society for Research in Child Development, New Orleans, 1977.

Gamble, Thomas J., and Edward Zigler. "Effects of Infant Day Care: Another Look at the Evidence." *American Journal of Orthopsychiatry* 56, no. 1 (January 1986): 26–42.

Garber, H., and R. Heber. "Modification of Predicted Cognitive Development in High-Risk Children Through Early Intervention." Paper presented at the meeting of the American Educational Research Association, Boston, April 1980. Published in *Intelligence* 4, no. 3 (1980).

Gardner, Howard. "Prodigies' Progress." *Psychology Today,* March 1981, 75ff.

————. "Composing Symphonies and Dinner Parties." *Psychology Today,* April 1983, 18ff.

Gardner, Martin. "Mathematical Games." *Scientific American,* April 1978.

Gerber, Magda. "Caring for Infants with Respect: The RIE Approach." *Zero to Three* (bulletin of the National Center for Clinical Infant Programs), February 1984, 1–3.

Goldenberg, Irene, and Herbert Goldenberg. *Family Therapy: An Overview.* Monterey, Cal.: Brooks/Cole, 1980.

Goleman, Daniel. "1,528 Little Geniuses and How They Grew." *Psychology Today,* February 1981, 28ff.

Gollin, Eugene S., ed. *Developmental Plasticity: Behavioral and Biological Aspects of Variations in Development.* New York: Academic Press, 1981.

Gordon, Ira J. *Human Development: A Transactional Perspective.* New York: Harper & Row, 1975.

Goren, C., M. Sarty, and P. Wu. "Visual Following and Pattern Discrimination of Face-Like Stimuli by Newborn Infants." *Pediatrics* 56 (1975): 544–9.

Greaves, Roger, trans. *Lao-Tzu and Taoism*. Stanford, Cal.: Stanford University Press, 1969.

Greer, John G., and Chris E. Wethered. "Learned Helplessness: A Piece of the Burnout Puzzle." *Exceptional Children* 50, no. 6 (1984): 524ff.

Harman, David, and Orville G. Brim, Jr. *Learning to Be Parents*. Beverly Hills, Cal.: Sage Publications, 1980.

Hess, Robert D. "Experts and Amateurs: Some Unintended Consequences of Parent Education." In *Parenting in a Multicultural Society*, edited by Mario D. Fantini and Rene Cardenas. New York: Longman, 1980.

Hinde, R. *Animal Behavior: A Synthesis of Ethology and Comparative Psychology*. New York: McGraw-Hill, 1966.

Hock, E. "Working and Nonworking Mothers with Infants: Perceptions of Their Careers, Their Infants' Needs, and Satisfaction with Mothering." *Developmental Psychology* 14 (1978): 37–43.

————. "Working and Nonworking Mothers and Their Infants: A Comparative Study of Maternal Caregiving Characteristics and Infant Social Behavior." *Merrill-Palmer Quarterly* 26 (1980): 79–102.

————, K. Christman, and M. Hock. "Factors Associated with Decisions About Return to Work in Mothers of Infants." *Developmental Psychology* 16 (1980): 535–6.

Huang, A. *Embrace Tiger, Return to Mountain*. Moab, Utah: Real People Press, 1973.

Illingworth, R. S. " 'Three Month' Colic." *Archives of Disease in Childhood* 29 (1954): 165–74.

Izard, C. E. *Human Emotions*. New York: Plenum Press, 1977.

————, et al. "The Young Infant's Ability to Produce Discrete Emotional Expressions." *Developmental Psychology* 16, no. 2 (1980); 132–40.

Jackson, Jane Flannery, and Joseph H. Jackson. *Infant Culture*. New York: Thomas Y. Crowell, 1978.

James, William. *The Principles of Psychology*. New York: Henry Holt, 1890.

Janov, Arthur. *The Feeling Child*. New York: Simon and Schuster, 1973.

Jones, Sandy. *Crying Baby, Sleepless Nights*. New York: Warner Books, 1983.

Kagan, Jerome. "Emergent Themes in Human Development." *American Scientist,* March–April 1976, 186–96.

————, R. B. Kearsley, and P. R. Zelazo. *Infancy: Its Place in Human Development.* Cambridge, Mass.: Harvard University Press, 1978.

Kirkland, John. *Crying and Babies: Helping Families Cope.* London: Croom Helm, 1985.

Klaus, M. H., and J. H. Kennell. *Parent-Infant Bonding.* St. Louis: Mosby, 1982.

Klein, Melanie. *Our Adult World and Other Essays.* London: Heinemann, 1963.

Kohlberg, Lawrence, and E. F. Zigler. "The Impact of Cognitive Maturity upon the Development of Sex-Role Attitudes in the Years Four to Eight." *Genetic Psychological Monographs* 75 (1967): 89–165.

Korner, A. F., H. C. Kraemer, M. E. Haffner, and E. B. Thoman. "Characteristics of Crying and Noncrying Activity of Full-term Neonates." *Child Development* 45 (1974): 946–58.

Kotelchuk, M. "The Infant's Relationship to the Father: Experimental Evidence." In *The Role of the Father in Child Development,* edited by Michael Lamb. New York: Wiley, 1976.

Lamb, Michael. "Fathers: Forgotten Contributors to Child Development." *Human Development* 18 (1975): 245–66.

————. "Interactions Between Eight-Month-Old Children and Their Fathers and Mothers." In *The Role of the Father in Child Development.* New York: Wiley, 1976.

————. "Father-Infant and Mother-Infant Interaction in the First Year of Life." *Child Development* 48 (1977): 167–81.

————. "The Father's Role in the Infant's Social World." In *Mother-Child, Father-Child Relationships,* edited by Joseph H. Stevens, Jr., and Marilyn Matthews. Washington, D.C.: National Association for the Education of Young Children, 1978.

————. "What Can 'Research Experts' Tell Parents About Effective Socialization?" In *Parenting in a Multicultural Society,* edited by Mario D. Fantini and Rene Cardenas. New York: Longman, 1980.

Laszlo, Ervin. *Introduction to Systems Philosophy.* New York: Harper Torchbooks, 1972a.

————. *The Systems View of the World.* New York: Braziller, 1972b.

Leman, Kevin. *The Birth Order Book: Why You Are the Way You Are.* Old Tappan, N.J.: Fleming H. Revell, 1984.

Leonard, George. *The Silent Pulse: A Search for the Perfect Rhythm That Exists in Each of Us.* New York: E. P. Dutton, 1978.

———. "Living with Modern Daughters." *Esquire,* June 1984, 181–91.

Levine, Melvin D., William B. Carey, Allen C. Crocker, and Ruth T. Gross, eds. *Developmental-Behavioral Pediatrics.* Philadelphia: W. B. Saunders, 1983.

Lewis, David. *How to Be a Gifted Parent.* New York: Berkley Books, 1979.

Lewis, J. M., W. R. Beavers, J. T. Gossett, and V. A. Phillips. *No Single Thread: Psychological Health in Family Systems.* New York: Brunner/Mazel, 1976.

Lewis, Michael, ed. *Origins of Intelligence.* New York: Plenum Press, 1976.

———, and C. Feiring. "Direct and Indirect Interactions in Social Relationships." In *Advances in Infancy Research,* I, edited by L. P. Lipsitt and C. K. Rovee-Collier. Norwood, N.J.: Ablex Publishing, 1981.

———, and S. Goldberg. "Perceptual-Cognitive Development in Infancy: A Generalized Expectancy Model as a Function of the Mother-Infant Interaction. *Merrill-Palmer Quarterly* 15 (1969): 81–100.

———, and Harry McGurk. "Evaluation of Infant Intelligence." *Science,* December 15, 1972, 1174–77.

———, and C. D. Wilson. "Infant Development in Lower-Class American Families." *Human Development* 15 (1972): 112–27.

Luce, Gay Gaer. *Body Time: Physiological Rhythms and Social Stress.* New York: Pantheon, 1971.

McCall, Robert. "Challenges to a Science of Developmental Psychology." *Child Development,* 1977, 333–44.

———. *Infants.* Cambridge, Mass.: Harvard University Press, 1979.

———. "Do Your Moods Affect Your Baby?" *Parents' Magazine,* June 1983, 80.

———. "Fathers Make Great Mothers." *Parents' Magazine,* October 1985, 200.

———, et al. "Transitions in Infant Sensorimotor Development and the Prediction of Childhood IQ." *American Psychologist,* August 1972, 728–48.

Macfarlane, Aiden. "Olfaction in the Development of Social Preferences in the Human Neonate." In *Parent-Infant Interaction,* edited by M. Hofer. Amsterdam: Elsevier, 1975.

MacLean, P. D. "A Mind of Three Minds: Educating the Triune Brain." In *Seventy-seventh Yearbook of the National Society for the Study of Education.* Chicago: University of Chicago Press, 1978.

Marshall, Megan. "Musical Wonder Kids." *Boston Globe Magazine,* July 25, 1981.

Maslow, A. H. *Toward a Psychology of Being.* New York: D. Van Nostrand, 1968.

————. *The Farther Reaches of Human Nature.* Harmandsworth, Eng.: Penguin Books, 1971.

Matthews, K. A. "Efforts at Control by Children and Adults with Type A Coronary-Prone Behavior Pattern." *Child Development* 50 (1979): 842–7.

————. "Antecedents of the Type A Coronary-Prone Behavior Pattern." In *Developmental Social Psychology,* edited by S. S. Brehn, S. M. Kassen, and F. X. Gibbons. New York: Oxford, 1981.

Montagu, Ashley. *Growing Young.* New York: McGraw-Hill, 1981.

Moore, Gaylen. "The Superbaby Myth." *Psychology Today,* June 1984, 6–7.

Morphett, Mabel, and Carleton Washburn. "When Should Children Begin to Read?" *Elementary School Journal,* March 1931.

Mussen, Paul H., ed. *Handbook of Child Psychology.* New York: Wiley, 1983.

Oster, Harriet. "Facial Expressions and Affect Development." In *The Development of Affect,* edited by Michael Lewis and L. A. Rosenblum. New York: Plenum Press, 1978.

Papousek, H., and M. Papousek. "Mothering and the Cognitive Head Start: Psychobiological Considerations." In *Studies in Mother-Infant Interaction,* edited by H. R. Schaffer. New York: Academic Press, 1977.

Paradise, J. L. "Maternal and Other Factors in the Etiology of Infantile Colic." *Journal of the American Medical Association* 197 (1966): 123–31.

Parke, Ross. *Fathers.* Cambridge, Mass.: Harvard University Press, 1981.

————, S. O'Leary, and S. West. "Mother-Father-Newborn Interaction: Effects of Maternal Medication, Labor and Sex of Infant." *Proceedings of the American Psychological Association,* 1972, 85–6.

Pelletier, Kenneth. "Healer." *Psychology Today*, February 1977, 35–83.

Piaget, Jean. *Psychology of Intelligence*. Paterson, N.J.: Littlefield, Adams, 1963.

————. *Intelligence and Affectivity*. Edited and translated by T. A. Brown and C. E. Kaegi. Palo Alto, Cal.: Annual Reviews, 1981.

Pines, Maya. "Good Samaritans at Age Two?" *Psychology Today*, June 1979, 66.

Plutchik, Robert. "Cognitions in the Service of Emotions." In *Emotion*, edited by Douglas K. Candland, et al. Monterey, Cal.: Brooks/Cole, 1977.

————. "A Language for the Emotions." *Psychology Today*, February 1980, 68–78.

Procaccini, Dr. Joseph, and Mark W. Kiefaber. *Parent Burn-Out*. New York: Doubleday, 1983.

Provence, Sally, "Infant Day Care: Relationships Between Theory and Practice." In *Day Care: Scientific and Social Policy Issues*, edited by E. F. Zigler and E. W. Gordon. Boston: Auburn House, 1982.

Ramey, C. T., and P. J. Mills. "Social and Intellectual Consequences of Day Care for High-Risk Infants." In *Social Development in Childhood: Day Care Programs and Research*, edited by R. A. Webb. Baltimore: Johns Hopkins University Press, 1977.

Rebelsky, Freda, and C. Hanks. "Fathers' Verbal Interaction with Infants in the First Three Months of Life." *Child Development* 42 (1971): 63–8.

Restak, Richard M. *Brain: The Last Frontier*. New York: Doubleday, 1979.

Robertson, J. "Mothering as an Influence on Early Development: A Study of Well-Baby Clinic Records." *Psychoanalytic Study of the Child* 17 (1962): 245–64.

Robinson, H. B., and N. M. Robinson. "Longitudinal Development of Very Young Children in a Comprehensive Day Care Program: The First Two Years." *Child Development* 42 (1971): 1673–83.

Rosenfeld, Albert. "The 'Elastic Mind' Movement: Rationalizing Child Neglect?" *Saturday Review*, April 1, 1978, 26–8.

Rubenstein, J. L., C. Howes, and P. Boyle. "A Two-Year Follow-Up of Infants in Community Based Infant Day Care." *Journal of Child Psychology and Psychiatry* 22 (1981): 209–18.

Safran, Claire. "How to Raise a Superstar." *Reader's Digest,* January 1985, 111–14.

Sander, Lou. "Infant and Caretaking Environment: Investigation and Conceptualization in a System of Increasing Complexity." In *Explorations in Child Psychiatry,* edited by E. J. Anthony. New York: Plenum Press, 1975.

Sanger, Sirgay, with John Kelly. *You and Your Baby's First Year.* New York: Morrow, 1985.

Scarr, Sandra. *Mother Care Other Care.* New York: Basic Books, 1984.

Schaefer, Earl S. "A Circumflex Model for Maternal Behavior." *Journal of Abnormal and Social Psychology* 59 (1959): 226–35.

Schaffer, H. R. *The Origins of Human Social Relations.* New York: Academic Press, 1971.

Schaffer, Rudolph. *Mothering.* Cambridge, Mass.: Harvard University Press, 1977.

Schuster, Clara Shaw, and Shirley Smith Ashburn. *The Process of Human Development: A Holistic Approach.* Boston: Little, Brown, 1980.

Sears, R. R., E. E. Maccoby, and H. Levin. *Patterns of Child Rearing.* Evanston, Ill.: Row, Peterson, 1957.

Siperstein, G. N., and E. C. Butterfield. "Neonates Prefer Vocal-Instrumental Music to Noise and Vocal Music to Instrumental Music." In *Oral Sensation and Perception,* edited by J. F. Bosma. Springfield, Ill.: Charles C. Thomas, 1972.

Skolnick, A. S., and J. R. Skolnick, eds. *Family in Transition.* Boston: Little, Brown & Co., 1971.

Sperry, R. W. "How a Developing Brain Gets Itself Properly Wired for Adaptive Function." In *The Biopsychology of Development,* edited by Ethel Tobach, Lester Aronson, and Evelyn Shaw. New York: Academic Press, 1971.

Spezzano, Charles. "Prenatal Psychology: Pregnant with Questions." *Psychology Today,* May 1981, 49–57.

Spock, Benjamin. *Baby and Child Care.* New York: Pocket Books, 1946.

———. *Baby and Child Care.* New York: Pocket Books, 1976.

Sroufe, L. Alan, and Jane Piccard Wunsch. "The Development of Laughter in the First Year of Life." *Child Development* 43 (1972): 1326–44.

————, and E. Waters. "Attachment as an Organizational Construct." *Child Development* 48 (1977): 1184–99.

Stern, Daniel, *The First Relationship: Infant and Mother.* Cambridge, Mass.: Harvard University Press, 1977.

————. *The Interpersonal World of the Infant.* New York: Basic Books, 1985.

Stern, G. G., B. M. Caldwell, L. Hersher, E. L. Lipton, and J. B. Richmond. "A Factor Analytic Study of the Mother-Infant Dyad." *Child Development* 40 (1969): 163–81.

Svejda, Marilyn J., Joseph J. Campos, and Robert Emde. "Mother-Infant 'Bonding': Failure to Generalize." *Child Development* 51 (1980): 775–9.

Thoman, Evelyn B., et al. "Neonate-Mother Interaction: Effects of Parity on Feeding Behavior." *Child Development* 41 (1970): 1103–11.

————, V. H. Denenberg, P. T. Becker, et al. "Analysis of Mother-Infant Interaction Sequences: A Model for Relating Mother-Infant Interaction to the Infant's Development of Behavior States." In *Maternal Infant Life Conferences,* Wisconsin Perinatal Center, 1974.

————. "Some Consequences of Early Infant-Mother-Infant Interaction." *Early Child Development and Care,* 1974, 249–61.

————. "Early Development of Sleeping Behaviors in Infants." In *Aberrant Development in Infancy: Human and Animal Studies,* edited by H. R. Ellis. New York: John Wiley, 1975.

————. "Sleep and Wake Behaviors in Neonates: Consistencies and Consequences." *Merrill-Palmer Quarterly,* 1975, 295–341.

————. "The Role of the Infant in Early Transfer of Information." *Biological Psychiatry,* 1975, 161–9.

————, et al. "Individual Consistency in Behavioral States in Neonates." *Developmental Psychobiology,* 1976, 271–83.

————, et al. "Modification of Responsiveness to Maternal Vocalization in the Neonate." *Child Development* 48 (1977): 563–9.

————, P. T. Becker, and M. P. Freese. "Individual Patterns of Mother-Infant Interaction." In *Observing Behavior.* Vol. I: *Theory and Applications in Mental Retardation,* edited by G. P. Sacket. Baltimore: University Park Press, 1978.

————, and S. Trotter, eds. *Social Responsiveness of Infants.* Hillsdale, N.J.: Johnson and Johnson, 1978.

———. "Changing Views of the Being and Becoming of Infants." In *Origins of the Infant's Social Responsiveness,* edited by Evelyn B. Thoman. Hillsdale, N.J.: Lawrence Erlbaum Associates, 1979.

———. "CNS Dysfunction and Nonverbal Communication Between Mother and Infant." In *The Neurological Bases of Language Disorders in Children: Methods and Directions for Research,* edited by C. L. Ludlow and M. E. Doran-Quine. NINCDS Monograph. Washington, D.C.: Government Printing Office, 1979.

———, and M. P. Freese. "A Model for the Study of Early Mother-Infant Communication." In *Maternal Influences and Early Behavior,* edited by R. W. Bell and W. P. Smotherman. New York: Spectrum, 1980.

———. "Affective Communication as the Prelude and Context for Language Learning." In *Early Language: Acquisition and Intervention,* edited by R. L. Schiefelbusch and D. Bricker. Baltimore: University Park Press, 1981.

———, C. Acebo, and P. T. Becker. "Infant Crying and Stability in the Mother-Infant Relationship: A Systems Analysis." *Child Development* 54 (1983): 653–9.

———, and C. Acebo. "The First Affectations of Infancy." In *Interfaces in Psychology, I: Developmental Psychobiology and Neuropsychology,* edited by R. W. Bell et al. Lubbock: Texas Tech University Press, 1984.

———, and S. Graham. Self-regulation of Stimulation by Premature Infants." *Pediatrics* 78, no. 5 (1986): 8555–860.

Thomas, Alexander, and Stella Chess. *Temperament and Development.* New York: Brunner/Mazel, 1977.

———. *The Dynamics of Psychological Development.* New York: Brunner/Mazel, 1980.

Thomas, Lewis. *The Lives of a Cell.* New York: Viking Press, 1974.

Thorpe, W. H. *Bird Song: The Biology of Vocal Communication and Expression in Birds.* Cambridge, Mass.: Harvard University Press, 1961.

Tronick, Edward, and Lauren Adamson. *Babies as People.* New York: Collier Books, 1980.

Trotter, Robert J. "Baby Face." *Psychology Today,* August 1983, 15–20.

Verny, Thomas, with John Kelly. *The Secret Life of the Unborn Child.* New York: Summit Books, 1981.

Wassersug, Joseph D., and Richard J. Wassersug. "Fitness Fallacies." *Natural History,* March 1986, 4, 34ff.

Weinraub, Marsha. "Fatherhood: The Myth of the Second-Class Parent." In *Mother-Child, Father-Child Relationships,* edited by Joseph H. Stevens and Marilyn Matthews. Washington, D.C.: National Association for Education of Young Children, 1978.

Weissbluth, Marc. *Crybabies.* New York: Arbor House, 1984.

Westin, Jeane. *The Coming Parent Revolution.* New York: Bantam Books, 1981.

Willemsen, Eleanor. *Understanding Infancy.* San Francisco: W. H. Freeman, 1979.

Wolff, Peter H. "Observations on Newborn Infants." *Psychosomatic Medicine* 21, no. 2 (1959): 110–18.

———. "Observations on the Early Development of Smiling." In *Determinants of Infant Behavior,* II, edited by B. M. Foss. London: Methuen, 1963.

———. " 'Critical Periods' in Human Cognitive Development." *Hospital Practice,* November 1970, 77–87.

———, and Richard I. Feinbloom. "Critical Periods and Cognitive Development in the First Two Years." *Pediatrics* 44, December 1969, 999–1006.

Yarrow, L. J. "Research in Dimensions of Early Maternal Care." *Merrill-Palmer Quarterly* 9 (1963): 101–14.

Yarrow, L. J., J. L. Rubenstein, and F. A. Pederson. *Infant and Environment: Early Cognitive and Motivational Development.* Washington, D.C.: Hemisphere (distributed by Wiley), 1975.

Yarrow, M. R., J. D. Campbell, and R. V. Burton. *Child Rearing: An Inquiry into Research and Methods.* San Francisco: Jossey-Bass, 1968.

Yutang, Lin, trans. and ed. *The Wisdom of Laotse.* New York: Modern Library, 1948.

Zukav, Gary. *The Dancing Wu Li Masters.* New York: William Morrow, 1979.

INDEX